The Social Life
of Trees

MATERIALIZING CULTURE
▪▪▪

Series Editors: Paul Gilroy, Michael Herzfeld and Danny Miller

Barbara Bender, *Stonehenge: Making Space*

Gen Doy, *Materializing Art History*

The Social Life of Trees

Anthropological Perspectives on
Tree Symbolism

Edited by

LAURA RIVAL

Oxford • New York

First published in 1998 by
Berg
Editorial offices:
150 Cowley Road, Oxford, OX4 1JJ, UK
70 Washington Square South, New York, NY 10012, USA

Paperback edition reprinted in 2001

Berg is an imprint of Oxford International Publishers Ltd.

Library of Congress Cataloging-in-Publication Data

A catalogue record for this book is available from the Library of
Congress.

British Library Cataloguing-in-Publication Data

A catalogue record for this book is available from the British Library.

ISBN 1 85973 923 7 (Cloth)
     1 85973 928 8 (Paper)

Typeset by JS Typesetting, Wellingborough, Northants.

This book is dedicated to the memory of
Alfred Gell, 1945–1997

Contents

List of Figures

List of Tables

Preface

This book is the outcome of an original question 'To which symbolic ends have trees been used?' put to a number of anthropologists in January 1996 at a conference on 'Trees and Wood as Social Symbols'. The goal of the conference was to address the social dimension of tree symbolism in different societies and cultures, and, more specifically, the extent to which trees are used as symbols of transgenerational continuity. Well aware of the condemnation of cross-cultural analysis of symbolic – or social – structures by both postmodernist and cognitive anthropologists who agree, albeit for very different reasons, that such endeavour can only result in arbitrary findings, we nevertheless felt that presenting detailed and original ethnographies of the ways in which trees are used to symbolise human existence and human society in various regions of the world was a useful intellectual exercise. By the end of the conference, we had, not a well-crafted cross-cultural comparative model describing tree symbolism and explaining its variation, but the clear picture of a recurrent theme, the vitality and power of self-regeneration of trees. Of course, what we loosely call 'tree symbolism' is a complex cultural representation composed of different kinds of knowledge. More detailed explorations of local systems of meaning, as well as comparative work, is needed to confirm the hypothesis that trees everywhere and at all times have been associated with the organic force of life.

The conference received the support of the Wenner Gren Foundation for Anthropological Research (Grant 189) and of the British Academy, gratefully acknowledged here. We would also like to thank the catering and conference staff of Wye College, at Wye, Kent, England, for their friendly hospitality and material support.

Participants, apart from the book's contributors, included Stephen Hugh-Jones, Nevill Colclough, and Leslie and Poranee Sponsel, Chris Hann and Phil Burnham, all of whom we warmly thank for their useful contributions to the discussion. Our thanks also go to John French, Ted Oakes, and the European graduate students enrolled at the Universities of Kent, Brussels, Montpellier and Paris under the EC-funded APFT (Pour l'Avenir des Peuples des Forêts Tropicales, For the Future of Rainforest Peoples) research programme, for their presence and lively participation in the debates on green activism.

Most of the editing involved in producing this volume has taken place at the University of Kent at Canterbury, where Jan Horn's invaluable administrative support has made the task manageable. Finally, I would like to thank Kathryn Earle for her patience and cooperation.

Laura Rival
Oxford, April 1997

Trees, from Symbols of Life and Regeneration to Political Artefacts

Laura Rival

T his book explores the symbolic significance of trees in a number
of contemporary cultures. From its beginnings, anthropology has
concerned itself as much with the ways in which natural processes are
conceptualised and the natural world classified, as with the ways in
which human societies interact with their natural environments and
use natural resources. Anthropologists have long debated the fact that
cultures as symbolic systems derive meanings largely from natural
elements. Ever since the seminal essay *De Quelques Formes Primitives de
Classification* by Durkheim and Mauss (1963 [1903]), they have pond-
ered on the social origin of human representations of natural categories,
as well as on the emergence of objective natural history. The present
book is part of this continuous effort to theorise interactions between
human societies and their natural environments. While much anthropological writing deals with animals, landscapes and domesticated
crops, very little concerns trees *per se*.[1] However, trees provide some of
the most visible and potent symbols of social process and collective
identity.

Tree symbolism, it might be argued, reflects the human urge to
express ideas through external and material signs, no matter what these
signs might be (Durkheim 1976 [1915]: 127). Anticipating some of the
recent theories developed within material culture studies, Emile Durkheim remarks that Australian Aborigines carve, tattoo or paint their
totems out of the need to represent the idea they form of their totems.
This desire 'to translate thought into matter' leads him to reflect on

the relevance of externalisation, materialisation and physicality for social theory, and to conclude that 'a collective sentiment can become conscious of itself only by being fixed upon some material object' (Durkheim 1976 [1915]: 236). The paradigmatic focus on the material constitution of society and the examination of material forms in terms of the social effects of their physical manifestation have proved very productive. We have now achieved a greater understanding of the dialectical relationship between, for instance, subject and object (Miller 1987), or the functional and the meaningful (Gell 1996). We are also in a better position to analyse modern social processes without resorting to either 'orientalism' or 'occidentalism' (Carrier 1995). However, the paradigm has its shortcomings. In material culture studies, anything material is treated as if it were object-like. But, as this collection amply illustrates, the physical presence of a tree is not that of an artefact; a tree is a living organism.

It could be argued, then, that trees are natural symbols. As defined by Mary Douglas (1970), for whom they are primarily derived from human physiology and bodily substances, natural symbols reflect the dual nature of humankind as both animal-like (the body) and god-like (the mind). This characterisation of natural symbols, not unlike numerous pre-Lévi-Straussian theories of totemism stressing the connection between totems and animal species, emphasises the polarity between residual, biological animality and developing humanity. Cast in this mould, animal symbolism is everywhere seen as an expression of the irreconcilability between, on the one hand, the organic body and its threatening bestiality, and, on the other, the mind, locus of morality and spirituality. With such a dualistic frame, the symbolic contribution of other life forms, particularly plants, whose social and metaphysical significance does not seem to lie in drawing an absolute distinction between nature and culture, but, on the contrary, in reaffirming the continuity of biological species within the living world, can only be devalued.

Some would argue that there is no need to study the symbolisation of trees, for trees represent little more than a background to activities. Places, rather than plants, have symbolic value; so trees would be better studied as part of a landscape. Of course, trees grow and change, but so do all elements in a landscape, be they natural or built. At once composite and historical, landscapes are permanently under construction (Ingold 1993), as well as open to reinterpretation (Bender 1993). The problem with the landscape approach, as William Cronon (1995: 20) so rightly puts it, is that 'nature' may to a large extent be a human idea, but, before all, it is a non-human thing. Cognitive anthropologists such as Pascal Boyer or Scott Atran would add that even if they have been endowed with cultural, historically changing meanings, natural kinds in the landscape, such as animal and plant species, are mentally apprehended through innate conceptual mechanisms quite unlike those triggered by landscapes, buildings, or any other human artefact.

If landscapes are essentially cultural and historical, the same could be said of the category 'tree', for a tree is not a biological species existing in the world previous to a work of recognition and classification. Atran (1990: 35), however, makes the convincing case that trees form a natural category, a life-form: 'The natural discontinuities apparent in the conception of tree pertain to processes of evolutionary convergence bound to ecological considerations in the competition for sunlight. People naturally tend to find trees phenomenally compelling because of their evident ecological role in determining local distributions of flora and fauna.' If the life-form 'tree' is an ontological category as defined by Boyer (1994), then it corresponds to elementary assumptions – and inferences that can be made – about what sort of thing a tree is, as well as to domain-specific principles that structure intuitive expectations concerning trees.

Although the authors of the contributions collected here have approached tree symbolism from very different perspectives, what comes out of the ethnographies is that trees are used symbolically to make concrete and material the abstract notion of life, and that trees are ideal supports for such symbolic purpose precisely because their status as living organisms is ambiguous. The rest of the chapter is devoted to developing and supporting this thesis. After a section on the necessity and danger of cross-cultural comparison, I discuss the role of tree symbolism in life cycle rituals and community politics. I then show that tree symbols revolve around two essential qualities, vitality and self-regenerative power, and conclude on the biological particularities which make trees so amenable to life-reaffirming and death-denying cultural representations.

The Comparability of Beliefs and Symbols

This collection belongs to the growing body of work showing dissatisfaction with the notion of 'culture', and with holistic analyses of cultural knowledge. The long tradition of interpretation of natural symbols as internal representations of external reality has come to a close. Mary Douglas (1996: Ch. 6) herself has somewhat disowned her classic analysis of Lele animal symbolism, on the ground that the identification between animal kingdom and social life works both ways. Natural symbols are not just projections or metaphors of social life. So, rather than looking for the correspondence of a particular social structure and a unique way of dividing up the continuous and undifferentiated biological world, she now suggests that we identify the theories that sustain the classification of animals and humans, and give meaning to the metaphors, for 'there is a more fundamental, non-metaphorical kind of connection between the way humans think of themselves and how they think of animals' (Douglas 1996: 138). Symbolic similarities, she continues, result from local theories about life and death, as well as from the practical and utilitarian knowledge of animals constituted in everyday interactions. By emphasising that theories must be seen as local and that meanings should be established with reference to use, Douglas (1996: 128) of course maintains that similarity is relative, variable and culture-dependent. But her – still functionalist – approach to similarity brings her, almost ironically, somewhat close to Frazer's law of similarity and principle that 'when customs are similar in different societies, we may then infer that the motives of the people performing them are also similar' (Ackerman 1987: 82).

Frazer, like other nineteenth-century scholars interested in comparative religion, was intrigued by the symbolic significance of trees in classical mythology, the religions of ancient civilisations, and many 'primitive' religious beliefs and rituals. To Frazer, primitive religions, whether animistic or totemistic, were first of all an attempt to make sense of, and control, the cycles of vegetational death and rebirth. He saw in tree worship the evidence that all religions had originated in the personification of nature. Early men worshipped trees and other life powers because 'everything was to them at once material and spiritual, the animate and inanimate being almost undistinguished' (MacLennan 1869: 414). Frazer spent his life compiling sources and accumulating facts on offerings to trees, propriation ceremonies preceding tree felling, ritual weddings between humans and trees, or beliefs in the mutual fertilising influences of human sexual intercourse and vegetational growth. Although clearly decontextualised and without much comparative force, his exhaustive collection of customs relating to trees should not be simply dismissed as speculative, arbitrary or overdetermined by Greek mythology. In the 1955 supplement to *The Golden Bough*, for example, a whole chapter is dedicated to the worship of trees and sacred groves. One hundred-and-fourteen beliefs and ritual practices from thirty-eight non-Western cultures are cited.[2] Such recurrences must be accounted for if we are to reassess the social determination of myths and symbols, and the comparability of beliefs (Strathern 1990).

Cross-cultural comparison remains the main task of anthropology, but to understand cultural specificity, that is, the ways in which historical and ecological processes have influenced the emergence and development of particular cultural forms, we need to have a clearer idea of the character of cultural regularities. We need to identify what human cultures share in common, what remains untouched by history, and why. Today's renewed interest in the way human thought is embodied (i.e. constrained by, and depending on, the body), as well as the extent to which experience shapes reason, has revived the debate about the generic psychic unity of humankind, particularly in the context of human thinking about the biological world. We clearly need to address the issue of recurrence in a new way, and this is precisely the task that a few cognitive anthropologists have set for themselves.

The commitment to analyse the interplay of universal physiological and psychological factors with specific cultural and historical ones has led Sperber and his followers (most prominently Boyer, Atran and Bloch) to rethink symbolism as a cognitive mechanism with specific functions in the construction of knowledge and the working of memory. Sperber (1996), for whom symbols are metarepresentations of hard-to-process beliefs, does not analyse symbolism as a cultural language, that is, a form of social communication which can be interpreted through exegesis and other semiological approaches. Atran (1990: 250) contends that symbolism, the goal of which 'is not to extend factual knowledge, resolve natural paradoxes or increasingly restrict the scope of interesting conceptual puzzles', 'goes the way of eternal truth, and is sustained in that path by faith in the authority of those charged with the task of continually reinterpreting the truth and fitting it to new circumstances'. He draws a sharp contrast between the 'ontological categories' of true, common-sense knowledge about the world, and symbolic representations. In other words, he establishes a radical and qualitative distinction between concepts such as biological species (i.e. living kinds), which are determined by innate cognitive dispositions, spontaneously learnable and highly similar across cultures, and forms of knowledge such as symbols and metaphors, which are only learnt through structured and directed tuition, or in specific social environments or contexts. Building on Sperber and Atran, Boyer (P. Boyer 1993a, b, 1994) offers a new interpretation of religious symbolism.

His analysis of religious symbols, like that of Victor Turner (1967), starts by acknowledging their intrinsic disparity. But whereas Turner speaks of ritual symbols as exhibiting a tension between two poles of meaning – one socio-moral, the other sensory – Boyer (P. Boyer 1994: 123–4) identifies two different kinds of knowledge in all religious represent-ations. One consists of common-sense elementary assumptions about the nature of the world, the other of counter-intuitive claims violating such common sense. The content of Boyer's elementary assumptions about the nature of the world (i.e. ontological categories) is richer than Turner's sensory perceptions. Innate and domain-specific, ontological categories are neither acquired through teaching, nor abstracted gradually from direct, physical experience in the world. And Boyer's counter-intuitive claims have no exact match in the socio-moral components of the social order (Turner's other pole), for Boyer is exclusively interested in the fact that the content of these religious assertions is conceptually distorted in a way that makes them at once intelligible and surprising, hence memorable. In any case, he does not, as Mary Douglas would, see them resulting from the free and unlimited playful exercise of the human imagination; they are, says Boyer (P. Boyer 1994: 59), strongly constrained by the properties of conceptual systems.

In a recent article, Pascal Boyer (1996) applies his cognitive theory of religion to Wendy James' (1988) ethnographic description of Uduk ebony oracles. Among the Uduk of Sudan, the causes of illness are divined through burning the young growths of the black heartwood babanus tree (*Dalbergia melanoxylon*), carefully selected from far-out woodlands. As James explains, the innate sensitivity of this wood, which burns 'bright and sharp', provides spontaneous information about the activities of witches, which can then be interpreted by diviners. This sensitivity of the wood, continues James (1988: 303), 'is a part of its wild nature, from the forest where it grows. It is a property of the species itself, the growing tree, to absorb sounds and other signals [. . .] from its surroundings, and reveal, in the consultation, what it has picked up.'

Boyer interprets this belief as a typical counter-intuitive projection of human attributes on to non-human domains. In his view, the religious idea that certain trees can overhear and record conversations is possible because of the basic innate conceptual knowledge that humans can do so. The Uduk 'listening ebony' divination is to him a perfect example of intentional psychology (P. Boyer 1996: 90). Why has he chosen to interpret what the Uduk see as the wood's property to absorb sounds and other signals as an anthropomorphic belief making the extraordinary claim that a tree can hear conversations? Would he account for the invention of tape-recorders as a manifestation of intentional psychology? My aim here is neither to discuss Boyer's theory of religion, nor its evolutionary underpinnings, but, more modestly, to stress that the corpus of ethnographies on which this book is based shows that what seems to drive tree symbolism is not so much the transfer of intentionality on to non-human living organisms, but, rather, the need to find within the natural environment the material manifestation of organic processes that can be recognised as similar to those characterising the human life cycle, or the continued existence of social groups.

Trees and Humans

Life Cycle Rituals

All over the world, rituals marking the life cycle make extensive use of trees. For the people of Nusa Penida and Bali, as Giambelli (Chapter 6) explains, the coconut palm is a central ingredient of birth, marriage and death rites. An exemplar of plant growth, the coconut palm symbolises all fruit-bearing trees. A coconut is planted when the first-born child cuts his or her first teeth. And, whereas a newborn is fed for the first few days of its life with the pulp of an immature coconut (prior to any breast-feeding), the first solid food a teething child eats is the kernel of an old coconut. The groom's family offers a shooting coconut to the parents of the bride during the wedding ceremony, and while an exhumed corpse is being cremated, a shooting coconut is momentarily placed in the grave. Uchiyamada (Chapter 8) mentions a very similar ritual in South India, where a funeral coconut tree, representing the life force of the ghost of the deceased, is planted either in the cremation pit or on the grave. Never watered or tended, the young tree usually dries out and dies, an expected outcome that signifies that the transformation from corpse to ancestor is progressing normally.

Tree symbolism among the Ankave of Highland Papua New Guinea is closely related to male initiation rites. Certain trees, such as the red pandanus, a woody palm-like plant locally classified as tree, provide vegetal substitutes for procreative substances. Men prepare an oily red juice with the red pandanus fruit, of which young boys undergoing initiation rituals must ingest large quantities. The juice is put in the same category as maternal blood. As Bonnemère (Chapter 5) demonstrates, this practice relates to Ankave ideas about maturation. The

Ankave conceptualise growth in foetuses and infants as being determined by a substantial increase of blood in the body. Bonnemère concludes that if the maturation of young Ankave male children into boys is, as in other Melanesian societies, directly dependent upon the ritual enactment of the process of gestation and birth by adult men, it does not involve their insemination with purely male substances. On the contrary, the ritual makes use of vegetal substances with feminine connotations.

Uchiyamada (Chapter 8), who describes South Indian funeral rites, interprets with great subtlety the complex symbolic uses of trees in a society deeply structured by hierarchical inequality and cross-cut by diverse cultural and religious traditions. Middle-caste Nayars bury the cremated remains of their dead relatives in funeral urns at the foot of jack-fruit trees. A year or so later, the urns are excavated, and the exhumed bones brought to the coast, where they are left to drift in the Arabian sea. After this ceremony the soul attains liberation and the deceased finally becomes an ancestor. The jack-fruit tree, which represents the life-span of the family (including the ascendants) and its ancestral house, is sacred. By contrast, the souls of dead Untouchables, considered inherently impure and polluted, never attain liberation. They remain attached to the soil, and become wandering lineage ghosts rather than proper ancestors. Milk trees (paala), which are extremely fertile but bring misfortune to the landed castes, grow on sites where Untouchables are said to have succumbed to violent treatment and died. Sacred groves often form and develop around milk trees. The contrastive fates of high-caste and untouchable spirits is further illustrated in the spatial organisation of lineage temples. High-caste deities are seated in hierarchical order around the temple's rectangular, paved, and neatly swept yard, at the centre of which stands a single sacred tree, whose name means 'soul transcending death'. At the back of the temple lies the sacred grove, peopled with evil deities of Untouchable origin. Whereas High castes view the sacred groves as a source of wild, dangerous and capricious powers, Untouchables represent them as their own lineage temples.

Alain Bouras' (1977) unpublished thesis on trees in Romanian folklore and material culture contains rich data on the association of fruit trees with marriage and death rituals. Whereas pine trees (metaphorically fruit trees) are symbolically wedded to the corpses of young men who died before having had a chance to marry, pine wood is used to make dowry chests, marital beds and coffins. Knight (Chapter 9) mentions a similar ritual association between marriage, death and fruit tree in

Japan. A fast-growing tree, planted when a daughter is born, is felled before her wedding to make a chest of drawers for her dowry. Her in-laws plant in her honour a fruit tree, symbol of fertility, that yields abundantly in the autumn. The tree is cut down when she dies, and its wood used to cremate her body. Examples of trees and woods linked to life crisis rituals abound, even in the modern European context. There is for instance a growing movement in parts of Europe to replace cemeteries and graves with 'peace forests'. For those who are promoting this new form of burial, the great advantage of trees over tombs is that only ashes and trees – if left undisturbed – last for ever. Trees are true symbols of life and eternity; graves are symbols of death and fading memory. Zelter (Chapter 10) mentions that the community to which she belongs has bought fifty-two acres of woodland in Norfolk to be used for the celebration of births, marriages, birthdays, anniversaries and deaths.[3] Finally, trees are commonly thought to be repositories of the souls of the dead awaiting reincarnation. The Daur Mongols, for example, consider trees to be places for nest-like containers of soul-eggs (Humphrey 1996). Finally, the afterbirth of humans (Mauzé, Chapter 11) or domesticated animals (Uchiyamada, Chapter 8) is very often tied to a tree, or buried at its foot.

Trees and the Human Body

The analogy between trees and human bodies is often quite explicit, and most contributions address the widespread symbolic correspondence between tree parts and body parts in its lexical manifestation. The inhabitants of Nusa Penida offer a particularly elaborate treatment of the parallelism between the coconut palm, its fruit and persons. As Giambelli remarks, the coconut tree life-span is roughly analogous to that of a human – sixty to sixty-five years. Moreover, the palm planted by a man for his child's first-tooth ritual starts producing in its tenth year, just a few years before the child reaches sexual maturity. In fact, says Giambelli (Chapter 6), the coconut tree becomes the child's *alter ego*. In some rituals, the coconut palm is presented with food offerings, clothed, and addressed like an ancestor. The homology is even more striking in the case of the coconut itself, whose five recognised stages of growth and maturation closely parallel the stages of human development. The full maturation of the fruit from flowering to harvest requires, just like human gestation, approximately nine months. The term for tree sap is identical to the term for blood,[4] and the term for breast milk is also used with reference to the sap of the inflorescence.[5]

The coconut is identified with the female breast not only lexically, but also in numerous symbolic representations, metaphors and stories. And, unsurprisingly, all life crisis rituals make use of the coconut shell as a ritual container for bodily remains, ranging from the afterbirth to the ashes of the dead.

Bonnemère (Chapter 5) also discusses the salient homology between palm trees and humans among the Ankave, who do not call the fruits of the two palms which play a central role in male initiation rites 'fruit', but 'body'. 'Veins', an 'eye', and a 'nose' are recognised on the areca nut. The areca palm is said to have originated from the head of a decomposed body. Bonnemère is careful to note, however, that in this context, lexical analogy is not motivated, as in Nusa Penida, by the fact that a seed grows and develops into a tree, but, rather, by the ritual intervention of men, who transform the fruit into vegetal blood, hence causing young male children to metamorphose into boys. Finally, she indicates that the Ankave use the word 'bone' for 'trunk' only in the case of trees that are ritually significant. The anthropomorphisation of tree species with particular cultural value, widespread in Melanesia, has been mentioned by numerous ethnographers. Calame-Griaule (1969: 22), for instance, points out that trees in many African folktales are considered living beings whose morphological features are comparable to those of humans. The resulting associations between, for example, sap and blood, leaves and hair, limbs and arms, bark and skin, or trunk and the human body should not be taken as merely analogical, for they establish a kind of identity between signifier and signified. The use of the same terms to name both body parts and tree parts is in fact very common in many human languages, including English.[6] The analytical difficulty of interpreting such lexical regularities will be taken up in the last section.

Another remarkable recurrence in the way tree symbolism is used in relation to human bodies is that trees are often believed to be hermaphrodite. Because of its pervasiveness in ancient and classical mythologies, the androgynous nature of trees has fascinated many commentators (see in particular Brosse 1989; Graves 1990; and Jung 1968). Far from being confined to archaic Western beliefs, cultural elaborations on tree androgyny have been reported by numerous ethnographers, including most contributors to this volume. It might well be that the uncertainty of trees' sexual identity constitutes a cultural limit to the homology between trees and humans widely found throughout the world. Such uncertainty might also explain why trees seem to offer excellent lived-in models (i.e. models based in sentient experience and practical knowledge) to symbolise the *reproductive couple*, that is, the genderless potential for self-regeneration conceived as comprising both female and male life principles.[7] Bloch (1992a), de Boeck (1994), Howell (1996), and Rival (1997 and in press/b) have presented rich ethnographic evidence of the occurrence of such symbolism in very different cultural contexts.

The personification of trees may be more metaphorical, as when kinship terms are extended to trees (Giambelli, Mauzé, Chapters 6 and 11), or more abstract, as in the case discussed by Uchiyamada (Chapter 8), where a tree stands not for the physical body, but for the soul. The analogy between tree and body may thus extend to less obviously material parts of the human person, such as the self, the spirit, the ghost, the personality, or the psyche. Jung's theory of personality development depicts the human psyche as undergoing successive phases of expansion, death and renewal. His vision of the natural growth and gradual transformation of the self is particularly explicit in his essay on the philosophical tree (Jung 1968), where the tree is an archetype of the human personality. Both are equally massive, erect and projective.[8] The association between tree and personality need not, however, be abstract and a-historical. The Japanese foresters studied by Knight (Chapter 9), for example, understand their professional involvement with trees in terms of personality formation. They control and direct tree growth tightly, so as to obtain trees imbued with Japanese temperament and moral qualities identified as typically Japanese, such as rectitude, endurance and sturdiness. And, as Mauzé (Chapter 11) observes, there is something of the same national archetype in the contemporary Northwest Coast Indian self-identification as 'People of the Cedar'.

Woods, Forests and Politics: Struggles for the Continuity of Sustainable Communities

Standing for Family Groups and Communities

Speculation over sexed individuation in trees triggers their use to represent not only the married couple but also, as Bonnemère and Giambelli (Chapters 5 and 6) show, the child–parent link. More generally, trees and plants make perfect natural models for genealogical connections.[9] A favourite guessing game among the Beti goes something like 'In my father's yard stands a tree whose wide limbs spread throughout the country', to which the audience must reply 'kinship'

(Calame-Griaule 1969). In addition to the famous milk tree of the Ndembu (Turner 1967), references to trees as symbols of kinship in Africa are countless (see de Boeck 1994 for a recent example). Leach and Fairhead (Chapter 12) indicate that silk cotton trees, said to have been planted by village founders (who are also the apex ancestors of chiefly lineages) become the material supports for rituals and offerings linked to ancestor worship. Knight (Chapter 9) shows how the continuity of the Japanese *ie* is both conceived of, and materially reproduced through, cycles of tree planting and harvesting over several generations. The longevity of such planted trees, concrete symbols of origin, vitality and fertility, is used to celebrate the reproductive capabilities that link people within webs of relationships.

Trees, however, do not exclusively express genealogical continuity. Giambelli (Chapter 6), for instance, contrasts the banyan tree, which represents the village community as a whole, with the coconut palm, which symbolises the life cycle of individuals. Planted at the centre of the village by a priest, it becomes the focus of village life and acquires its sacred character only after having reached maturity, that is, when aerial roots appear on the buttressing trunk. Traditionally a community symbol, it is now the major symbol of national unity, used as emblem by the largest Indonesian political party. State officials regularly plant banyan trees in public ceremonies. Like Humphrey (1996: 95–8), who notes that tree groves among Daur Mongols symbolise the health and vigour of the community, Howell (Chapter 7) argues that vivacious community relations obtain among the Lio through the use of mild drugs made from palm products during transformative life-giving rituals. And if the ritual she discusses stresses the making of relationships in the present, it in no way neglects links with the past. Although the agricultural ritual she analyses establishes discontinuity between a former hunting-and-gathering way of life and the present semi-sedentary horticulturist mode of subsistence, it secures continuity between new and old village sites through the transplanting activities of priest-leaders.

Trees and Social Groups: Jural and Political Interlockings

When used to symbolise political collectivities, as in the case of the Northwest Coast Indian tribal councils examined by Mauzé (Chapter 11), or to give a ritualistic dimension to political activities such as those described by Zelter (Chapter 10), or even to draw sustainable management plans and implement conservation policies such as those analysed by Leach and Fairhead (Chapter 12), and Sivaramakrishnan (Chapter 13), trees are systematically associated with environmental health, community welfare and prosperity.[10] The chapters by Leach and Fairhead, Mauzé and Sivaramakrishnan examine the differing discourses and contested meanings that arise when localities become entangled in hierarchical relations with powerful external political and economic forces. In each case we are presented with a local population that thinks of trees mainly in terms of continuity and reproduction, but is now faced with economic development and forest conservation policies based on political and legalistic (re-)definitions of trees, forests and forest-dwelling people. Such discourses and policies often emanate from decision-makers who perceive themselves (and the societies to which they belong) as alienated from forests, and who see the regeneration of world forests, that is the re-establishment of their health and vitality damaged by pollution and indiscriminate logging, as the solution to the crises that threaten the continuation of life on the planet.[11]

Sivaramakrishnan (Chapter 13) carefully excavates the historical discourses linked to state intervention in South-west Bengal, India, and the forestry policies that have moulded native landscapes into commercial forests and constructed local populations as targets of economic and social development. What appears to the locals as a continuous landscape shaped by a wide range of agro-forestry practices has been politically and legally reinterpreted and simplified by colonial powers into two contrastive areas, forests and rice fields, which correspond to two entirely distinct managerial regimes; forests are owned by the state, and trees classified as timber. The local view of trees as crops within an agroforestry economic complex is dismissed by experts as non-scientific, and so is the current indigenous preference for exotic tree species, for native tree species have come to play an essential role in state-making. Like Latour's (1993) hybrids, they have become the social agents through which modernity, progress, the erasure of the colonial past, and the close partnership between state and community are articulated. Sivaramakrishnan also addresses the problem of cultural continuity. Transformations in the landscape greatly undermine the transmission of indigenous tree symbolism embedded in direct experience and implicit knowledge. As transmission now relies more on story-telling than on phenomenological engagement with the forest ecosystem, tree symbolism gets easily displaced by the rigid categorisations of trees and other natural elements that pervade education and politics, and regulate social life. When not discarded, indigenous beliefs are subject to processes of fixation, normalisation and incorporation not dissimilar to those affecting native tree species.

New policies on sacred groves, such as those recommended by Mitra and Pahl (1994), are a case in point. These two authors argue that sacred groves, real sanctuaries of biodiversity, are unique examples of ecological understanding and management, and that 'social fencing' religious beliefs that have encouraged people to protect vast tracts of virgin forests for centuries should be encouraged or reintroduced through government legislation. There is little understanding in their recommendation of the intricate micropolitics discussed by Sivaramakrishnan, or of the nature of people's fear of sacred groves and resident gods' wrath examined by Uchiyamada (Chapter 8). Uchiyamada's rich ethnographic data not only shed light on the shortcomings of Mitra's and Pahl's 'deifying conservation', but also illuminate the fact that the same notion of vitality and regenerative power equally underlies traditional Hindu beliefs about, and modern environmentalist views on, sacred groves. One could apply the same line of reasoning to Mehta's (1995) denunciation of 'the dendrophobia of Western culture', based on his reinterpretation of Hindu traditional beliefs in trees in the light of present-day anxiety about pollution and deforestation. Trees in Hindu thought cleanse pollution and sin. To illustrate this idea, Mehta describes the ritual marriage between a *manglik* girl (a bride-to-be whose horoscope reveals that she will bring misfortune on her prospective in-laws) and a tree. The 'wedding' purifies the girl from her ill fate; she can then marry 'secure in the knowledge that she is bringing only good luck to her husband's house' (Mehta 1995: 31). Popular green writings are full of such parallels between traditional religious beliefs and ecological wisdom (Guha 1989).

In the case of the Kissia people of the Guinean Republic, the conservation and development policies implemented by the French colonial powers throughout the nineteenth century, and by international aid donors today, trigger a different type of recategorisation. In this case, what are taken to be the remnants of original forests are in fact anthropomorphic environments resulting from daily subsistence and domestic activities. The Kissia forest islands studied by Leach and Fairhead (Chapter 12) have not preceded human settlements, but have been caused, directly or indirectly, intentionally and non-intentionally, by human occupation and local practices encouraging tree growth and forest regeneration. The two authors thus argue that the original landscape *is* savannah, not forest. Consequently, conservation policies based on the assumption that forest islands must be protected from human encroachment, predation or mismanagement are entirely wrong-headed and counter-productive. By recategorising such highly socialised environments as natural and wild (Cronon 1995), colonial administrators and present-day developers demonstrate how oblivious Westerners can be of the fact that the natural world is intricately entangled with human history, and that what we call forest today is, to a large extent, a human construction. The Kissia's implicit, practical and physical construction of forest patches within the landscape stands in marked opposition to the colonial construction of an imaginary forested wilderness and to the management plans drawn up to exploit it rationally; yet, all these representations equally refer to trees as sources of fertility, vitality and health.

Mauzé (Chapter 11), while exploring in similar ways the tensions between indigenous and Western ways of thinking about trees, adds a new dimension to the debate. She examines the changing use of tree symbolism by Northwest Coast Indians now deeply involved in ethnic and green politics, and highlights the political processes undergone by Northwest Coast Indians, whose cultures are changing from 'wood-oriented' to 'tree-obsessed'. As with the Kissia, implicit cultural meanings and traditional metaphors interlocking the life cycles of social groups and trees become explicit symbols employed to articulate competing interests as well as new politicised collective identities. For Mauzé, such a transformation must be understood in the context of influential Western discourses on forests and nature, and in relation to the wider political struggle of ethnic minorities within the Canadian nation-state. The alliance between Greens and Indians to save British Columbia's old growths is very complex. Northwest Coast Indians are seen as natural extensions of the forest,[12] and the traces of their historical presence in the rainforest, such as the trees culturally modified by their forebears, naturalised. Of course, to be granted a 'natural culture' or an inherently 'ecological' ethnic identity is advantageous in political negotiations. This, however, should not automatically imply that indigenous leaders are simply tuning their political rhetoric to new Western green ideologies. The commonality of discourse may well have to do with a shared perception of trees as sources of welfare and vitality. Anthropological studies of the impact of deforestation on indigenous communities are numerous, but very few link politico-economic analyses with changing cultural meanings and symbolism.[13] Only by doing so can we grasp the complex status of a culturally transformed tree, at once as alive as any ancient tree and as object-like as a totem pole. And, even more striking, these culturally modified trees are symbols of vitality, welfare and well-being in *both* traditional and modern belief systems.[14]

Western Tree Activism

Arboreal imagery in Western green politics is based on strikingly similar uses of trees and forests to signify environmental health and social vitality. Phrases like 'Without trees there would be no life' or 'trees are the lungs of the world' indicate that trees symbolise the regeneration of life. Moreover, as a large number of other organisms – particularly animals – depend on them, trees, even when planted, are seen to represent wilderness: 'they stand for nature' as one environmentalist remarked. I am in no way pretending to offer a thorough account of what trees mean in England today. Nor am I trying to present a detached account of the consciousness and actions of people who do something for the environment; this would inevitably reduce their certitude to a mere social construction (Brosius 1996). Although I have not carried out systematic ethnographic research on trees in England, my notebook is full of thoughts, remarks and quotations gleaned in the course of reading and conversing with a wide range of people. I find it remarkable that these snippets of recorded conversation and fragments of texts, despite the curious amalgam of scientific information, common sense, partial memories of old customs and folk beliefs, and poetic imagery, neatly cluster around a few key symbolic expressions not unlike those found among non-Western peoples. Here, too, trees are identified with humans, and admired for their great proportions, old age, potency and self-regenerating energy. With modernity taken to be the primary cause of deforestation, trees further symbolise anti-modern (i.e. anti-urban, anti-consumerist and anti-industrial) values, and, as Angie Zelter's contribution (Chapter 10) exemplifies, stand in opposition to manufactured objects, particularly to arms and cars, the symbols of death and decay.

A leading green activist, Angie Zelter eloquently expresses the evocative power of trees, which, for a non-negligible section of the Western population, stand not only for life, but also for social justice and public space. The inclusion of an activist's piece in a scholarly book may surprise some readers, but it highlights the force of tree symbolism far more effectively than many current analyses of Western environmentalist movements. The style of 'Grassroots Campaigning for the Forests' is simple and straightforward, without rhetoric or elaborate poetry. Yet the power of the message (for example, that powerful destructive forces such as war and social injustice can be resisted and healthy communities recreated) is firmly rooted in the energising morality inspired by 'the living presence of a tree'. We are reminded here of Jim Fernandez' thesis (Chapter 4) that trees provoke the moral imagination into valuing and assessing the health of human bodies and corporate communities. Trees in Angie's and her companions' political imaginary are not mere metaphorical images. Their material presence is unmistakably physical and concrete. Angie and her companions scatter the seeds of their favourite trees around the fences and over the gates of military bases. When European or North American armies are reported to have attacked and killed civilians in enemy territory, they plant trees in their backyards or on community woodlands. During anti-road protests, they protect ancient trees from destruction with their own bodies, and while camp-aigning against the arms trade, hold in their fists 'acorns germinating into little oak trees'. Not unlike the Asturians discussed by Jim Fernandez in this volume, they are engaged in the politics of presence. Their political engagement has a physical dimension that goes beyond speech. Trees are meaningful not only for what they represent, but also in themselves, as sources of actual and sensual involvement with the world. Performance, the ritualisation of theatrical, symbolic actions such as burning and burying one's car and planting a tree on the 'grave', or damaging road tarmac to plant sprouting plants in the interstices, is key to political actions that address the materiality of the world and take life as a primary issue for political intervention.

The political activist is inspired; more, she identifies with the tree. Both share the same moral qualities: patience, strength, determination, and the power of changing the surrounding landscape peacefully. Trees are models of self-regeneration and self-sufficiency, the essential qualities of modern sustainable living. As a tree campaigner told me 'both human beings and trees are composed of cells, our DNA is 95 per cent the same. The environment we both share is becoming unsuit-able for our cellular survival. We both eat the earth and drink from the earth. What affects one affects the other. We both face the same problem.' He added that, like good ecologists, trees use only solar and wind power to pull water and minerals from the earth into their bodies, using only what they need to grow and reproduce; the rest they pass into the atmosphere. Moreover, unlike the growing number of unrooted, displaced humans driven by modern urges to constantly rush about from one place to another, they are, he remarked, beings who stand in one place for hundreds of years. No wonder, then, that trees are sub-merged within human politics; their fate and the fate of disempowered human communities are one and the same. Tree campaigners do not always get involved in forest campaigns because trees mean something special to them, or because they include all classes of sentient beings within the same moral community. Not all of them would say that trees are like humans, like ancestors, relatives, or friends. Their political ideal (social justice) still firmly grounded within the human sphere, they may say that what they fight for are the human rights of forest-dwellers and local communities.[15] But even then arboreal imagery is widely used, and healthy human communities are compared to buoyant forest biodiversity. This is perhaps due to the fact that '[T]o us as to the ancients the tree is still the patron of fertility, as those have discovered to their cost who have bared the country of its forests. To us as to them it is still the thing of all things living that is endowed with the most enduring life, the most persistent vigour.' (Philpot 1994 [1897]: 91).

Europeans and North Americans have created a staggering number of associations all around the world to save trees and forests.[16] If only a few engage, like 'Reforest the Earth' to which Angie Zelter belongs, in direct action, most are involved in some kind of campaigning, and almost all have tree planting schemes. Many schools and countless local associations and church groups in England are – or have been – involved in planting trees. Local governments (parish councils, district councils and county councils) have all planning officers or councillors responsible for trees.[17] The popularity of tree planting is such that it cannot simply be explained in terms of people wanting to 'do something for the environment'. For environmental awareness takes the form of a *life-giving action*, which, as Sinden (1989: 12–13) puts it, often turns into an obsession for planting trees and then forgetting about them. This is why, he adds, 'something like half the newly planted trees in urban areas die within ten years from lack of care [i.e. lack of water and nutrients]', or simply 'because they have been badly planted'. Knight (Chapter 9) discusses the negative effects, not of indiscriminate planting, but of neglecting planted trees. Interestingly, popular mis-judgements about what giving life to trees actually amounts to are matched by serious misapprehensions of what death is for trees. For Oliver Rackham (Milner 1992: 154) most of the fifteen million trees blown down during the great storm of October 1987 ended up discarded as waste because of people's ignorance of trees. As he remarks, '[T]he majority of storm-damaged trees remained alive. Most trees were killed by clearing-up operations, not by the storm. An uprooted tree, left alone, probably had a greater chance of survival than the tree trans-planted to replace it.'

Both scholarly[18] and popular writings stress that trees in the West symbolise historical continuity, and, as such, provide a visible symbol of human society (Thomas 1984: 216). Euroamerican consciousness and sense of identity is deeply marked by the fact that they outlive human beings. Trees are ancient organisms, 'the oldest living things in our landscape'. Those estimated to be between 500 and 15,000 years old, 'ancient witnesses of events that no human now living has seen' (M. Boyer 1996:34) are visited, photographed, and regularly written about.[19] In Simon Schama's (1995) words, they have become the living and enduring memorials of historical heroes and great historical events. By extension, trees encompass human history as living links not only to the past, but also to the future. 'Trees locate us in time and place [. . .] they are our past and our future [. . .] the key to our survival' (Sinden 1989: 9), the signs of social peace, security and confidence in the future (Daniels 1988). Schama (1995: 18) contends that trees have embodied social memory in Europe for centuries, and nature myths persisted to this day, for 'the cultural habits of humanity have always made room for the sacredness of nature'. Destruction and denial have always come with worship (an idea, incidently, well supported by the Japanese case presented by Knight). Moreover, natural environments are still used to express the virtues of, and give a sense of identity to, particular political communities.

Biopolitics and Religious Symbolism

Arboreal imagery is as central to the representation of the political processes and socio-economic relations examined here as it is in the rituals discussed in the previous section. These in turn are far from being devoid of political undertones. The use of tree products in the Ankave initiation ritual, which articulates existential concerns about birth, growth and maturity with the political economy of gender difference and clan membership, is unmistakably political. On Nusa Penida and Bali, high-status families traditionally exercised mono-polistic rights over local coconut production. Therefore, 'newcomers', their clients, entirely depended on their good will to access the large supplies of coconuts needed for the performance of life crisis rituals. Furthermore, given that the generative power of these rituals is closely related to the use of coconut water, which expresses favourable ancestral dispositions toward the living, newcomers are blessed with the water, not of their own ancestors, but of their 'patrons'. For the Lio, palm wine, betel, areca nuts, and sugar palm branches are politically signif-icant as products triggering communal feelings and expressing collective identity.[20] Moreover, the Lio agriculturalist mode of subsistence in some way becomes a political charter. In the Japanese case, the homology between the stem family, the house and the forest plantation is most strongly associated with wealthy landowning families. A number of recent African ethnographies (for example, Argenti 1996; de Boeck 1994; Feeley-Harnick 1991; van Beck and Banga 1992) could also be mentioned for their focus on the political dimension of tree symbolism.

The significance and widespread character of tree symbolism become immediately apparent when religious representations and political discourses are juxtaposed. And so does the fact that the religious and political symbolism examined in this book is primarily concerned with the notions of life and death applied to individual bodies and corporate identities. For instance, the loss of biodiversity and forest cover is simultaneously perceived by many as scientific information and as loss of vitality and regenerative power. Both aspects have influenced policy-making. Two questions, thus, must be asked: Why are trees so recurrently used to symbolise life and vitality? What types of knowledge constitute the basis on which such symbolic constructs are elaborated?

The Vitality and Self-regenerative Powers of Trees

Trees as Givers of Energy

Trees fill Angie Zelter with peace, strength, and the energy to fight. She and many campaigners feel that trees communicate spiritual energy. In a dichotomised symbolic field, trees stand on the side of life, while roads represent death and *anomie*. Various contributions to this book explore the recurring connection between trees, vitality, strength, and self-generating power. Traditionally, Northwest Coast Indians (Mauzé, Chapter 11) absorbed the inner force of trees (particularly of cedars, which they called the 'trees of life') simply by touching the bark. For many indigenous communities, ancient forests threatened by loggers have become symbols of strength, renewal, historical continuity and welfare. Balinese people locate the vital energy of the coconut palm in its seed (Giambelli, Chapter 6), while, for the Bunaq of East Timor, the potential for life and growth is located in the root, considered the most alive part of a plant (Friedberg 1990). Humphrey (1996: 95–8) notes that the Daur Mongols use the same word for root, growth point, ancestor, shaman and spirit. They think of trees as energy-giving, and plant evergreens in their cemeteries. For the Ankave (Bonnemère, Chapter 5), who locate the energy of ritual trees in the fruit juice men prepare, vitality is not a natural given, but the product of male intervention. Japanese foresters admire the determination to survive and the vigour of trees whose roots penetrate through rocks to find soil nutrients (Knight, Chapter 9).

In South India, the vitality of trees is seen as emanating from the supernatural life force of ghosts, the wandering spirits of the recently dead (Uchiyamada, Chapter 8). When properly controlled by the living, the life force is transitory and transforming, and the trees associated with it (the coconut planted on the cremation pit, the jack-fruit tree under which the funerary urn is buried, or the pipal-mango tree in the temple yard) sacred and harmless. But when dead spirits are prevented from transforming, hence remaining ghosts for ever (a common fate for Untouchables), their life force engenders trees that grow wild, and give rise to highly fertile, but extremely dangerous, sacred groves. The life force Uchiyamada examines in such great detail is frightening and highly ambivalent. Its regenerative power comes from the dead. In the other examples, the vitality of trees is not ambivalent, but uncertain and open to speculation. The regenerative power may be located in the roots, in the fruit, in the buds, or in the sap. Planted trees may be seen as having less vitality than trees growing wild. In her seminal article on Trobriand canoe making, Nancy Munn (1977) presents an extreme manifestation of the 'tree paradox'. Here trees do not envigorate humans, but humans give life to slow, heavy and immobile trees by transforming them into swift, vigorous and slippery canoes. The wooden artefact is more alive than the tree. The youths who decorate a canoe instil their vigour into it. It is human labour that renders the artefact animate, and makes it similar to the human body.

Wood as Living Matter

If either roots, buds, leaves, fruit, or bark may stand for vitality, regeneration and growth, the symbolisation of wood, a substance understood to be at once living and lifeless, is usually far more ambiguous. Wood, particularly of the trunk, is often equated with bone. A coconut palm, once cut, receives a different name on Nusa Penida, not, as Giambelli (Chapter 6) explains, to establish a contrast between 'alive' and 'dead', but, rather, to distinguish the fruit-bearing tree from the tree that no longer produces coconuts but is still alive as wood. In other words, once cut, the tree is not dead, but sterile. Traditionally, Northwest Coast Indians did not fell trees for wood, but used fire to remove large planks from standing cedar or fir trees. Thanks to the natural preservative oils in the heartwood and to their fungicidal properties

(Peattie 1991), these trees, known today as 'culturally modified trees' or CMTs, would not decay; more, they continued to live and grow. Mauzé (Chapter 11) notes that bark collection did not impede the continuous growth of cedar trees either. She adds that objects made of wood were considered alive because the wood, although transformed, remained basically the same, a living substance. Interestingly, today's indigenous communities seem to grant far more symbolic power to culturally modified trees (CMTs) than to wooden artefacts.

The idea that wood and wooden objects are 'alive' because trees are living organisms is extremely widespread.[21] Japanese foresters say that wood 'breathes' as it absorbs and expels atmospheric humidity. They also explicitly state that to transform a tree into wood is to give the tree a second life, which will generally be of the same duration as the first one. So a tree that has stood for a hundred years produces wood for house beams that will last a hundred years; a tree that has stood for a thousand years produces wood for temple foundations that will last a thousand years. But a tree can live a second life only if cut in its full maturity. This is why, as Knight (Chapter 9) reports, foresters are critical of both modern forestry practices and modern conservation policies. Trees in forest plantations are cut too early, i.e. before having reached their optimum age. And environmentalists who protest against the felling of old trees are in fact advocating their decay and corruption. However, despite the belief that tree-cutting is a life-giving action, foresters and other professionals involved in the timber industry see themselves as life-takers who must ask forgiveness of and propitiate the spirits of the trees they have destroyed by sponsoring religious rituals and offerings.

The Uncertain Nature of Life in Trees

The fact is that plants in general and trees in particular die very slowly. The contrast with animal death, a much more sudden business, is evident. Even if animal death is somewhat processual, there is a clear-cut, definite and irreversible passage from the moment when the animal moves and breathes to that when it stops moving and breathing; from the moment when its heart beats, to that when the bloodstream stops running. A live body is warm, a dead one stiff and cold. Botanists agree that trees do not have a 'natural' life-span like animals; this is why many species take as long to decline as to grow. Raynal-Roques (1994: 168–72) notes that the trunk of a tree may be intensely alive, but is composed of a mixture of dead and live tissues. And, as the ecologist Patrick Blandin (1995: 70) so judiciously puts it, if 'trees live a long life [. . .], they, in some ways, start dying while keeping on living'.[22] A Californian Bristlecone pine may be 5,000 years old, but parts of its slow-growing trunk and roots already died centuries ago. With only a small section of the root system still functioning, water is sent up 'through a single sector of healthy sapwood to a few needled limbs while the rest of the tree has become lifeless' (Milner 1992: 122). Wood comprises both dead and live cells. Under certain conditions cut branches stuck back into the soil can root (Raynal-Roques 1994: 294–5). Fairhead and Leach (Chapter 12) mention that Kissia people make indirect use of this biological property in their forest management practices. Until further research is undertaken, the question as to whether such utilitarian practices may be related to beliefs surrounding the transformation of the Cross into a living tree (Brosse 1989; Guénon 1931), or to folktales about wooden artefacts that transform back into fruiting trees (Bouras 1977), cannot, of course, receive a satisfactory answer.

If in some cultural representations trees are alive but inanimate (Humphrey 1996: 95; Munn 1977), in others they may be seen as animate but not quite alive, or as the dwelling places of spirits who are alive. In all cases, however, trees appear to be potent symbols of vitality precisely because their status as living organisms is so uncertain. Life travels in them from seed to fruit to seed (see Giambelli, Chapter 6, for a particularly rich and developed example) without full individuation. Trees do not have a life, they propagate life.

Symbols of Life or Obscure Objects of Knowledge?

The ethnographic materials so far examined indicate a strong correlation between the symbolic significance of trees and speculations about death and life. As seemingly everlasting biological organisms, trees appear to transcend death because they are not really alive in the first place, at least not in the same way as animals are. However, the symbolic representations presented here play with this ambiguity only to reaffirm one-sidedly that trees stand for life, vitality and self-regeneration. To what extent do symbolic systems make use of the strange biological destiny of trees, and how are we to interpret the fact that trees 'physicalise' the human wish for transcendence? No definite answers are offered to these questions by Bloch, Fernandez and Ellen, whose chapters (Chapters 2, 4 and 3 respectively) explore alternative, and to some extent complementary, avenues. Instead of propounding a single interpretative framework, this book presents tree symbolism from the standpoint of three major fields of analysis of natural symbols, symbolic anthropology (Fernandez, Chapter 4), ethnoscience (Ellen, Chapter 3), and cognitive anthropology (Bloch, Chapter 2). Whereas Bloch discusses the ambiguous status of trees as living organisms with reference to the concept of life, Ellen approaches the issue of tree symbolism by focusing on the curious prototypicality of palms. Fernandez, for whom language, experience and the power of imagination are central to social life, stresses the links between tree metaphors and the moral values they evoke.

Life-giving Plants, the Power of Imagination and the Concept of Life

In their chapters, Bloch, Fernandez and Ellen all explore, with various degrees of explicitness, the difficulties encountered in applying cognitive theory to an anthropological understanding of tree symbolism. As the ethnographic examples I presented illustrate, tree symbols materialise the living process at three levels: that of individuals, that of communities and social groups, and that of life itself.[23] The conceptual status of trees is far from being self-evident. Moreover, and as a number of chapters dwelling upon the intricate interlockings of human life cycles and the life cycles of trees or forest succession suggest, it is often impossible to decide what belongs to human history, and what pertains to ecological conditions. Mounting evidence from historical ecology research (Balée 1994; Crumley 1993; Fairhead and Leach 1996, and Rival in press/a) and studies in environmental history (for example, Cronon 1991 and Rackham 1986) tend to show that trees and forests are not naturally given categories; they result from the dialectical unfolding of historical and ecological processes. Finally, the symbolic use of trees as signs of vitality, life, growth and fecundity, the focus of this volume, is primarily manifest in figures of speech and ritual actions that cannot be interpreted from one exclusive standpoint.

Ellen (Chapter 3) chooses to explore the functional value of a special kind of woody plant, palms. He invites us to wonder why palms appear to be symbolically treated as if they were trees, which they are not in either botanical or folk-botanical terms. He examines their classificatory status with a view to offering a more general reflection on the central role of prototypes and life forms in biological classifications. Ellen applies himself to identifying the utilitarian considerations that underpin the symbolic centrality of palms as exemplary trees, and concludes that the position of palms in ethno-botanical classifications is largely defined by social functions. If pragmatic interest is what drives the classification of palms, their symbolic power should be primarily influenced, not by specific and innate cognitive abilities to categorise nature, but, rather, by their economic and cultural prominence. For him, therefore, natural symbols arise within, and change through, historical processes, a position which leads him to be equivocal about Atran's (1990) assertion that trees constitute a 'life form' corresponding to innate ecological knowledge. In answer to Ellen, Atran (Medin *et al.* in press) would almost certainly insist that the category 'tree' is not defined with reference to the use and function of an artefactual product (timber), but to specific biological properties. He might add that, if goals and interests do affect the classification of species (because words merge concepts and lexical entries together),[24] they do not affect reasoning about species and their underlying, essential properties. Though Ellen argues that palms are treated as symbolic trees because they are 'life-giving plants' of enormous use-value, he would also maintain that wood/tree polysemy suggests that the great economic and material importance of wood in most human societies must play some role in enhancing the life form.

What strikes Fernandez (Chapter 4), who refuses to separate the emotional from the intellectual, or the poetic from the cognitive, is that in many societies and cultures trees express health and vitality. As the empirical world gets symbolically elaborated, it is used in the creation of moral orders and moral communities. Tree symbolism helps giving meaning to social life, and facilitates the imagining of corporate bodies full of vitality. Like Bachelard, and against Atran, Fernandez takes common sense to be intrinsically symbolic because rooted in experience, that is, in perceptions that are both phenomenal and sensible. This leads him to contend that interpreting tree symbolism without analysing the power of words and the force of experience is self-defeating. Language structures the way we think religiously about the natural world. Language, essentially a historical process,[25] blurs all distinctions between everyday knowledge of the world and religious representation; the two become inseparable in a word like 'cedar tree' for Northwest Coast Indians, or 'coconut palm' for the Balinese. This is why Fernandez opposes the reductionist view of Deleuze and Guattari (1987), who see tree metaphors as inherently Western and patriarchal; the tree of knowledge (Maturana and Varela 1992), for example, has nothing to do with hierarchy. But this is also why political discourses, legal definitions and institutional categorisations fix and essentialise the nature of trees in relation to social groups, ending all speculation about their ambiguous status. What matters analytically for Fernandez, however, is that social action is motivated by the power, force and vitality of the verb; and the tree is a potent symbol because of its power to evoke – and hence mobilise – beyond our intuitions about trees in the world, and beyond our scientific knowledge of trees, the social energy out of which moral communities are constituted.

The constitution of moral communities through the use of tree metaphors is, in a sense, precisely what Bloch (Chapter 2) aims at explaining. Bloch, for whom all religious morality has the propensity to supersede organic life, argues that if trees are ubiquitous symbols of life, a cross-cultural analysis of tree symbolism must start with an examination of local theories of life and death.[26] For life, far from being an unproblematic quality or essential property, is a notion open to speculation, which gets communicated through semantic channels shaped by the politics of performance and persuasion. In other words, the 'concept' of life is not a cognitive issue. In his comparative study of the symbolism of initiation rites and sacrifice, Bloch (1992b) identifies a recurring ritual structure through which the symbolic reproduction of human society and of all the organisms on which it depends is achieved through the rejection of natural life-processes such as the biological cycles of growth and decay (and death), and the promotion of conquering forms of transcendental vitality and mystical fertility. In their endless elaboration of the difference between living beings and other types of objects, religious representations, he continues, do not draw closely on concepts, but, rather, relate to other mental representations.[27] They can, therefore, never be entirely and definitely interpreted – a conclusion also reached by Sperber (1996:100). Bloch shares Boyer's thesis that religious representations combine explicit counter-intuitive principles with implicit biological ones – the latter constraining the former – but departs from his (as well as Sperber's and Atran's) implicit assumption that the difference between a living organism and an artefact, or between a live and a dead organism, is ontological. Life, Bloch argues, is not something we intuitively know about, by simply using our common sense. The distinction between life and death, far from being clear-cut, is graded, and always uncertain.

Going back to trees, as the ethnographic chapters amply illustrate, that trees serve as concrete and material representations of life, from its most physical to its most abstract connotations, has been amply demonstrated. Tree symbolism is, however, paradoxical. Like human beings, trees are, on the one hand, subject to processes of growth and maturation. But, on the other hand, the life of trees, with its enduring quality that transcends the finality of human life, never really ends, or seems to continue under a different form. Religious beliefs about these extraordinary plants do not really violate rational understanding and common sense, but, rather, elaborate on, and play with, their ambiguous status. Trees are dubious candidates as living organisms, and wood is not object-like; both are at once somewhat alive, and somewhat dead. This is, perhaps, the key to the correct interpretation of wood/tree polysemy. Metarepresentations such as 'trees symbols of life' do not necessarily violate intuitive expectations about trees, or entertain counter-intuitive claims about them. What they convey, rather, is that life is really mysterious and awe-inspiring; it is not fully understood, it is never entirely interpreted, and it can never be essentialised. Neither life nor death constitute natural, innate conceptual categories. And this is the case for trees as for humans.

Notes

1. Recent authoritative contributions on animal symbolism are Willis (1990), Ingold (1988), Clutton-Brock (1989), and Morphy (1989). Two edited volumes proposing to approach landscapes from an anthropological perspective are Hirsch and O'Hanlon (1995) and Bender (1993). On domesticated crops, my personal and limited selection from a vast and rich body of literature includes the classic essays by Haudricourt (1962, 1964), the monographs of Descola (1994) and C. Hugh-Jones (1979), and the two recent edited volumes by D. Harris and G. Hillman (1989), and D. Harris (1996).

2. Although all his sources are secondary, many are based either on ethnographic accounts, or on colonial and missionary sources equally used by anthropologists. The cultures he cites are located in Sudan, Nigeria, India, Burma, Formosa, Afghanistan, and the Solomon Islands, as well as various other regions of Africa, South Asia and South-east Asia.

3. The longest period of peace one could reasonably expect for one's bodily remains in the average conventional urban cemetery is thirty years, after which graves are cleared to make room for new corpses. In Ueli Sauter's forest cemetery, a 'tree of life' costs between 3,000 and 7,000 Swiss Francs. Those who cannot afford it may purchase for 750 Swiss Francs a plant or shrub to be planted on the perimeter of the 'peace forest' (Klett 1994: vi). Many thanks to Klauss Seeland and Christin Kocher-Schmid for making this information available.

4. See Humphrey (1996), who notes that the Daur Mongols believe that blood comes out of old trees (especially birches), which then become spirits.

5. Juillerat (1986: 46,67) explains that for the Yafar the coconut inflorescence symbolises the woman's body; its sap is called the 'flower's blood'. He adds that Yafar belonging to the 'female moiety', whose totem is the coconut palm, are called the 'children of the vagina's blood', while those belonging to the 'male moiety', whose totem is the sago palm, are called the 'children of the penis' blood'.

6. For Melanesia, see among others Munn (1977 and 1986), Juillerat (1986), Herdt (1987), Damon (1996), Coiffier (1994), Gell (1973). For other regions, see in particular Calame-Griaule (1969 and 1980), Feeley-Harnick (1991), de Boeck (1994), Bloch (1992a), Argenti (1996).

7. This is a point entirely missed by Judith Butler (1993: 31) in her etymological discussion of the Greek term for matter and wood (timber), *hyle*.

8. It is not impossible that Deleuze and Guattari's (1987) well-known opposition between the Western arborescent model and the Eastern rhizomorphic model took its origin in their rejection of Jung's ideas. Maturana and Varela (1992), Bouquet (1996), and Strathern (1995) have all commented on the centrality of logical trees in the representation of thought processes, understanding and relationships. Any of these authors could be used to show how reductionist Deleuze's and Guattari's dualism is. See also Fernandez' discussion of non-hierarchical tree metaphors (Chapter 4) and Ellen's comments on Deleuze and Guattari (Chapter 3) in this volume.

9. For an insightful analysis of plant metaphors and ties of filiation see Fox (1971) and Gell (1973).

10. The welfare of a forest estate often becomes the material expression of a community's health; so tree-cutting can mirror social disorder, as Pamela Leonard's ethnography of China's Sichuan region (Leonard 1995) so well illustrates. In the three historical periods she examines (the Great Leap Forward, the Cultural Revolution, and the present day), the treatment of trees is caused by, and reflects, society's orderly or disorderly state. Villagers explain the massive destruction of trees in the late 1950s as a reaction to the 'Old Society'. The aim of the revolution was to destroy old ways, including the peasant conservation ethic and concern for kin and descendants. See Knight (Chapter 9, this volume) for a comparable case in Japan, where the social chaos caused by massive upland out-migration is reflected in environmental disorder, particularly well expressed by the condition of abandoned forest plantations.

11. See for example the UKFN Forests Memorandum and Forest Charter (UKFN 1994). For a similar, albeit more utopian, political message, see the pamphlet of the 'Movement for Compassionate Living' written by Kathleen Jannaway (1991), which advocates the complete phasing out of animal farming

and the release of pastures to forests. The rationale for this is that trees, unlike other crops, can meet nearly all human needs while at the same time performing an essential ecological role. Morover, a tree-based culture would automatically generate self-reliant, sustainable and democratic village communities. It is proposed that the 'coming age of the tree', a new age of abundant living and peace, should be the alternative to the 'present wasteful and destructive lifestyles of the dominant culture'.

12. Slater (1995: 130) talks about ecological discourses which represent the Kayapos as embodying the Amazon forest.

13. For an excellent survey of the current literature on the topic, see Sponsel, Bailey and Headland (1996). Turner (1967: 21–2), who argues that the milk tree, the emblem of the Ndembu, signifies the unity and continuity of Ndembu society both as a religious and a political symbol, and mentions that young literate Ndembu compare the milk tree to the British flag displayed above colonial headquarters, would almost certainly give much importance to the symbolic dimension of present-day environmental discourses and forest conservation policies.

14. For a comparative case in Oregon, see Proctor (1995). For an alternative indigenous position see the Canadian contributions to the special issue of *Cultural Survival Quarterly* edited by Bray and Irvine (1993).

15. For a discussion of the closely related notion of environmental justice, see Di Chiro 1995.

16. To name just a few in Britain: World Rainforest Movement, World Forest Action, Trees for Survival, Trees for Life, Tree Spirit, Tree People, Tree Group, Task Force Trees, Society for the Preservation of the Rain Forest Environment, Save the Forests Save the Planets, Replanting Vietnam, Reforest the Earth, The Reading Tree Club (Milner 1992: 161–70). Some of these tree organisations combine campaigning and tree planting with more recreational and spiritual activities. They may organise visits and tours of the country's tree heritage. Others are more inclined to educational and cultural activities, such as reviving old, traditional tree festivals, or creating new ones to celebrate the beauty and value of local trees.

17. Legislation for the protection of trees (resulting in a great many trees being covered by more than one form of legal protection) comprises: (1) wild life legislation and civil law; (2) TPOs (Tree Preservation Orders); (3) designated Conservation Areas; (4) conditions attached to planning permission; and (5) felling licence control (Sinden 1989).

18. The historical and cultural origins of Western ideas about, and attitudes towards, trees is the subject of outstanding scholarship, from which the following are unmissable landmarks: Schama (1995), Cosgrove and Daniels (1988), Thomas (1984), Cronon (1983, 1991, 1995) and Harrison (1992).

19. She adds: 'This memory is what touches us even more than a tree's extreme age, its species or its beauty. [. . .] As soon as a tree lives beyond [its] age, [it] becomes a parable for the passing of time, an image of the living and yet petrified memory' (M. Boyer 1996: 38).

20. For a similar use of palm wine among the Gour of Ivory Coast, see Haxaire (1996).

21. This point has been made by a number of authors working on art and material culture. See for instance Küchler (1993) and Argenti (1996). Giambelli, this volume, Chapter 6, makes similar observations. In our own Western context, the common idea that wood is a 'noble' matter (like leather) implies that it is alive and 'breathes'. But in the oppositional discourse of environmentalists, wood and wooden artefacts are considered dead objects expressing consumer values. Only standing trees (particularly the oldest ones) are perceived to be alive.

22. My translation from the French: 'les arbres vivent longtemps, mais, d'une certaine manière, ils commencent à mourir tout en restant vivants'.

23. The latter, a far more abstract notion mainly found in mythologies attached to the cosmic tree, is not discussed in this book. The cosmic tree, also known as the tree of life or *axis mundi* has been the subject of a vast body of philosophical, theological and mythological writings. See Brosse (1989) for an excellent overview. For ethnographic examples, see Hastrup (1981) and Rival (1997).

24. In the same vein, Sperber (1996: 199) notes that 'in certain conditions, the mere fact of labelling a living object modifies the way in which the child will categorise this object'.

25. As Humphrey (1996: 108) puts it, history enters into cognition through giving names to pre-linguistic concepts.

26. Schama (1995: 15) and Harrison (1992, 1995) have shown the historical depth of the symbolic connection between trees and human mortality in Western consciousness. According to Harrison, Euroamericans see the human condition as being defined by an ecology of finitude, from which they desperately try to escape: 'Nature knows how to die, but human beings know mostly how to kill as a way of failing to become their ecology. When we do not speak our death to the world we speak death to the world' (Harrison 1992: 249). So, '[W]hen we surpass ourselves the most, we reach out towards our death, we in fact reach out toward nature, for nature, ultimately, is the place where our death is at home' (Harrison 1995: 436).

27. Lakoff and Turner (1989) explore this phenomenon through the multiplicity of metaphors used to express the meaning of death and life, both in poetic and ordinary language. As they remark, '[L]ife and death are such all-encompassing matters that there can be no single conceptual metaphor that will enable us to comprehend them' (Lakoff and Turner 1989: 2).

References

Ackerman, R., *J. G. Frazer, his life and work*, Cambridge: Cambridge University Press, 1987

Argenti, N., The material culture of power in Oku, North West Province, Cameroon, unpublished doctoral dissertation, University of London, 1996

Atran, S., *Cognitive foundations of natural history*, Cambridge: Cambridge University Press, 1990

Balée, W., *Footprints of the forest, Ka'apor ethnobotany. The historical ecology of plant utilization by an Amazonian people*, New York: Columbia University Press, 1994

Bender, B. (ed.), *Landscape. Politics and perspectives*, Oxford: Berg, 1993

Blandin, P., 'Dans la forêt des idées reçues', in D. Meiller (ed.), *La forêt, les savoirs et le citoyen*, Paris: ANCR, 1995

Bloch, M., 'What goes without saying: the conceptualization of Zafimaniry society', in A. Kuper (ed.), *Conceptualizing society*, London: Routledge, 1992a

—— *Prey into the Hunter. The politics of religious experience*, Cambridge: Cambridge University Press, 1992b

Bouquet, M., 'Family trees and their affinities: the visual imperative of the genealogical diagram', *Journal of the Royal Anthropological Institute* 2(1), 1996, pp. 43–66

Bouras, A., La place de l'arbre dans les fêtes écologiques et sociales roumaines, MS, Paris, 1977

Boyer, M. F., *Tree-talk, memory, myths and timeless customs*, London: Thames & Hudson, 1996

Boyer, P., 'Cognitive Aspects of Religious Symbolism', in P. Boyer (ed.), *Cognitive Aspects of Religious Symbolism*, Cambridge: Cambridge University Press, 1993a

—— 'Cognitive constraints on cultural representations: natural ontologies and religious ideas', in L. A. Hirshfeld and S. Gelman (eds), *Mapping the mind: domain specificity in cognition and culture*, Cambridge: Cambridge University Press, 1993b

—— *The naturalness of religious ideas. A cognitive theory of religion*, Cambridge: Cambridge University Press, 1994

—— 'What makes anthropomorphism natural: intuitive ontology and cultural representation', *Journal of the Royal Anthropological Institute* 2(1), 1996, pp. 83–98

Bray, D. and D. Irvine (eds), 'Resource and sanctuary. Indigenous peoples, ancestral rights and the forests of the Americas', special issue of *Cultural Survival Quarterly* 17(1), 1993

Brosius, P., 'Analyses and interventions: anthropological engagements with environmentalism', San Francisco: Paper presented at the Annual Meeting of the American Anthropology Association, 1996

Brosse, J., *Mythologie des arbres*, Paris: Payot, 1989

Butler, J., *Bodies that matter. On the discursive limits of 'sex'*, New York: Routledge, 1993

Calame-Griaule, C., *Le thème de l'arbre dans les contes africains*, Paris: CNRS, 1969

—— 'L'arbre et l'imaginaire', *Cahiers Orstom* (série sciences humaines) XVII (3-4), pp. 315-20, 1980

Carrier, J. (ed.), *Occidentalism. Images of the West*, Oxford: Clarendon Press, 1995

Clutton-Brock, J. (ed.), *The walking larder. Patterns of Predation, Pastoralism and Predation*, London: Unwin Hyman, 1989

Coiffier, C., *L' Ecorce et la moelle du rotin. Conception iatmul de l'univers*, unpublished doctoral dissertation, Paris: EHESS, 1994

Cosgrove, D. and S. Daniels (eds), *The iconography of landscape*, Cambridge: Cambridge University Press, 1988

Cronon, W. (ed.), *Changes in the land: Indians and colonists and the ecology of New England*, New York: Hill & Wang, 1983

—— *Nature's metropolis: Chicago and the Great West*, New York: Norton, 1991

—— *Uncommon Ground. Rethinking the human place in nature*, New York: Norton, 1995

Crumley, C. (ed.), *Historical ecology. Cultural knowledge and changing landscapes*, Santa Fé: School of American Research Press, 1993

Damon, F., 'Selective anthropomorphization: Trees in the Northeast Kula ring', San Francisco: Paper presented at the Annual Meeting of the American Anthropology Association, 1996

Daniels, S., 'The political iconography of woodland in later Georgian England', in D. Cosgrove and S. Daniels (eds), *The iconography of landscape*, Cambridge: Cambridge University Press, 1988

de Boeck, F., 'Of trees and kings: politics and metaphor among the Aluund of Southwest Zaïre, *American Ethnologist* 21 (3), 1994, pp. 451-73

Deleuze, G. and F. Guattari, *A thousand plateaus. Capitalism and shyzophrenia*, London: The Athlone Press, 1987

Descola, P., *In the society of nature. A native ecology in Amazonia*, Cambridge: Cambridge University Press, 1994

di Chiro, G., 'Nature as community: the convergences of environmental and social justice', in W.Cronon (ed.), *Uncommon Ground. Rethinking the human place in nature*, New York: Norton, 1995

Douglas, M., *Natural symbols. Explorations in cosmology*, New York: Vintage Books, 1970

—— *Thought styles. Critical essays on good taste*, London: Sage, 1996

Durkheim, E., *The elementary forms of the religious life*, London: Allen & Unwin, 1976 [1915]

Durkheim, E. and M. Mauss, *Primitive classification*, trans. Rodney Needham, London, Cohen and West, 1963 [1903]

Fairhead, J. and M. Leach, *Misreading the African landscape: society and ecology in a forest–savanna mosaic*, Cambridge: Cambridge University Press, 1996

Feeley-Harnick, G., *A green estate: restoring independence in Madagascar*, Washington, DC: Smithsonian Inst. Press, 1991

Fox, J., 'Sister's child as plant. Metaphors in an idiom of consanguinity', in R. Needham (ed.), *Rethinking kinship and marriage*, London: Tavistock, 1971

Frazer, J., *Aftermath. A supplement to the golden bough*, London: Tavistock, 1955

Friedberg, C., *Le savoir botanique des Bunaq: percevoir et classer dans le Haut Lamaknen (Timor, Indonésie)*, Paris: Museum National d'Histoire Naturelle, 1990

Gell, A., *Metamorphosis of the cassowaries*, London: Athlone, 1973

—— 'Vogel's net. Traps as artworks and artworks as traps', *Material Culture* 1(1), 1996, pp. 15–38

Graves, R., *The white goddess*, London: Faber & Faber, 1990

Guénon, R., *Le symbolisme de la croix*, Paris: Gallimard, 1931

Guha, R., *The Unquiet woods. Ecological change and peasant resistance in the Himalaya*, New Delhi: Oxford University Press, 1989

Harris, D. (ed.), *The origin and spread of agriculture and pastoralism in Eurasia*, London: UCL Press, 1996

Harris, D. and G. Hillman (eds), *Foraging and Farming. The Evolution of Plant Exploitation*, London: Unwin Hyman, 1989

Harrison, R., *Forests, the shadow of civilization*, Chicago: Chicago University Press, 1992

—— 'Toward a philosophy of nature', in W. Cronon (ed.), *Uncommon Ground. Rethinking the human place in nature*, New York: Norton, 1995

Hastrup, K., 'Cosmology and society in medieval Iceland', *Ethnologia Scandinavia*, 1981, pp. 13–78

Haudricourt, A., 'Domestication des animaux, culture des plantes et traitement d'autrui', *L'Homme* II, 1962, pp. 40–57

—— 'Nature et culture dans la civilisation de l'igname: l'origine des clônes et des clans', *L'Homme* IV, 1964, pp. 93–104

Haxaire, C., 'Le vin de palme et la noix de kola: nourritures paradoxales', in C. M. Hladik *et al.* (eds), *L'alimentation en forêt tropicale. Interactions bioculturelles et perspectives de développement*, Vol. II, Paris: Unesco, 1996

Herdt, G., *The Sambia. Ritual and gender in New Guinea*, New York: Holt, Rinehart & Winston, 1987

Hirsch, E. and M. O'Hanlon (eds), *The anthropology of landscape. Perspectives on place and space*, Oxford: Clarendon Press, 1995

Howell, S., 'Many contexts, many meanings? Gendered values of the northern Lio of Flores, Indonesia', *Journal of the Royal Anthropological Institute* 2, 1996, pp. 253–69

Hugh-Jones, C., *From the milk river. Spatial and temporal processes in Northwest Amazon*, Cambridge: Cambridge University Press, 1979

Humphrey, C. with U. Onon, *Shamans and elders. Experience, knowledge and power among the Daur Mongols*, Oxford: Clarendon Press, 1996

Ingold, T. (ed.), *What Is an Animal?*, London: Unwin Hyman, 1988

Ingold, T., 'Temporality of the landscape', *World Archaeology* 25, 1993, pp. 152–74

James, W., *The listening ebony: moral knowledge, religion and power among the Uduk of Sudan*, Oxford: Clarendon Press, 1988

Jannaway, K., *Abundant living in the coming age of the tree*, Leatherhead, Surrey: Movement for Compassionate Living, 1991

Juillerat, B., *Les enfants du sang. Société, reproduction et imaginaire en Nouvelle Guinée*, Paris: Maison des Sciences de l'Homme, 1986

Jung, C., *Alchemical studies*, London: Routledge and Kegan Paul, 1968

Klett, R., 'Im "Friedwald" auf ewig dem Leben verbunden' *Südkurier* 95, 26.04.1994, p. vi

Küchler, S., 'Landscape as memory: the mapping of process and its representation in a Melanesian society', in B. Bender (ed.), *Landscapes. Politics and perspectives*, Oxford: Berg, 1993

Lakoff, G. and M. Turner, *More than cool reason: a field guide to poetic metaphors*, Chicago: Chicago University Press, 1989

Latour, B., *We have never been modern*, translated by C. Porter, New York: Harvester Wheatsheaf, 1993 [1991]

Leonard, P., The political landscape of a Sichuan village, Unpubl. PhD Thesis, University of Cambridge, 1995

MacLennan, J. F., 'The worship of animals and plants – Part I', *The Fortnightly Review* 6, 1869, pp. 407–27

Maturana, H. and F. Varela, *The tree of knowledge. The biological roots of human understanding*, Boston: Shambhala, 1992

Medin, D., E. Lynch, J. Coley and S. Atran, 'Categorization and reasoning among tree experts: do all roads lead to Rome?', *Cognitive Psychology*, in press

Mehta, G., 'A culture of trees', *Resurgence* 168, 1995, pp. 31–5

Miller, D., *Material culture and mass consumption*, Oxford: Basil Blackwell, 1987

Milner, J. E., *The tree book*, London: Collins & Brown, 1992

Mitra, A. and S. Pahl, 'The spirit of the sanctuary', *Down to Earth*, 31, 1994, pp. 21–36

Morphy, H. (ed.), *Animals into Art*, London: Unwin Hyman, 1989

Munn, N., 'The spatiotemporal transformation of Gawa canoes', *Journal de la Société des Océanistes*, 33, 1977, pp. 39–52

—— *The fame of Gawa: a symbolic study of value transformation in a Massim (PNG) society*, Cambridge: Cambridge University Press, 1986

Peattie, D. C., *A natural history of western trees*, Boston: Houghton Mifflin, 1991 [1953]

Philpot, J.H., *The sacred tree, or the tree in religion and myth*, Felinfach: Llanerch Pub., 1994 [1897]

Proctor, J., 'Whose nature? The contested moral terrain of ancient forests', in W. Cronon (ed.), *Uncommon Ground. Rethinking the human place in nature*, New York: Norton, 1995

Rackham, O., *The history of the British countryside*, London: Dent, 1986

Raynal-Roques, A., *La botanique redécouverte*, Paris: Belin, 1994

Rival, L., 'The Huaorani and their Trees: Managing and Imagining the Ecuadorian Rain Forest', in K. Seeland (ed.), *Nature is Culture. Indigenous Knowledge and Socio-Cultural Aspects of Trees and Forests in Non-European Cultures*, London: Intermediate Technology Publications, 1997

—— 'Domestication as a Historical and Symbolic Process: Wild Gardens and Cultivated Forests in the Ecuadorian Amazon', in W. Balée (ed.), *Principles of Historical Ecology*, New York: Columbia University Press, in press/a

—— [*Forthcoming*] 'Marginality with a Difference: How the Huaorani Remain Autonomous, Preserve their Sharing Relations and Naturalize Outside Economic Powers', in M. Biesele and P. Schweitzer (eds), *Hunters and Gatherers in the Modern Context: Conflict, Resistance and Self-Determination*, Oxford: Berghahn Books of Providence, R.I., in press/b

Schama, S., *Landscape and memory*, London: Harper Collins, 1995

Sinden, N., *In a nutshell. A manifesto for trees and a guide to growing and protecting them*, London: Common Ground, 1989

Slater, C., 'Amazonia as edenic narrative', in W. Cronon (ed.), *Uncommon*

Ground. Rethinking the human place in nature, New York: Norton, 1995

Sperber, D., *La contagion des idées. Théorie naturaliste de la culture*, Paris: Odile Jacob, 1996

Sponsel, L., R. Bailey and T. Headland, 'Anthropological perspectives on the causes, consequences and solutions of deforestation', in L. Sponsel, T. Headland and R. Bailey (eds), *Tropical deforestation. The human dimension*, New York: Columbia University Press, 1996

Strathern, M., 'Out of context: the persuasive fictions of anthropology', in M. Mangarano (ed.), *Modernist anthropology. From fieldwork to text*, Princeton, NJ: Princeton University Press, 1990

—— 'The relation. Issues in complexity and scale', *Prickly Pear Pamphlet* No. 6, Cambridge: Prickly Pear, 1995

Thomas, K., *Man and the natural world: changing attitudes in England 1500–1800*, London: Allen Lane, 1984

Turner, V., *The forest of symbols*, Ithaca: Cornell University Press, 1967

UKFN, *Forests memorandum and forest charter*, Norwich: UKFN, 1994

van Beck, W. and P. Banga, 'The Dogon and their trees', in E. Croll and D. Parkin (eds), *Bush base, forest farm: culture, environment and development*, London: Routledge, 1992

Willis, R. G. (ed.), *Signifying Animals. Human Meaning in the Natural World*, London: Unwin Hyman, 1990

Part I

Why Trees Are Good to Think

Why Trees, Too, Are Good to Think With: Towards an Anthropology of the Meaning of Life

Maurice Bloch

Trees are used as major symbols all over the world, and the purpose of this chapter is to present a tentative explanation of why this should be the case. The most obvious way of approaching this question is to consider what it is about trees and the way they are conceptualised that makes them such suitable objects for symbolisation; and, indeed, this will be my concern. However, to do this, and to leave it at that, would be to forget what Victor Turner taught us (but also often forgot!): that ritual symbols are part of a process. It is not simply in the evocative capacity of the conceptualisation of one of the objects concerned that we find an explanation of their presence at a particular stage in a ritual, but in their transformative potential during the process of ritual (Turner 1968). The ritual process is always focused on a special type of substitution, where one thing 'becomes' another, in the same way as wine 'becomes' the blood of Christ during the mass (Lévi-Strauss 1962: Ch. 8). These transformations are not arbitrary. When one thing is changed into another, it is clear that some sort of empirical connection between the two states still exists. It is this commonality that is to be the channel for the achievement of ritual. The famous flutes of Melanesian and South American rituals gain their power from the fact that the same material object, long and hollow, can be shared by something that is, at one moment, represented as a penis and, at another, as a vagina.

Ritual transformations depend, therefore, on a connection that links different states, and on a difference sufficiently obvious to make the transformation worth while and arresting. Transforming wine into blood is typical of ritual; transformations of wine into whisky would not do. I view such transformative potential as the central fact of ritual symbolism, and shall argue here that the symbolic power of trees comes from the fact that they are good substitutes for humans. Their substitutability is due to their being different, yet continuous with humans, in that they both share 'life'. This distant commonality is intriguing, problematic and uncertain. Thus, both the shared element – life – and the uncertainty and distance between humans and trees must be considered and understood.

The Need for a General Theory of Tree Symbolism

In *The Savage Mind*, Lévi-Strauss (1962) argues that animals are good as tools with which to think about human society, though his argument could – and does – apply to plants and many other things as well. According to him, this usefulness does not come from the nature of animals as such, but, rather, from the way they can be classified in contrastive sets and hierarchies that are then used to represent analogically socially and/or culturally created similarities and differences. He has been criticised by a number of anthropologists, who point out, in different ways, how, implicitly or explicitly, the uses of animal symbolism, including the critical contrasts that different cultures stress between species, are not arbitrary, as he suggests, but dependent on the recognition of what is known to be shared between animals and humans (Descola 1992). The point was that animals were good to think for humans because animals were alive in a way that was perceived to be similar to that of humans (Fortes 1966; Tambiah 1969), and because animals and people were ecologically linked in the food chain, as well as in other less obvious ways (Dahl and Hjort 1976).

Not only do all cultures seem somehow to recognise this kinship and mutual dependence between animals and humans, but some greatly dwell on it, and on the ethical problems it poses (Arhem 1996; Descola 1996; Karim 1981; Rival 1996). In the field of symbolism, the recognition of commonality and interdependence between people and other animals is not just a matter of mythical contemplation for human beings; it very often becomes also the very basis of certain ritual practices. In such rituals, what comes to the fore is the implicit unity of life: the fact that it involves such practices as eating, digesting and excreting, growing and withering, and, above all, being born and dying. Rituals thus exploit the parallels and connections established by the partly shared life processes of humans and non-humans in order to link dramatically the former with the latter. This is most often done through substitution and the subsequent killing of the animal, performed to bring about beneficial results for the human ritual partner, such as, for instance, curing, renewal, or even a form of immortality (Bloch 1992a).

If life and its processes are what are recognised as linking animals and humans, should this not also suppose an equal and similar role for plants in ritual and symbolism? In fact, a rapid survey of the comparative ethnography reveals that plants too are important, though, as Rival notes in her introductory chapter, they have rarely been the object of such theoretical interest and scrutiny as has been directed towards animals. Perhaps the reason is that the killing of plants in ritual, though it occurs (Rappaport 1968), is a less spectacular subject for ethnographic films than the essential staple of animal sacrifice that characterises this form of entertainment. However, the general questions raised by the symbolic use of plants are just as interesting as those concerned with animals; indeed, they are similar, though not identical.

One such question comes from an observation that the use of plants in ritual forces on us even more strongly than does animal symbolism, i.e. that such use depends as much on the similarity plants are perceived to share with humans, as on the salient differences that clearly exist between these two kinds of living things. In the case of animal sacrifice, for example, similarities between animals and humans are usually used as starting-points for practices that emphasise – even define – the gulf between people and other animate things. This is particularly true of rituals that stress that one species eats the other and not vice versa, or that one species has the ability to speak while the other does not (Bloch 1992a: Ch. 3). Thus animals may be sacrificed as substitutes for human beings precisely because they are both like and also fundamentally different from people. The ubiquity and repetitious nature of animal symbolism is to be explained by the fact that the same feature demonstrates a salient commonality between humans and animals, i.e. life, while the same differences between them are picked out from the limited list of possibilities that the real world offers to real people, among which lack of speech, promiscuous sexuality, edibility and lack of ancestors seem to be the most common. The basis of this type of symbolism therefore involves both the principles that govern the cognition of what living kinds have in common, and those that govern what differentiates them.

The same kind of argument can be made to apply to plant symbolism in general. The similarity stressed between plants and humans is basic-ally the same as that between animals and humans, that is, the fact that both are alive, though, as we shall see, this common condition is somewhat less obvious when we are dealing with the vegetable world. The differences stressed are, however, totally different for plants and animals. For example, for plants, the focus is often on rootedness. When we turn to that sub-section of the vegetable world that we can loosely call 'trees', further, more specific, differences between them and humans become symbolically salient. In earlier articles on a group of Malagasy slash-and-burn cultivators called the Zafimaniry, who put extraordinary emphasis on the significance of trees, I showed how what was symbol-ically stressed about trees was the greater durability and hardness they display when compared with people (Bloch 1992b, 1993).

To be more specific, the Zafimaniry stress three types of connection between trees and people. First, that both are alive. Second, that humans rely on trees for: making houses; making the earth fertile and weed-free; producing heat for cooking and warmth; obtaining cash from outsiders by selling timber; and, last but not least, providing raw material for most artefacts and, as the Zafimaniry make a kind of bark cloth, even clothing. Finally, they stress that certain trees, because of their heartwood, have 'bones'. By contrast, in their symbolic represent-ations, they emphasise four differences between trees and people: (1) the fact that trees and humans have different life-spans;[1] (2) the fact that trees transform themselves into a lasting material, wood, out of which durable artefacts such as houses can be made; (3) the fact that, although alive like animate beings, trees are immobile, and become fixed and associated with specific locations, in a way that is normally typical only of features of the landscape; and (4) the fact that the 'bones' of trees (by which is meant the lasting heartwood of the trunks) continue to increase as a proportion of the whole throughout the life of the organism, whereas the bones of people, once they have reached maturity, remain as no more than a small part of their bodies, and, indeed, seem to 'shrink' as they rot in the grave after death (Bloch 1992b). I have explained these ideas, and put them in the wider context of the general symbolism specific to the Zafimaniry, in a number of earlier publications. Indeed, with a degree of familiarity with the cult-ures concerned, it is relatively easy to give this kind of ethnographic, i.e. hermeneutic, interpretation of such local systems. To leave the matter there, however, as most contemporary anthropologists seem to want to do, is also, in a certain way, perverse. This is because the similarities of a system such as that of the Zafimaniry with many others cry out for more general explanations that are not tied to a single instance.

Anthropologists, nowadays, seem to have given up on any attempt to supply more general explanations, but this has simply led to other scientists' trying to do so in their stead and, in the process, often repeating some of the discipline's past errors – errors that it has subsequently learnt to avoid. There is a need for anthropologists to go beyond particularities, since, as glancing over this book's contributions amply confirms, the same themes come up again and again all over the world. This, of course, does not mean ignoring the equally important fact that similarities between symbolic systems are accompanied by a fundamental variability that it would be methodologically misleading to forget. This is indeed a common situation in anthropology, and, for that matter, in other social sciences as well, where the realisation of the co-presence of both obvious cross-cultural regularities and no less obvious cultural specificities has led to violent lurches between, on the one hand, theories that stress the irreducible particularities of specific cases, explicable only by a specific and unique history, and thereby forget the striking regularities across human cultures, and, on the other hand, theories that emphasise extra-cultural or extra-historical factors such as ecology, economy, or constraints coming from the nature of human cognitive capacities, and that often, in the process, become ridiculously reductionist. However, it is in understanding the combination of (1) constraints coming from the world as it is, and as it presents itself as an opportunity for human production, together with (2) the particular cultural history of groups or individuals, and (3) the nature of human psychology, that we can begin to give reasonable epistemological accounts of our data. These may not always be achievable in practice, since, in many cases, the enterprise is impracticable, so that we are forced to give partial accounts, usually from a single one of these three perspectives. But if we do give such partial accounts, we must make the provisional character of our explanations clear, and present our explanations in such a way that they can be compatible, and 'wait for' combination with, the other two types of constraints. In other words, we must not construct theories that seem to exclude the recognition of either historical specificities, or cross-cultural regularities. The remainder of this chapter is one such theoretical attempt. It looks at what might be the cognitive constraints that would explain cross-cultural recurrences in tree symbolism; but it does this in a way that 'awaits' combination with an ecological and a historical analysis.

Cognitive Constraints on Tree Symbolism

The psychological literature on the cognition of plants offers a limited amount of choice from which to build theories that might explain recurrences in the symbolism of trees. In fact nowhere do psychologists or ethno-botanists begin to consider what is the central question of this chapter, and is, indeed, the central concern of this book generally, i.e. what is it about such cognition that makes plants, and more specifically trees, particularly suitable for religious symbolism?

What we do have is relatively rich work on classification. The work of Brent Berlin and his associates (Berlin *et al.* 1973) has enabled us to discover important constants in plant and animal classification in different cultures. In particular, they have shown that living kinds tend to be ranked in terms of five ranks, though this does not include the overarching category of 'living kinds' itself, which seems to be taken for granted. They show that there is always a general level of class-ification for plants, although this may not be named, as is indeed the case for the Zafimaniry, and that trees are often an immediate subdivision of plants.[2] Implicit also in their work is an assumption that, as far as I know, has been unchallenged in both the psychological and anthropological literature, that all cultures, and therefore all people, have a concept of 'life'. Writers such as Berlin, and a number of sub-sequent psychologists, also argue that such classifications are anchored to a 'basic level', often resembling the scientific 'species level'. Finally, they stress that natural kinds, and especially living kinds, are thought of in terms of essences; that is, that people believe that below empirical features, such as colour, shape, smell or sound, there lies an essence that remains unchanged even if some typical empirical features norm-ally associated with a particular species are lacking. Thus an albino leopard is still a leopard.

This point concerning the fundamental and universally unique way by which natural kinds and artefacts are conceptualised forms the basis of Atran's (1990) bold hypothesis that there is something innate about our cognition of living kinds, something that leads us to construct a specific 'living kinds' domain. To argue for a specific domain is to argue that a certain type of thought is relatively isolated from other types of thought, and that it is governed by principles of organisation that are different from those applying to other areas of cognition. It is often argued, as in this case, that such a domain-specific module is invoked for dealing with a specific type of phenomena existing in the world. Atran then goes on to take two further, but not logically necessary, steps. First, that such a cognitive domain is governed by a distinct area in the nervous system. Secondly, that such an area is produced by a common human genetic heritage. Atran is therefore arguing, *inter alia*, that we have a dedicated device, the product of our genetic make-up, that enables us to recognise living things as such, to cognise them in a special and different way from, for example, artefacts, and to make presuppositions about them. Living kinds do not result from learned experience, but from innate human predispositions. One of Atran's main illustrations of this proposition is the essentialism with which species are understood. Thus everybody knows, that is, people in all cultures and all children after a certain age, that a tiger made to look like a lion is still, *really*, a tiger. It must also follow that, for Atran, all human beings in some way know and similarly understand what 'life' is, though he does not make this point explicitly.

Atran's work is very useful in two ways. First, it moves the discussion of classification away from a mere consideration of structure, towards a discussion of the cognitive processes by which classification is formed both ontologically and phylogenetically. Secondly, he, like a number of other authors, makes us reflect, not simply on the structure of classificatory systems, but also on the *way* living kinds are categorised. In particular, he stresses how living kinds always seem to be conceptualised as having a distinctive essence, which distinguishes them from other non-natural kinds. There are, however, a number of problems involved in Atran's approach, some of which concern his psychological theories, while others are of an anthropological nature. The anthropological objections are of three sorts. The first one is that in his enthusiasm to stress the universal features of classification systems, Atran underplays the very real and very great differences existing between cultures, between individuals, between adults and children, and between children of different ages. In fact, he seems to be at pains to discount all evidence for such variability. The second concerns the fact that, although he is more interested than most writers in the ethnobotanical field in the beliefs concerning the entities classified, he goes nowhere as far in this matter as most anthropologists would like; the folk ontology of people is only a small part of an anthropologist's concern, since she or he is mainly interested in how people use and speculate about different species. The third objection concerns the rigidity with which Atran imagines people's cognition. He seems unable to account for the tentative nature of so much of culture, for the degree of disagreement and doubt that is found in the field, or for the obvious significance of context.

The 'hardness' of his view of taxonomy is particularly significant here, since it is linked to one of the psychological problems implicit in his work. Atran, in his enthusiasm to stress the unique and universal understanding of living kinds, refuses the prototype theories of concepts initially developed by Eleonor Rosch, at least in so far as these theories apply to plant and animal kinds. This is because the prototype theory, with its emphasis either on best exemplars or on family resemblances, seems to negate the idea of an underlying essence. In order to criticise the prototype view of such concepts, Atran (1990: 55) is forced to move to a highly restrictive definition of folk classification, and even of *meaning*. One effect of these restrictions is not only to beg the question, since it only considers the 'meaning' of living-kind terms in relation to classificatory definitions, but also to exclude any possibility of understanding the ways in which the core meanings of concepts are exploited and extended that might explain the regularities observed in plant and animal symbolism.

It is the capacity of prototype theory to make us grasp the subtlety of the uses of concepts and their associated words in, for instance, metaphors, that has turned writers such as George Lakoff (1987) into supporters of this theory of the nature of concepts. Lakoff rightly stresses the value of this perspective for his own concerns. Atran, however, also has a point. There is now extensive evidence, both ethnographic and psychological, to show that adults, if not children as well, universally attribute something special and different to living things: that they possess an essential irreducible core. Such evidence cannot be ignored; but it cannot be all there is to the matter. If living kinds are as special as Atran argues, then it must also follow, either implicitly or explicitly, that what they have in common, i.e. *life itself*, must also be conceptualised. Atran's theory, like all other theories about living kinds, implicitly requires knowledge and understanding of life, even though the precise nature of this knowledge and understanding is rarely examined.

It is here that some recent developments in the work on concepts might come to our aid. A number of writers, amongst them Frank Keil (1992), have modified our view of concepts in general by stressing that, at least in the case of living things, concepts contain at their core implicit 'theories'. Such writers, in this way similar to those advocating the prototype view, are able to recognise both the looseness of concept extensions and the significance of their rich and unpredictable associative fringe, while still retaining the key element, stressed by Atran, that adults believe, rightly or wrongly, that there is a strong essential theoretical core to living kinds. Unlike classical concept theory, Keil's formulation defines this core, not in terms of empirical features, but in terms of 'theories'. When applied to living kinds, such formulations are problematic in so far as what is meant by 'essence' could refer to two entirely different sorts of things. It could simply concern the 'dogginess' of dogs, in which case the core theory would be about this 'dogginess'. Or, alternatively, the conceptualisation could imply an understanding of living kinds as *living*, and a belief in an underlying essence. It would then be because dogs are *alive* that people believe that, in spite of their bewildering variety, they all share dogginess. In this case, the core theory is about life itself and in general, and the essentialism of particular living kinds is a mere epiphenomenon. In other words, if living kinds are understood by adults, whether implicitly or explicitly, as 'living', then what we need to uncover is their 'theory of life'. It seems to me that both Atran and Keil are endorsing both the alternative positions outlined in the previous paragraph at the same time, without really distinguishing them. This is clearly unsatisfactory.

It is important to be clear that, for the purpose of this chapter, I am only concerned with the question raised by the second alternative, since, whatever the virtues or otherwise of the former, it is the latter position that seems well supported in both the anthropological and psychological literature. The key questions are: (1) What do lay people, implicitly and explicitly, understand by life? and (2) How can the nature of this concept help us to understand such phenomena as the use of plants in general, or trees in particular, in symbolism and ritual? Writers such as Atran or even Keil, who hardly discuss the concept of life itself, seem of little help in answering either of these two questions. They probably believe that the concept of life is not constructed, but innate, and that, consequently, little can be said about it in cognitive terms. Whether they are right in this is ultimately a matter for research; but, as we shall see, their position has not gone unchallenged in psychology.

From an anthropological viewpoint, the necessary corollary to the innatist hypothesis (that all human beings recognise unproblematically certain kinds as living and others as not living), is also suspicious. Anthropologists have shown that the way in which lay people seem to consider these matters is highly tentative, discursive and complex. I am not arguing against a writer such as Atran that the core concept of life is culturally variable. It seems to me that, on this matter, the ethnographic record backs him completely (Ellen 1996; Descola 1996). What is at issue is different. Both Atran and Keil stress the fundamental difference between living kinds and artefacts,[3] to such an extent that being alive or not is assumed to be a clear-cut issue. Atran (1990) is particularly extreme in this matter. On page 56, he tells us that in lay taxonomy 'every natural object is either a living kind or not', presumably for all people, at all times. The anthropological record contradicts such strong assertion; indeed, Atran himself admits that such objects as lichens and fungi are only doubtfully recognised as being alive by Itza Maya,[4] as they also are by the Zafimaniry, according to my own knowledge of the ethnography.

If we turn to the Zafimaniry and to the limited insight into conceptualisation that vocabulary provides, we see how difficult to maintain an assertion such as that of Atran would be, and how what evidence there seems to be, points in the other direction. The Zafimaniry, like other Malagasy, have a word for living, *velona*, that applies to all living kinds, as well as to certain stones (for example quartz), clouds, motor engines, and so forth, without any indication that these are metaphorical uses. The word for dead, *maty*, is even more promiscuous, since it can apply to almost anything that does not work or is broken. To make matters even more complicated, another form of the same root, *faty* (literally 'that which has died', or 'corpse') only applies to humans and a few animals. Thus, a tree can be *maty*, but what remains of it is not its *faty*. Other key words, such as those for 'bearing progeny' or 'being sick', are used for plants as well as for humans and animals; but such usage seems metaphorical, in that several informants with whom I discussed the matter explicitly said that in spite of common usage rice, for example, 'does not *really* have children'. Thus, the tentative evidence that the examination of the lexicon provides is best understood as meaning that animals are the 'best examples' of being *alive*, while other beings, such as humans, plants and, perhaps, kinds 'we' would consider as definitely not alive, such as clouds, are less typical, and things like mushrooms are on the far periphery of the life prototype.[5] Not only does this seem to me the situation for the Zafimaniry but, on purely anecdotal evidence, it seems also to be the case for many other cultures, including European ones. And it is, of course, also the case described by a number of psychologists for very young American children. I wonder, however, whether in contexts less formal than experimental situations, such a lack of sharp boundary and clarity would not still be implicitly present in the knowledge of adults (Descola 1996). It is because of such ethnographic observations that the psychological theories of Atran and Keil seem ultimately to be unsatisfactory.

The rival, but related, theories of another psychologist, Susan Carey, somewhat modified for anthropological purposes, seem much more appropriate to the data. In addition, they enable us to advance in our understanding of the *content* of the concept of life. Carey's starting-point is similar to that of Atran and Keil. It is the general cognitive theory of domain-specificity, as set out most recently by Sperber (1994). The most telling reason for positing that the entire human nervous system is modular and that it is innately differentiated into discrete domains for the understanding of specific kinds of data is the speed with which children learn about these phenomena. Chomsky convincingly argues that children could not possibly learn natural language as fast as they do without being biologically predisposed for it; this explains the fact that all natural languages share a common deep structure. There must therefore be, according to him, a different domain for language, ready-made for this use, and quite different from other mental capacities. In a similar fashion, Sperber and Atran argue that the speed with which children learn about living kinds, and the cross-cultural universality of this knowledge, suggest the existence of an innate disposition for understanding this kind of thing in a special way that is organised differently from other types of knowledge.

Carey agrees that the speed of learning and the universality of the knowledge about living kinds suggest an element of innate predisposition and domain-specificity, but she differs from the writers discussed above in that she rejects the evidence for an innate domain for folk biology as such. Instead, and basing herself on considerable experimental work, she argues that the construction of a living-kind domain in children is a gradual and entirely learned phenomenon, made possible by another, better documented and, in this case, probably innate domain, labelled variously by different writers as the 'folk psychology domain', the 'naive psychology domain', the 'theory of mind domain', or the 'metarepresentational domain' (Sperber 1994 and 1996). The naive psychology involved in such a domain is the ability to interpret animation as the sign of intentionality, or, in other words, the imaginative attribution of a mind to other beings. Such an ability enables very young children, as young as two hours old, to distinguish between self-motivated and non-self-motivated phenomena, and to behave quite differently to those to which a 'mind' is attributed. This faculty lies at the very basis of all forms of communication, especially with other humans (Premack and Premack 1994). For Carey, it is the gradual development of such an innate ability that leads to the later construction of the living-kind domain (Carey 1985 and 1996).

The process of this construction according to Carey is roughly as follows. At first, the attribution of a 'mind' to animate, and only animate, objects is very uncertain, leading to the kind of phenomena that Piaget labels 'childhood animism'. Later, this attribution gets anchored to humans and animals and, in an uncertain way, gets transformed into a 'theory of life'. This too is, at first, uncertain, and Carey stresses the difficulty young children have in grasping the meaning of, for example, death. Are statues dead in the same way as grandfathers are? . . . The child is not too sure. Later on, such things get fairly thoroughly sorted out, as does the distinction between humans and other animals, but, at first, this too is not entirely clear. Then, later, perhaps as late as ten, the notion of 'living things' gets expanded from animals to people, and so as to include plants, and presumably trees, so that, in the end, the adult idea of 'life' is fully formulated.

Carey is particularly interesting for anthropologists because such a developmental process actually turns our attention to the *content* of the cognition of 'life'. First, she stresses the recognition of intentionality in other animate beings as its *fons et origo*, thereby ensuring a permanently peripheral position to plants. Secondly, she studies the inductions made by children about what it is to be alive. For example, if children are told rabbits have an organ with an invented name, will they also believe that cats, humans, daisies and motorcars also have such an organ? The result of this work demonstrates that even adults hold a graded notion of life – i.e. that objects are 'more or less alive'. This graded view is particularly clear in the case of children, though with growing maturity the type of inductions made by Carey's subjects come to resemble more the scientific view, though never becoming identical with it. This means that people's notion of 'life' is much more ragged and provisional than we would imagine from the writings of, for example, Atran.

The significance of such a finding, and the reason why it is so attractive to field-working anthropologists, is that, although Carey's work is concerned with American children and adults, anecdotal evidence suggests that it corresponds well with what we find in other societies, and therefore it makes ethnographic observations, such as those described above for the Zafimaniry, much more comprehensible and likely. The value of such a position is not only that it gives real insight into the content of what is understood by the concept of being alive; it also explains the much more tentative and graded picture we find in the kind of ethnographic data most anthropologists have recorded.

There is a difficulty in Carey's argument. American children after the age of ten have constructed a hard and fast 'living kind domain' capable of sustaining exactly the same intuitions that Atran or Sperber consider universal and innate, while Zafimaniry adults are tentative in this matter in a way that seems to resemble the approach of American seven-year-olds. We should be wary, however, in arguing from this that Zafimaniry adults are like American children. Rather, it is quite obvious to me that, in matters biological, the average Zafimaniry, with her or his closer involvement with the forest and agriculture, is far more knowledgeable than the average American.

However, there might be another interpretation of Carey's – and others' – findings regarding the systematicity of biological knowledge in older American children than one couched merely in term of cognitive development. By the age of ten, and perhaps sometimes even seven, American children are thoroughly formally schooled in biology. And since the test situation in Carey's experiments must be very reminiscent for those who undergo it of the formal education with which they are familiar, it would not be surprising that they should respond in such situations as they would in school, and therefore produce a quasi-scientific version of their understanding of 'life'. This would in no way exclude their retaining, in informal and practical contexts at least, a conceptualisation that reflects more closely the tentative process by which a living-kind domain has been established for them. This sort of situation has, indeed, been shown to exist for the understanding of physics amongst American college students. It seems therefore quite possible that the tentative and gradual process uncovered by Carey continues to characterise adult American knowledge in less formal contexts.

This hypothesis is supported by the fact that most Westerners, including Americans, can sympathise with and even assent to such 'unscientific' statements as 'plants are less alive than butterflies', even though they have been taught to *know* better. If this is so, Westerners would, in informal contexts, be very similar to the Zafimaniry, and the developmental story told by Carey would underlie many of the nuances, subtleties and uncertainties that we find in the ethnographic data and in the informal intuitions of everyone.

In particular, it would explain the peripheral 'living kind' status of plants in general, and that of trees in particular, in all cultures. This is due to the fact that plants are apparently inanimate, and that it is therefore difficult, or paradoxical, to attribute intentionality to them, while this attribution of intentionality remains, for everyone, the core theory of the concept 'life'. Understood in this way, Carey's work concords well with the ethnographic data discussed above and, for that matter, with such observations as the fact that Western animal rights protesters are more concerned with cruelty towards sheep than towards spiders, and very rarely feel strongly about the killing of moulds. In fact, such a graded picture of life does more; it suggests a possible explanation of the symbolical uses of plants and trees.

The Symbolical Functions of Plants and Trees

The starting-point of this chapter was the observation that symbolism used in ritual is to be understood in terms of conceptual analogies, which are based on perceived continuities and discontinuities, and that, in the case of living kinds, the continuity we find most often stressed is the presence of life, while the discontinuities may be such things as the inability to speak, promiscuous sexuality, or differences in life-spans. In rituals, these continuities and discontinuities are exploited as avenues for establishing connections and operating disconnections. This is because rituals have a purpose: to cure, for example. This purpose is achieved by connecting related entities, which therefore must have an apparently 'real' and convincing unity between them, e.g. animals and people, and then disconnecting them, because of their 'real' and convincing difference. During the disconnection (for example, killing), transformations are carried out or recognised in the symbol that cannot be carried out on the principal entity. Then, the original connection is re-established once again because of its 'real' and convincing character, so that those for whom the ritual is carried out can benefit from the results of the operations carried out on the symbolic entity. This is done by demonstrating their apparent unity. Ritual practices depend, therefore, on the complex demonstrable 'real' and convincing proximity, and on the 'real' and convincing distance of the symbols and the subjects of the ritual. They must be neither too close, nor too distant and, in fact, the more ambiguous, yet convincing, the relationship, the more it can be evoked and used in this game of 'one moment I am here, the next I am not'. Animals that are clearly alive, but not human, serve well in this game, in which the ambiguities are played out around their problematic intentionality. Thus, not surprisingly, it is precisely upon the problem of the attribution of intentionality to beings more or less distant from humans, imaginary or not, who are more or less 'alive', that so much of religion hinges (Boyer 1994; Sperber 1994).

The same sort of games can be played with plants, where, again, the difficult relation of the presence and absence of intentionality and life is stressed. In the case of trees, a further element can be introduced: games around the issue of the presence of life itself, because of the uncertainty of whether plants and trees are fully alive or not. This is certainly the motor of Zafimaniry symbolism, and it depends on the fact that, for them, being alive is not a clear-cut matter as would be implied if we followed Atran, but is, in the case of trees, a questionable *theory*, as Carey suggests it is for children, and as I argue it probably is also for all adults.

Psychological theories such as Carey's are of relevance, therefore, for the discussion of recurrences in the nature of religious symbolism, because these studies concern the cognitive bases out of which such symbolism is built. They can explain the opportunities that such cognition offers for religious constructions (as does here the 'more or less' character of the conceptualisation of life) and, to a certain extent, account for them. If, as in this case, there is a good reason to believe that the type of cognition in question is not culturally variable, we then have the added benefit that such studies inevitably suggest a credible explanation for the regularities in the symbolism we find in different cultures. It is the universality in the conceptualisation of 'life' that explains the universal aspects of plant and tree symbolism, the presence of which will strike the reader of this book as he or she reads about so many specific cases. However, drawing attention to this cognitive anchoring does not, and cannot, fully account for the phenomena themselves. If it pretended to do so, it would ignore the very great element of variation that is also just as present as the regularities. But, in fact, this is no real problem for the theoretical position adopted here, which can accommodate variation as well as recurrence. First of all, the cognitive anchor proposed is itself a shifting anchor, since it consists, not of a simple categorical 'theory of life', but of a 'theory of life' that applies differentially and contextually to different types of beings. Secondly, it is essential for understanding the theoretical thrust of the argument to remember that it can only be *one* explanatory element 'awaiting' to be combined with ecological and historical explanations before a fuller account of particular ethnographic cases can be given, even if, in practice, this remains an impossible goal.

Notes

1. A difference that the Zafimaniry elaborate further by finding finer discriminations between the life-spans of different tree species, and using them analogically to compare and comment on different types of people.

2. For a discussion of whether this is legitimate, see *inter alia* Atran 1990: 67.

3. Often forgetting about non-living natural kinds.

4. See the footnote to Carey 1996: 275.

5. Such an assertion is anecdotal, inasmuch as all anthropological statements of this sort are; they would merit more systematic study.

References

Arhem, K., 'The cosmic food web: human–nature relatedness in the Northwest Amazon', in P. Descola and G. Palsson (eds), *Nature and Society*, London: Routledge, 1996

Atran, S, *Cognitive Foundations of Natural History*, Cambridge: Cambridge University Press, 1990

Berlin, B., J. Breedlove and P. Raven, 'General principles and nomenclature in folk biology', *American Anthropologist* 75, 1973, pp. 214–42

Bloch, M., *Prey into Hunter: The Politics of Religious Experience*, Cambridge: Cambridge University Press, 1992a

—— 'What goes without saying: the conceptualization of Zafimaniry society', in A. Kuper (ed.), *Conceptualizing society*, London: Routledge, 1992b

—— 'Domain specificity, living kinds and symbolism', in P. Boyer (ed.), *Cognitive Aspects of Religious Symbolism*, Cambridge: Cambridge University Press, 1993

Boyer, P., *The Naturalness of Religious Ideas*, Cambridge: Cambridge University Press, 1994

Carey, S., *Conceptual Change in Childhood*, Cambridge, Mass.: MIT Press, 1985

—— 'On the origin of causal understanding', in S. Carey and D. Sperber (eds), *Causal Understanding*, Cambridge: Cambridge University Press, 1996

Dahl, G. and A. Hjort, *Having Herds: Pastoral Herd Growth and Household Economy*, Stockholm: University of Stockholm, 1976

Descola, P., 'Societies of nature, and the nature of society', in A. Kuper (ed.), *Conceptualizing Society*, London: Routledge, 1992

—— 'Constructing natures: symbolic ecology and social practice', in P. Descola and G. Palsson (eds), *Nature and Society*, London: Routledge, 1996

Ellen, R., 'The cognitive geometry of nature: a contextual approach', in P. Descola and G. Palsson (eds), *Nature and Society*, London: Routledge, 1996

Fortes, M., 'Totem and Taboo', *Proceedings of the Royal Anthropological Institute for 1966* (1962)

Karim, W.-J., *Ma'Bedisek Concepts of Living Things*, London: Athlone Press, 1981

Keil, F., *Concepts, Kinds, and Cognitive Development*, Cambridge, Mass.: MIT Press, 1992

Lakoff, G., *Women, Fire and Dangerous Things*, Chicago: Chicago University Press, 1987

Lévi-Strauss, C., *La Pensée Sauvage*, Paris: Plon, 1962

Premack, D. and A. J. Premack, 'Moral belief: Form versus content', in L. Hirschfeld and S. Gelman (eds), *Mapping the Mind*, Cambridge: Cambridge University Press, 1994

Rappaport, R., *Pigs for the Ancestors*, New Haven: Yale University Press, 1968

Rival, L., 'Blowpipes and spears: the social significance of Huaorani technological choices', in P. Descola and G. Palsson (eds), *Nature and Society*, London: Routledge, 1996

Sperber, D., 'The modularity of thought and the epidemiology of representations', in L. Hirschfeld and S. Gelman (eds), *Mapping the Mind*, Cambridge: Cambridge University Press, 1994

—— *La Contagion des Idées. Théorie Naturaliste de la Culture*, Paris: Odile Jacob, 1996

Tambiah, S., 'Animals are good to think and to prohibit', *Ethnology* 8, 1969, pp. 423–59

Turner, V., *The Forest of Symbols: Aspects of Ndembu Ritual*, Ithaca: Cornell University Press, 1968

Palms and the Prototypicality of Trees: Some Questions Concerning Assumptions in the Comparative Study of Categories and Labels

Roy Ellen

Iwish to open up for discussion the question as to just how universal and prototypical the image and category of tree might be in human psychology and culture, and to explore as a special test case the position of palms in ethnobotanical classifications and symbolic arrays. Palms, as a group of plants (by which I mean here standing palms, not rattans), are of comparative ethnosemantic interest, as they are sometimes formally classified as trees in folk and scientific classifications and sometimes not; sometimes labelled as a separate group of plants and sometimes not. Nevertheless, in anthropological studies (as exemplified by this present collection of essays), in which particular emphasis is placed on their symbolic role, palms appear to function as exemplary members of the category tree. I believe it would be useful to explore whether this is simply a consequence of ethnocentric assumptions on the part of the ethnographer, or whether there is a fundamental and widespread cultural ambiguity in the status of palms as trees.

Palms in European Folk Classifications and in Science

In European languages palms are nowadays unproblematically described as trees (for example 'palm trees', *palmier (arbre)*, *die Palme (der Baum)*, *palm boom*, etc.), but they are definitely not prototypical cognitively. This is what one would expect in a geographic area where they are non-endemic, infrequent or at the extremes of their range. Nevertheless, it is difficult to place them in any other life-form (or other macro-category) of temperate plants, and so they are, in a sense by default, designated 'trees', though trees, it must be admitted, of a very special kind.

The position in scientific taxonomy and botany broadly reflects what we find in the European folk classifications, and this we would broadly expect given what is known of the history of those classifications. 'Palm' as an ethnobotanical term is derived from Latin *palma*, so-called because of the resemblance of the leaves to the outspan of a human hand (Skeat 1953 [1879–82]: 425). The Latin, but not the cognate Greek word *palame*, also signifies 'palm' (plant). Although distinct types of palm were known from the Roman world, the most likely developmental sequence is that the term (as with its Greek and Phoenician predecessor, 'phoenix') prototypically referred to the date palm (*Phoenix dactylifera*). It was the date palm that the Greeks had sanctified to Apollo, and that became an emblem of victory or triumph (Corner 1966: 324–5, OED 1933 v. VII: 400–1). Hebrew 'tamar' (also 'to be erect') refers to the date palm. It is unclear whether this word was ever extended to include the other endemic palm of west Asia, *Borassus flabellifer* (Hastings 1963: 656–7).

During the early period of European expansion (1450–1650), when many previously unknown species were being reported, introduced and recognised as economically important, palms were not labelled as a single group, nor were they necessarily considered trees. Perhaps this is not surprising. There is some evidence for the appearance of a tentative and covert collective identity for palms by the end of this period. Thus, the pre-Linnaean botanist Rumphius (who had seen many types of palm at first hand in the Moluccas between 1653 and 1702) coined names for some thirteen. Two of these contained the root 'palm': 'Palma indica nucifera' (*Cocos nucifera* L., the coconut palm), and 'Palma indica vinoria' (*Arenga pinnata* (Wurmb) Merr.); while 'Sagus' (sago: *Metroxylon* spp.) is included by extension (Peeters 1979: 154–6); we also find the expression 'vinum palmeum', the labelling of rattans by affinity as 'Palmijuncus', and a tree fern (*Cyathea rumphiana* (v. A. v. R.) Merr.) named 'Palmifilix alba'. Linnaeus himself had only seen one living palm at the time of the publication of *Systema Naturae* in 1735, and it was not until 1789 that Antoine de Jussieu (in his *Genera Plantarum*) first designated a single botanical family to encompass all plants we would now describe as palms, the Palmae (Arecaceae).

By the nineteenth century, with the routinisation of the palm category in scientific botanical usage, with the discovery of many hundreds of new species as a consequence of European exploration and imperial consolidation, and the presence of more species of living palm in Europe following the development of greenhouses, botanic gardens and the fashion for exotics in gardening (see for example Jellicoe *et al.* 1986: 419–20), the status of 'palm' as a distinct type of plant, and as a label delineating many particular kinds, was firmly established. Despite the morphological similarities between different palms (Uhl and Dransfield 1987: 161), their collective identity appears to have had much to do with their tremendous usefulness as a source of food and materials. Rumphius had classified palms on the basis of their respective wine-giving and nut- and meal-yielding properties, giving coconut pride of place, 'the captain of the Ambonese herbal' (van Slooten 1958: 333–6, Rumphius, Liber 1, *Herbarium Amboinense*). This emphasis on economics in the definition of palms is interesting in the context of debates about the role of utility versus morphology in plant classification (Hunn 1982; Randall and Hunn 1984), and it links up with what I wish to say below about palms in the folk classifications of tropical subsistence cultivators.

The acceptance of palms as trees in European folk classifications appears to have accompanied their recognition as a distinct type of plant. Modern botanical illustrations of the different habits of standing palms (Figure 3.1) indicate the wide range of types, extending from the undeniably tree-like to something altogether more shrubby in appearance. If we look at early European representations of palms (Figures 3.2a–c) here also their tree-like qualities are not immediately apparent; indeed, they are distinctly suspect. By the nineteenth century, however, representations had definitely become more tree-like (Figure 3.2d). The transition could never be complete, as the key defining features of palms in relation to other trees are distinctly ambiguous. Of course, 'tree' is not, anyway, a proper phylogenetic category, though there are botanists who are inclined to give it some weight in classification. Generally speaking, there exists a common-sense botanical definition of palms as something like 'evergreen trees, unbranched (or dichotomously branched), usually erect . . .'. However, botanists persuaded more by formal syllogistic logic and a sense of consistency object that, since palms are monocotyledonous and without regular secondary thickening, they cannot be trees. They will point to the fact that, instead, the stem or trunk produces from its apex successive leaves one at a time, with the leaf base entirely sheathing the stem, that

Figure 3.1 Habits of various standing palms. Modified from Uhl and Dransfield, *Genera Palmarum* (1987: 556), with permission.

branching is uncommon, that there is no cambium, and that root systems bear little resemblance to those of other trees. In between, we find taxonomists who will only designate as trees amongst the mono-cotyledons, palms and that group that was once accepted as being most closely related to palms taxonomically, the pandans (Mabberley 1987: 635). Those who specialise in palms seem more broad-minded in their definition of trees. So, for example, Corner (1966: 7) is quite emphatic in placing palms, along with screwpines, traveller's palms, tree-lilies, grass-trees, and bamboos, and along with various bromeliads, aroids, orchids, sedges and rushes, in a category of 'monocotyledonous trees without a unifying and familiar designation', which he describes collect-ively as 'sword trees'.

Figure 3.2 European representations of palms. 2a. The coconut palm (*Cocos nucifera*) and (2b) the talipot (*Corypha umbraculifera*); both from van Rheede's *Hortus Malabaricus* [16]; 2c. 'Fontes fluvii Paraguay' with *Mauritia* palms, from Martius' *Flora Brasiliensis* [19]. All reproduced from Corner 1966.

Palms in Tropical and Sub-tropical Folk Classifications

In the tropics (and to a lesser extent in the sub-tropics) the situation in which potential human classifiers of palms find themselves is different. As we move from the poles to the Equator so the number of palm species increases dramatically (Henderson, Galeano and Bemal 1989), with only two genera reaching Europe compared with thirty-nine in Brazil (139 species). Such abundance might be thought to translate into perceptual salience and thence collective categorisation and labelling, and to more obvious incorporation into the life-form 'tree'. However, on both counts we find the opposite to be the case.

Palms are rarely classified or labelled by folk biologists in the tropics as trees in explicit formal terms. In the cases listed in Table 3.1, selected it is true on the basis of the clarity of the data rather than statistical typicality, there are only six examples of explicit inclusion, as opposed to sixteen of explicit exclusion or ambiguity in status. In some languages, some palms are included and others excluded; in others, the term for tree may be applied to individual stands, but there is a distinction between a 'stand' and 'wood' (where 'wood' is also polysemously 'tree'), as in Malay or standard Indonesian *pohon* versus *kayu*. Thus, the term *pohon kelapa* (coconut tree) is frequently encountered, while *kayu kelapa* is rare. Claudine Friedberg (1990: 213–18) reports that in Bunaq (a Papuan language from Timor) there is a term for tree (*hotel*) that includes palms, collectively termed *lepu pol* (where *lepu pol* in turn is part of *hotel upan guha*), and these are together close to pandans and bananas in their classification. But in addition there is a current Austronesian term, *ai*, that never refers to palms.

It is also the case that palms are rarely grouped under a single collective term (Table 3.2), though the supporting data here are more restricted. However, the family resemblances between different kinds of palm may be acknowledged through overlapping and polythetic groupings, which receive varying degrees and types of lexical recognition. Thus, amongst the Brunei Dusun (Bernstein and Ellen, in press) *benjiru* (*Licuala*) is a kind of *pinang* (*Areca catechu*), or *Licuala* is likened to *piasau* (*Cocos nucifera* L). For the Tasek Merimbun Dusun, *Licuala* palms form a covert grouping, and perceived resemblances between a broader range of palms may mean that in some cases we might speak of palms more generally forming a covert category. Among the Palawan of the Philippines (Revel 1990: 146) palms appear to be grouped into sago-producing plants (*Arenga, Caryota, Metroxylon*) and cabbage and fruit palms (*Areca, Pinanga* and *Veitchia*). The coconut is classified quite separately. This would appear to reflect a more widespread contrast between soft-centred and hard-centred palms. More unusually, Yopno in the Huon peninsula area of Papua New Guinea (Kocher Schmid 1991: 176–86) label all palms collectively as *dsopang silep* and pandans as *kiyang silep* (*silep*, family or household; *dsopang, Heterospathe* spp. and *kiyang, Pandanus brosimos, P. julianettii*). In other words, both palms and pandans collectively are labelled with respect to their most proto-

Table 3.1 The status of palms as trees in selected languages of tropical and sub-tropical peoples*

Population	Location	Term for tree	Notes	Status of palms	Source
Aga	Luzon, Philippines	+		excluded	Brown 1984: 153
Akawio	Guyana	+		excluded	Brown 1984: 181
Alune	Seram, Indonesia	+		excluded	Florey, pers. comm.
Bunaq	Timor, Indonesia	+		ambiguous	Friedberg 1990: 213–18
Carapana	Colombia	+		excluded	Brown 1984: 183
Dusun	Brunei, Borneo	+	large woody plants	excluded	Bernstein 1996: 442–4
Hanunóo	Mindoro, Philippines	+	wood, shrub	included	Conklin 1954: 260–3 and *passim*
Isirawa	Irian Jaya, Indonesia	+	= wood	excluded	Brown 1984: 177
Kalam	highlands, New Guinea	+	= wood	excluded	Bulmer 1974
Koiwai	Irian Jaya, Indonesia	+	large plant, vines	included	Brown 1984: 160
Lotuho	southern Sudan	+		included	Brown 1984: 198
Mokilese	Carolines, Micronesia	+	= wood	included	Brown 1984: 186
Nimboran	Irian Jaya, Indonesia	+	= wood	included	Brown 1984: 179
Nuaulu	Seram, Indonesia	+		excluded	Ellen, field data
Semelai	Malaysian peninsula	+	includes coconut, excludes *Licuala*	ambiguous	Gianno 1990: 54–5
Spanish	Puerto Rico	+		excluded	Brown 1984: 174–5
Sri Aman Iban	Sarawak, Malaysia	+		excluded	Christensen, unpubl.
Tequistlatec	Oaxaca, Mexico	+	= wood, includes coconut	ambiguous	Brown 1984: 184
Tobelo	Halmahera, Indonesia	+		excluded	Taylor 1990: 87–119
Waodani	eastern Ecuador	+	includes banana, yucca, bush	ambiguous	Brown 1984: 167
Wola	New Guinea highlands	+	woody plants	excluded	Sillitoe 1995: 204, 208
Yopno	Huon peninsula, New Guinea	+	excludes cultivated trees	excluded	Kocher Schmid 1991: 187
Zapotec	Oaxaca, Mexico	+	includes erect cactus	included	Brown 1984: 158

* *Note:* I include here only sources that make explicit reference to the categorical relationship of palms to trees. References to Brown 1984 as a source indicate his own field materials plus data acquired through personal communication and access to unpublished sources.

typical and salient member. Among the Alune in west Seram (M. Florey, pers. comm.) palms are not clearly grouped as an overt category, and probably not as a single covert category either. 'Moreover, the lexemes for palm morphology (most importantly the terms for inflorescence) differ between kinds of palm.' Sub-tropical Tzeltal in the Chiapas province of Mexico (Berlin, Breedlove and Raven 1974: 161, 419) variously classify palms amongst trees or as unaffiliated covert plants (for example *Chamaedorea*), but have neither a general overarching term nor a covert category. Overall, whether palms are considered trees, and the extent to which they are given distinct categorical recognition, appears to transcend any broadly-based genetic classification of languages, or classification by geographic region or habitat.

Although palms are rarely labelled as a group of plants separate from any other group in ethnobotanical classifications (though they may exhibit degrees of covert recognition), they do appear to have a utilitarian and symbolic status that exceeds that of the average dicotyledonous timber or fruit-producing tree. Thus, there is a very strong link between classificatory status and function. Most prototypical trees do not provide a basic source of carbohydrate, or food, though it is always possible to list important exceptions, such as *Canarium*, breadfruit, or *Ricinodendron* (Harris 1977). By contrast, palms commonly provide a major starch staple (Ruddle *et al.* 1978), nourishing fruits (Rival 1993: 638–9), edible apical 'cabbage', alcoholic beverages, and stimulants such as betel (Ellen 1991); and may have a wide variety of multiple uses as construction materials, to the extent that they may become culturally dominant in particular economies and life-ways. For the Nuaulu of Seram (Ellen 1977: 110; 1988) sago palms (*Metroxylon sagu*) are not only the most important source of edible starch, eaten at every meal, but also a source of proteinaceous grubs of the weevil *Rhynchophorus bilineatus*, which are extracted from rotting stumps; of thatch (leaves), of walling (woody leafstalks) and of an adaptable manufacturing material (woody leaf sheaths) for the making of containers and other utensils.[1] Fox (1977: 26) provides a similar exhaustive list for the role of *Borassus* amongst the Rotinese. No wonder, then, that palms should also have an important symbolic role. Examples of palm symbolism are provided in several of the chapters in this book (those by Bonnemère, Giambelli and Howell, Chapters 5, 6 and 7), and the literature on the material and symbolic role of palms is substantial.

Table 3.2 Presence or absence of generic terms for standing palms in selected languages

Population	Location	Overarching term for standing palms	Total no. of locally named palms[2]	Source
Alune	Seram, Indonesia	—	8	Florey, pers. comm.
Dusun	Brunei, Borneo	—	8	Bernstein, 1996: 442–4, Bernstein and Ellen, in press
Hanunóo	Mindoro, Philippines	—		Conklin 1954
Nuaulu	Seram, Indonesia	—	14	Ellen, unpubl. field data
Palawan	Palawan, Philippines	—	6	Revel 1990: 146
Tzeltal	Chiapas, Mexico	—	4–5	Berlin, Breedlove and Raven: 1974: 161–411
Tobelo	Halmahera, Indonesia	—	15	Taylor 1990: 156–7
Wola	New Guinea highlands	±[1]	9	Sillitoe 1995: 204, 208
Yopno	Huon peninsula, New Guinea	+	9	Kocher Schmid 1991: 176–86, 316

1. optional: 2. at basic (generic) level: does not include rattans.

Are Palms Symbolic Trees?

Not only are palms economically and symbolically important for many tropical peoples, they somehow appear to become exemplary trees in ritual discourse and practice, even though they may not be formally classified as such. We can summarise this paradox in a simple diagram. Figure 3.3a summarises the conceptualisation of palms as an exemplary kind of tree in symbolic schemes; Figure 3.3b illustrates the conceptualisation of palms as peripheral in ethnobiological classifications based predominantly on plant morphology.

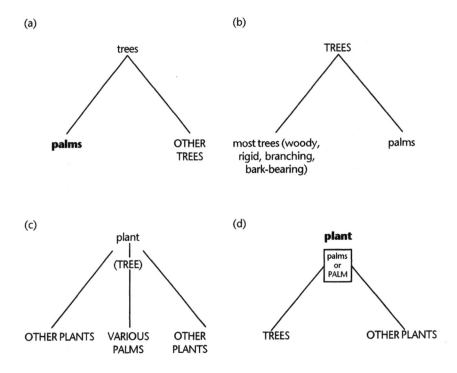

Figure 3.3 Relationship between palms and the category 'tree' in (3a) symbolic and (3b) morphological classifications. In the first, palms are conceptualised as an exemplary kind of tree; in the second they are peripheral. 3c illustrates the relationship between 'palms', 'trees' and 'plant' in terms of lexical and ethnobiological salience for a hypothetical palm society. 3d illustrates the relationship between 'palm', 'tree' and 'plant' in terms of symbolic focus for a hypothetical palm society. In the diagrams, UPPER CASE letters indicate lexically-expressed categories, **boldface** indicates conceptual salience and lower case indicates covertness.

In their chapters, Bonnemère, Giambelli and Howell (Chapters 5, 6 and 7) all understand the connection between palms and trees on the basis of metaphorical and symbolic evidence rather than on the basis of language or ethnobiological classification in the conventional sense. In the case of both the Lio of Flores and the Balinese there exists a metaphorical repertoire that unites palms and trees generally. This is something which is well documented for eastern Indonesia, especially the imagery of trunk – base, source, origin, beginning, cause – and tip – treetop, shoot, buds (see for example Traube 1986: 14–15). Thus, for the Rotinese (Fox 1975: 119) *tuu* (lontar palm) appears to function as a tree in symbolic terms. But this function is not necessarily restricted to a single symbolically dominant palm. In his account of Umeda symbolic life in the Sepik, Alfred Gell (1975: 123–33) shows how *Areca*, coconut, sago and *Caryota* are all important, with coconut as a kind of symbolic *primus inter pares* (cf. the 'Palmyra indicum' of Rumphius, and also the ethnobiological status of the coconut among the Palawan, discussed above). But Gell (1975: 237) is also very clearly suggesting that all these palms are somehow standing in for some unspoken abstract image of 'treeness' especially when we are invited to see clear metalinkages between trees as symbols and humans as symbolic vehicles. In Bonnemère's account of the Ankave-Anga in the New Guinea highlands, not only is *Areca* (a palm) treated as an exemplary tree, but so are pandans, *Cordyline* (a shrub), and *Ficus* (a strangling fig), all of which are problematically peripheral in most definitions of the tree category.

This is all very puzzling and confusing. Why should palms – and other doubtful tree types – rarely be labelled as a separate group in the classifications of tropical and sub-tropical peoples, why should they seldom be explicitly classified as trees, and yet at the same time they be honorary trees in symbolic terms? Is there a connection between these three observations? Certainly, palms appear to have an inter-mediate status, almost mediating between trees and other plants. This intermediate status can plausibly be explained partly in terms of general vegetational diversity, and in terms of the diversity of palms in part-icular. Thus, in the tropics the distribution of plant types is more continuous than in temperate areas, at least as far as the minds of ordinary humans are concerned. Botanists may be different. There are various intermediate and ambiguous groups (tree-ferns, pandans, rattans), while the number of kinds of palm is greater, and they are distributed more widely. In some areas, palms may be dominant (as in sago swamp, *Nypa* coastal fringes, and plantations), while a greater

proportion of all palms are domesticated or semi-domesticated compared with other forest trees. Palms themselves also vary in their
properties and potential, although their overall morphology is the same.
Some are soft-centred, some are hard. Soft-centred palms are often
sources of food (sago flour, lontar syrup); hard-centred ones can be
used for wood (*Oncosperma*). Both kinds provide cabbage and fruits.

In short, the argument favouring palms as 'prototypical examples'
(Rosch 1977) of the category 'tree' is weak, and neither are they an
immediately recognisable *gestalt* (Atran 1985: 309). Where they obtain
a collective categorical status this appears to be almost in opposition
to prototypical trees, and through culturally-enhanced salience as a
special-purpose grouping. In this respect the category 'palm' is a bit
like the animal life-form 'mammal'. Both, in effect, are only unambig-
uously labelled in scientific classifications, though they incipiently exist
to varying degrees in different folk schemes. Both comprise a number
of highly-salient and functionally important species, which in the case
of mammals in European societies has made them exemplary animals.
Their common distinctive features stem not so much from simple
exterior morphology, as from an aggregate of anatomical and growth
features that rarely become indicators for folk-biologists. As a group,
palms do not possess some of the key qualities that make trees good
symbols: they certainly produce food (and in abundance) but they do
not usually have the branches, timber-producing woody trunks or roots
that match the imagery widely associated with prototypical trees. Thus,
the category 'palm' and the various covert and labelled groups that
sub-divide and cut across it are excellent examples of (depending on
your theoretical predisposition) either the intersection of mundane and
symbolic classifications, or the difficulty of finding operative ethnobiological classifications for particular peoples that exclude significant
cultural criteria.

Tree as Label, Cognitive Prototype and Symbol

Our discussion of the classificatory status of palms would be almost
complete at this point were the classificatory status of trees as a whole
more straightforward. What I wish to demonstrate in the final section
of this chapter is that our understanding of palms as objects in
classifications and as symbols cannot be separated from a fundamental
paradox in the classificatory status of trees. Thus, according to
Witkowski, Brown and Chase (1981), following Berlin (1972: 66–9), a
general term for tree is a recent addition to languages, recent that is in

terms of the evolution of language. On the other hand, if tree is a historically recent term this confounds other evidence from cognitive and developmental psychology that 'tree' is a basic image prototype (see for example Boster 1996), together with the implicit evidence of much ethnography that it is what Fox (1975) has called a 'primary symbol'.

For Witkowski, Brown and Chase the appearance of a discrete tree life-form is a response to a corresponding decline in what Bousfield (1979: 203–4) has called 'semantic contact'. By this is meant that as people are removed from the world of plants, as societies become larger and more complex, with greater division of labour reflected in functional access to living and growing organisms, so the need for general life-form terms increases and the need for specific terms decreases. Occasionally tree terms may only refer to a specific type of tree, as in the much-cited case of 'cottonwood tree' for 'tree' (Trager 1939) in the native languages of the American southwest. Indeed, Brown and his associates argue that several thousand years ago, terms for 'tree' were either absent or encoded only as 'a low salience category'. Where a tree concept is recognised, suggests Brown (1977), this necessarily implies a second life-form, that is 'herb', where the main discriminating dimension is size rather than ligneousness. Indeed, there is complementary evidence from child language acquisition studies that the first distinction to emerge is between large and small plants (Dougherty 1979). This orthodoxy appears now to have superseded earlier assumptions of distinctive feature analysis employed classically by Charles Frake (1980 [1962]: 12) in his description of Subunan botanical life-forms, where categories are determined by the presence or absence of just two features in a contrast set: woodiness (W) and rigidity (R)L. Thus, *gayu* 'woody plants' = W,R; *sigbet* 'herbaceous plants' = $\bar{W}$R, and *belagen* 'vines' = $-\bar{R}$.

The late acquisition of a 'tree' term is consistent with other evidence regarding the difficulty of isolating a natural cognitive prototype in the visual landscape (Brown 1990: 31–2; Hunn 1987: 148). Thus, Figure 3.4 illustrates in outline the form of twelve species selected for the range of habits that trees display; but these in turn are drawings of ideal trees standing in isolation. Although tree germplasm is genetically programmed to generate a phenotypically particular structure (with its distinctive branching pattern, erectness of growth, consistency of trunk thickness, form of canopy, overall symmetry and so on), this is seldom achieved as a result of ecological constraints. Although they conform to precise architectural principles and provide models that

Figure 3.4 Tree forms, selected to indicate range of types. Based on original illustrations by John White in Phillips 1978. Not drawn to scale.

have taxonomic integrity, trees growing in clumps or in forest rarely have the same appearance as those growing individually in the culturally modified spaces of settlements, tree-lined avenues or botanic gardens.

Similarly, it is difficult to establish a clear boundary between trees and non-trees in the visual landscape (Figure 3.5); trees, bushes and shrubs all merging imperceptibly, displaying varying degrees of size and woodiness and multiplicity of stem. What we describe as a tree is not 'due to phylogenetic relatedness but to evolutionary convergence in response to common adaptive challenges constrained by laws of form' (Hunn 1987: 148). At the same time, trees as individuals elide with trees as a collectivity; individual 'stands' (to take a British English example) becoming 'clumps', clumps becoming 'copses' (coppices), copses becoming 'woods', and woods becoming 'forest'. Indeed, in some languages the word for 'tree' is the same as that for 'forest' (see for example Morris 1976). Forest trees are, therefore, simultaneously singular and groupy; while trees as things are not completely separate from the environment in which they exist. Unlike animals, which are visually autonomous and can wander around as individuals, trees are like rocks and hills, not simply in the landscape but of it as well. Their literal rootedness and groupiness only highlight this. No wonder we cannot see the wood for the trees.

And when Brown suggests that early tree terms were encoded as 'a low salience category', he also proposes that this was through semantic extension from 'wood'. This is why wood/tree polysemy is so widespread. Indeed, some wood terms do appear to have emerged before tree terms (see for example Blust 1974: 5, 11–12). Such polysemy disappears as societies become more complex. Thus, the less inclusive item, the reference of which appears to have been extended, is an item that acquires its salience from cultural use rather than from intrinsic

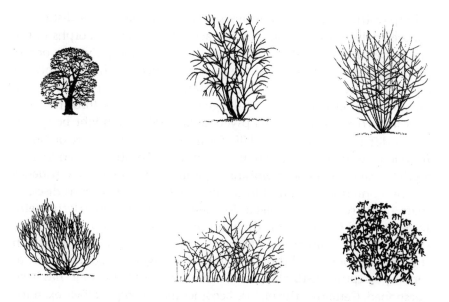

Figure 3.5 Plant morphotypes, selected to indicate continuity between recognisably tree forms and shrubby herbs. Based on original illustrations by Jan Masek in Lawrence 1985. Not drawn to scale.

perceptual qualities: wood as a material with many technological applications exemplifying trees in general; or (as in Austronesian bird/chicken
polysemy) chickens as domesticates that have co-evolved closely with
human populations and that provide food and sacrificial items
exemplifying birds as a whole (Ellen 1993: 81). In either case, the
conceptual identity is expressed by using the same word.

All this brings us back to some well-worn utilitarianist versus
universalist arguments (Hunn 1982; Randall and Hunn 1984). We need
not go over old theoretical ground here, but of particular relevance is
the claim by Atran (1985: 306) that there is an inconsistency between
Brown's claim for the definition of tree in terms of size, and his functional definition in terms of wood. Atran (1985: 307) continues:

> [I]t will not do to argue that referential expansion simply consists in
> relaxing the functional component of the definition and stressing only
> the perceptual component . . . The perceptual features attaching to the
> artifact "timber" and the living kind "tree" are quite different in nature:
> those that attach to "tree" are virtual properties that include pheno-
> menally typical attributes of trees, whereas the only perceptual logically
> characteristic of "timber" relate to being wooden and cut.

Despite the persistent controversies surrounding formal distinctive
feature analysis, the continuous character of vegetative morphs in the
landscape, the implication that wherever wood/tree polysemy occurs
'tree' has a low saliency, and the heat generated by the functionalist
arguments, 'tree' *is* always the first botanical life-form to be encoded,
judging from evidence of cross-language comparisons (Brown 1977).
This in turn suggests that its psychological saliency might be qualitatively different from botanical life-forms such as 'vine', 'grass' or 'bush'.
If, indeed, some life-forms are more natural than others, then 'tree' is
a prime example. Some promising experimental cross-species evidence
for this contention is found in the observations that pigeons discrim-
inate trees from other objects in their field of vision (Hernnstein,
Loveland and Cable 1976), though presumably they do not contrast
them with other botanical life-forms. However, the extent to which
this implies conceptual thought rather that vague 'imaginal' codes, or
innate perceptual distinctions rather than learned behaviour, has been
questioned. Certainly, the picture becomes more complex if we examine
recent work on primates, where phylogenetic similarities with humans
are closer (Cheney and Seyfarth 1990: 86–91). What evidence we do
have points to visual environmental stimuli being organised more

according to function (food sources, potential predators, nesting sites, tool-making materials) than in terms of abstract proto-lifeforms. Nevertheless, there are at least some data to support the theoretically plausible view (Boster 1996: 276–80) that a number of features of 'natural' classification might be a consequence of co-evolution and natural selection, though the evidence does not extend to the lexical tagging of such apparently universal images.

There is also an additional body of evidence – a set of compelling theoretical propositions, as well as some strong intuitive reasons – for supposing that 'tree' must have been from a very early time a major metaphoric vehicle for the classification of other kinds of more abstract relations, as is evident in kinship discourse and the widespread use of the tree partonyms 'root', 'branch' and 'trunk' in everyday as well as symbolic language. In his work on Rotinese ritual language, Fox (1975: 113–15) locates seven linkages between 'tree' (*ai*) and other primary symbols, making it the most connected and, presumably, the most salient Rotinese symbol. In addition, tree (*ai*), fruit (*boa*), leaf (*dok*), and trunk (*huk*) all occur in an inner core of symbols. And that such usages need not be tied to words rather than to unlabelled culturally-informed images is supported by increasing evidence that down-plays the linguistic model of culture (Bloch 1992, 1993). Cultural variation, nevertheless, must have a considerable impact on the form of 'tree' metaphors. Analogical correspondence or consubstantiality between tree (or plant) and human development, reproduction, longevity and relatedness (Fox 1971) is more widespread than the occurrence of trees that symbolically mediate between houses and people (as in 'heartwood' for 'bone', or tree/housepost interchangeability), or that express the animate/inert ambiguities of timber. Indeed, it might be tentatively suggested that wood/tree polysemy emerges only where houses are more than temporary shelters and their construction is a significant cultural activity. There is some evidence to suggest that non-agricultural nomadic forest-dwelling populations not only recognise fewer basic terms for plants, but especially fewer terms for wood-producing trees (Ellen, in press).

So, although not all life-forms are 'natural', in the sense employed by Berlin, Boster and by Atran (1985: 311), some are more natural than others (Randall 1987: 143). The obvious configurational qualities of trees make them, at the very least, in Eugene Hunn's apposite phrase, 'perceptually compelling', and 'it is not hard to understand why folk biologists almost everywhere should be motivated to give trees nomenclatural recognition' (Hunn 1987: 148). Even if 'the tree' as an abstract icon – something that bears no particular relation to any one species – is a complex cultural simplification (Ohniki-Tierney 1981), and there is no 'natural' basis for the *gestalt* property of treeness, such properties need not always be associated with continuities in nature. They might, instead, be associated with deductive discontinuities (Brown 1990), permitting perceptual continuities such as 'tree <> woody shrub <> shrubby herb <> herb' to be effectively sub-divided. In this case, a better bet might be a propositional model for prototypic trees (see for example Wierzbicka 1985: 182–3): trees produce fuel, wood for construction, shade, substances (nuts, fruits, seeds that can be eaten by humans and others); are taller than people; have trunks; grow for a long time. These specifications need not be equally weighted, and 'when tree categories are consolidating in languages, utilitarian properties of prototypic trees are by far more significant than specifications entailing size, appearance, growth, and so on' (Brown 1990: 31–2). Brown continues:

> Those botanical entities in nature that produce wood which can be used as fuel or in construction, and *also* provide shade for creatures the size of people, and *also* produce substances which can be eaten by people and/or other creatures, tend strongly to include an array of things that happen to share certain perceptual properties: trunks, bark, leaves or needles, branches, large size (bigger than people), and so on. These particular things constitute a segment of a botanical continuity which people focus on because all things associated with that segment have *all* the utilitarian properties listed above [. . .] This segment is singled out for special attention when a name or label is assigned to all those botanical things having all of the noted utilitarian properties. It just so happens that most botanical things so named also share a number of perceptual properties. As a consequence, naming produces or, better, imposes a discontinuity on the world which, in fact, is not naturally there. This, of course, is a deductive discontinuity. The deductive discontinuity relating to 'tree', then, underlies the consolidation of a Gestalt property of 'treeness'.

If we now return to Figure 3.3, we can see illustrated in (c) the relationship between 'palm', 'tree' and 'plant' in terms of lexical and ethnobiological salience for a hypothetical society where palms are salient economically and ritually. In many societies there is no general term for plant (Berlin 1992), nor for palm (as we have established). The only degree or level of categorical inclusion which is lexically expressed is 'tree'. This would be a perfectly accurate description of, say, the Nuaulu case. However, lexical expression may be a poor guide to symbolic significance, and if we stress general metaphoric and symbolic usages the plant image may be more important than trees in general (Figure 3.3d), except when idioms of longevity, durability and hardness, exemplified by trunk, and shade, by canopy, are required. Palms can sometimes fulfil these symbolic requirements, but not always. Compelled by a taxonomic logic of transitivity that is common in the literate cultures of the West we tend to emphasise a logical-sentential string of the kind: a palm is a kind of tree, and a tree is a kind of plant. Given what we now know of the ambiguous character of the category 'tree', the middle term in this transitive proposition may be redundant, or at least only relevant in certain places for certain purposes. Thus, when it comes to symbolic considerations, what is most important is not that palms are 'trees', exemplary or not, but that they are salient life-giving 'plants'. In certain cultural settings, anyway, the symbolic force of the 'arborescent' motif may therefore have been overstated.[2]

Acknowledgements

Some of the material discussed in this chapter draws upon two recent research projects funded by the British Economic and Social Research Council with which I have been involved: 'The ecology and ethno-biology of human–rainforest interaction in Brunei (a Dusun case study)'[R000 23 3088]; and 'Deforestation and forest knowledge in south central Seram, eastern Indonesia', [R000 23 6082]. I would like to thank Margaret Florey and Hanna Christensen for permission to use unpublished material, and John Dransfield of the Royal Botanic Gardens, Kew, for his helpful suggestions.

Notes

1. Some palms even provide fuel and wood for construction, contradicting one of the key features that overall would appear to separate them from dicotyledonous trees. For the Nuaulu, the hard wood of *panuke* (*Oncosperma tigillarium*) is the favoured material for the manufacture of arrow mid-shafts, door-bolts and longbows. See also the role of *Bactris gasipaes* amongst the Huaorani of Amazonian Ecuador (Rival 1993: 639–43).

2. As it has been by Deleuze and Guattari (1987).

References

Atran, S., 'The nature of folk-botanical life forms', *American Anthropologist* 87, 1985, pp. 289–315

Berlin, B., 'Speculations on the growth of ethnobotanical nomenclature', *Language and Society* 1, 1972, pp. 51–86

—— *Ethnobiological classification: principles of categorization of plants and animals in traditional societies*, Princeton, NJ: Princeton University Press, 1992

Berlin B., D. E. Breedlove and P. H. Raven, *Principles of Tzeltal plant classification: an introduction to the botanical ethnography of a Mayan-speaking people of highland Chiapas*, Academic Press: New York, 1974

Bernstein, J. H. and R. F. Ellen [in press], '*Licuala* palms in Brunei Dusun ethnobotany', *Brunei Museum Journal*

Bloch, M., 'What goes without saying: the conceptualisation of Zafimaniry society', in A. Kuper (ed.), *Conceptualising society*, London and New York: Routledge, 1992

—— 'Domain specificity, living kinds and symbolism', in P. Boyer (ed.), *Cognitive aspects of religious symbolism*, Cambridge: Cambridge University Press, 1993

Blust, R., 'Proto-Austronesian syntax: the first step', *Oceanic Linguistics* 13, 1974, pp. 1–15

Boster, J., 'Human cognition as a product and agent of evolution', in R. F. Ellen and K. Fukui (eds), *Redefining nature: ecology, culture and domestication*, Oxford: Berg, 1996

Bousfield, J., 'The world seen as a colour chart', in R. F. Ellen and D. Reason (eds), *Classifications in their social context*, London: Academic Press, 1979

Brown, C. H., 'Folk botanical life-forms: their universality and growth', *American Anthropologist* 79, 1977, pp. 317–42

—— *Language and living things: uniformities in folk classification and naming*, New Brunswick, NJ: Rutgers University Press, 1984

—— 'A survey of category types in natural language', in S. L. Tsohatzidis (ed.), *Meaning and prototypes: studies in linguistic categorisation*, London and New York: Routledge, 1990

Bulmer, R., 'Folk biology in the New Guinea highlands', *Social Science Information* 13 (4–5), 1974, pp. 9–28

Cheney, D. and R. Seyfarth, *How monkeys see the world: inside the mind of another species*, Chicago: University of Chicago Press, 1990

Corner, E. J. H., *The natural history of palms,* London: Weidenfeld and Nicolson, 1966

Deleuze, G. and F. Guattari, *A thousand plateaus: capitalism and schizo-phrenia* (trans. Brian Massumi), London: Athlone, 1987

Dougherty, J., 'Learning names for plants and plants for names', *Anthropological linguistics* 21, 1979, pp. 298–315

Ellen, R. F., 'The place of sago in the subsistence economics of Seram', in Tan Koonlin (ed.), *Sago-76: papers of the first international sago symposium*, Kuala Lumpur: Kemajuan Kanji, 1977

—— 'Foraging, starch extraction and the sedentary lifestyle in the lowland rainforest of central Seram', in J. Woodburn, T. Ingold and D. Riches (eds), *History, evolution and social change in hunting and gathering societies*, Oxford: Berg, 1988

—— 'Nuaulu betel chewing: ethnobotany, technique, and cultural significance', *Cakalele: Maluku Research Journal* 2(2), 1991, pp. 97–122

—— *The cultural relations of classification: an analysis of Nuaulu animal categories from central Seram*, Cambridge: Cambridge University Press, 1993

—— 'The cognitive geometry of nature: a contextual approach', in P. Descola and G. Pálsson (eds), *Nature and society: anthropological approaches*, London: Routledge, 1996

—— [in press] 'Modes of subsistence and ethnobiological knowledge: between extraction and cultivation in southeast Asia', in D. Medin and S. Atran (eds), *Folk-biology: a synthesis*, Cambridge, Mass.: MIT Press

Fox, J., 'Sister's child as plant: metaphors in an idiom of consanguinity', in R. Needham (ed.), *Rethinking kinship and marriage*, London: Tavistock, 1971

—— 'On binary categories and primary symbols', in R. Willis (ed.), *The interpretation of symbolism*, London: Malaby, 1975

—— *Harvest of the palm: ecological change in eastern Indonesia*, Cambridge, Mass.: Harvard University Press, 1977

Frake, C. O., 'The ethnographic study of cognitive systems', in A. S. Dil (ed.), *Language and cultural description: essays by Charles O. Frake*, Stanford: Stanford University Press, 1980 [1962]

Friedberg, C., *Le savoir botanique des Bunaq: percevoir et classer dans le haut Lamaknen (Timor, Indonesie)*, Mémoires du Museum National d'Histoire Naturelle, Botanique, Tome 32, Paris: MNHN, 1990

Gell, A., *Metamorphosis of the cassowaries: Umeda society, language and ritual*, London: Athlone, 1975

Gianno, R., *Semelai culture and resin technology*, Memoir 22, New Haven, CT: Connecticut Academy of Arts and Sciences, 1990

Harris, D. R., 'Alternative pathways toward agriculture', in C. A. Reed (ed.), *Origins of agriculture*, The Hague: Mouton, 1977

Hastings, J., *Dictionary of the Bible, Vol. 3*, London: Clark, 1963 (2nd edn)

Hays, T. E., 'Plant classification and nomenclature in Ndumba, Papua New Guinea highlands', *Ethnology* 18, pp. 253–70

Henderson, A., G. Galeano and R. Bernal, *Field guide to palms of the Americas*, Princeton: Princeton University Press, 1989

Hernnstein, R. J., D. H. Loveland and C. Cable, 'Natural concepts in pigeons', *Journal of Experimental Psychology: Animal Behavior Processes* 2, 1976, pp. 285–302

Hunn, E. S., 'The utilitarian factor in folk biological classification', *American Anthropologist*, 84, 1982, pp. 830–47

—— 'Science and common sense: a reply to Atran', *American Anthropologist* 89, 1987, pp. 146–9

Jellicoe, G., S. Jellicoe, P. Goode and M. Lancaster (eds), *The Oxford companion to gardens*, Oxford: Oxford University Press, 1986

Kocher Schmid, C., *Of people and plants: a botanical ethnography of Nokopo village, Madang and Morobe provinces, Papua New Guinea*, Basle, Switzerland: Basler Beitrage zur Ethnologie, Band 33, 1991

Lawrence, E. (ed.), *The illustrated book of trees and shrubs*, London: Octopus, 1985

Mabberley, D. J., *The plant-book: a portable dictionary of the higher plants*, Cambridge: Cambridge University Press, 1987

Morris, B., 'Whither the savage mind?: notes on the natural taxonomies of hunting and gathering people', *Man* 11, 1976, pp. 542–57

Ohniki-Tierney, E., 'Phases in human perception/ conception/symbolization processes: cognitive anthropology and symbolic classification', *American Ethnologist* 8, 1981, pp. 451–67

Peeters, A., 'Nomenclature and classification in Rumphius's *Herbarium Amboinense*', in R. F. Ellen and D. Reason (eds), *Classifications in their social context*, London: Academic Press, 1979

Phillips, R., *Trees in Britain, Europe and North America*, London: Ward Lock, 1978

Randall, R., 'The nature of highly inclusive folk-botanical categories', *American Anthropologist* 89, 1987, pp. 143–6

Randall, R. and E. Hunn, 'Do life-forms emerge or do uses for life? Some doubts about Brown's universals hypotheses', *American Ethnologist* 11, 1984, 329–49

Revel, N., *Fleurs de paroles: histoire naturelle Palawan. Vol. 1, Les dons de Nägsalad*, Paris: Editions Peeters, 1990

Rival, L., 'The growth of family trees: understanding Huaorani perceptions of the forest', *Man* 28(4), 1993, pp. 635–52

Rosch, E., 'Human categorisation', in N. Warren (ed.), *Studies in cross-
cultural psychology*, London: Academic Press, 1977

Ruddle, K., D. Johnson, P. Townsend and J. Rees, *Palm sago: a tropical
starch from marginal lands*, Honolulu: University Press of Hawaii, 1978

Sillitoe, P., 'An ethnobotanical account of the plant resources of the
Wola region, southern highlands province, Papua New Guinea',
Journal of Ethnobiology 15(2), 1995, pp. 201–35

Skeat, W. W., *An etymological dictionary of the English language*, Oxford:
Clarendon Press, 1953 [1879–82]

Slooten, D. F. van, 'Rumphius as an economic botanist', in H. C. D. de
Wit (ed.), *Rumphius memorial volume*, Baarn: Hollandia N.V., 1959

Taylor, P. M., *The folk biology of the Tobelo people: a study in folk classification*, Washington DC: Smithsonian Institution Press, 1990

Trager, G. L., '"Cottonwood" = "tree": a southwestern linguistic trait',
International Journal of American Linguistics 9, 1939, pp. 117–18

Traube, E. G., *Cosmology and social life: ritual exchange among the Mambai
of east Timor*, Chicago: University of Chicago Press, 1986

Uhl, N. and J. Dransfield, *Genera Palmarum: a classification of palms
based on the work of Harold E. Moore*, Lawrence, Kansas: The L. H.
Bailey Hortorium and the International Palm Society, Allen Press,
1987

Wierzbicka, A., *Lexicography and conceptual analysis*, Ann Arbor: Karoma
Publishers, 1985

de Wit, H. C. D., 'A checklist to Rumphius's *Herbarium Amboinense*', in
H. C. D. de Wit (ed.), *Rumphius memorial volume*, Baarn: Hollandia
N.V., 1959

Witkowski, S. R., C. H. Brown and P. K. Chase, 'Where do tree terms
come from?', *Man (NS)* 16, 1981, pp. 1–14

Trees of Knowledge of Self and Other in Culture: On Models for the Moral Imagination

James W. Fernandez

Prowling around Trees in Search of Enlightenment

In the sacred grove there grew a certain tree round which at any time of day and far into the night a grim figure might be seen to prowl.

The Golden Bough (Chapter I:1)

Introduction

It is not hard for me to commune with trees. In my years of ethnographic fieldwork in Equatorial and Tropical Africa and on the Cantabrian, sea-facing slope of northern Spain I have lived among people who live in or next to forests upon which they have long, in important part, depended both economically and symbolically. And I have done some prowling with them around their salient trees. These are people who, from this traffic, have become quite knowledgeable about trees. And they have been, almost always, very happy to talk about that subject and impart their knowledge. If I had worked exclusively among Eskimo or Aymara I could hardly have contributed to this book. Or any chapter I might have written would surely have been a more austere one. Ecological circumstances alter cultural cases. The cultural icons of such barrens and steppe people are necessarily quite different. I have worked among forest-dwellers and forest margin people. In this chapter I will be interested in the use they make of this landscape and of these trees to aid and abet their understanding and as repositories of their knowledge . . . particularly their knowledge about social relationships.

Arboreality and the Moral Imagination

Trees have been fruitful leitmotifs in my fieldwork in Africa and Europe, and they are powerful images, both imitative and contagious, which do significant work in the local imagination. And it is some of that work that I would like to attend to here. True to this ethnographic presence and beyond the engagement with the writing of this chapter I could hardly escape making trees a leitmotif in my ethnography generally.

About the place of trees in culture, of course, we Indo-Euro-Americans know quite a lot. At the very least Frazer's *Golden Bough* informs us, in a compendious way, of the centrality of trees in this great family of cultures. We recall how he began his massive associationist *oeuvre*, whose own leitmotif was the 'struggle for succession' in culture, in the fateful happenings at Diana's oak grove at Nemi. Thereafter the reader is led on to hundreds of pages on nature worship, vegetation rites and, in particular, tree spirits and tree worship in Europe. To be sure Europeans already knew from the Paradise Myth that the knowledge of good and evil, of yea and nay, of the pleasures and perditions of being fruitful and multiplying, of struggling and failing or struggling and succeeding are fruits of the tree, the tree of knowledge, the bearer of bitter fruit AND the abode of the serpent. We also know from Frazer's *Golden Bough* the manifold polyvalence of trees. In the beginning of that massive *opus* the tree harbours something akin to the political power of perpetuity, and determined but mortal men who pretend to the priesthood of that power must ceaselessly prowl around the dubiously fruitful tree of life in defence of it until autumnal fore-shortening of nutrient flow and the falling leaves of time bring about the recurring tragic replacement.

> Those trees in whose dim shadow
> The ghastly priest does reign,
> The priest who slew the slayer,
> And shall himself be slain!
>   Macauley

But hundred of pages later our imaginations are captured by less sombre scenes, in relation particularly to spring ceremonies, with their Maypole or May Tree around which men and women dance to guarantee the perpetuity that lies in the annual renewal of fertility of nature and human kind alike.

These figures, whether Diana's hunter king, circling around, and in some sense gaining his power from the fruitful overarching tree, with its eternal golden bough – whose immortality contrasts so ominously with his own mortality – or these May Tree dancers, are but versions of the archetypal figure, who beneath or in close association with a tree of enlightenment or re-invigoration attains to special power and insight: Augustine, who in his long agony of indecision flings himself down under a fig tree in his garden and is finally and fully converted (*Confessions*, Book VIII. 12). Newton, whose powerful mind is, the myth has it, under an apple tree, inspired to convert, by force of gravity, a God-given but disorderly universe into an orderly one. Not to mention, outside the Western tradition, what came to Bodhisattva, the Buddha, under the Bo tree.[1] Of course, anthropologists do not have to go so far afield. For Victor Turner it was the *mudyi* tree, we remember, that inspired him to one of his most insightful analyses and one of the most basic formulating statements of his symbolic theory.[2] Men contemplate trees and shake them that their fruits may fall to their profit, but men and women, in the presence of trees, find their imaginations shaken into new understandings of their selves and the universe and of the relation between the two. What power in and over the imagination trees have seemed to have, and what an apt leitmotif they have contributed to orienting thought in culture. Trees of knowledge, indeed!

Frazer was fertile in analogy and sustained reiterative allusions, and trees were among the most sustained and allusive of analogies in his *oeuvre*. But analogies and allusions to what purpose? For purposes mainly, in a Victorian age, we may hazard, of exciting the 'moral imagination' by images more evocative of human attitudes and the verities of the human condition than Victorian platitudes might allow. It is that Darwinian image of man not only as 'the slayer who must be slain' if human life is to live on, but who must also and otherwise, in a plethora of apparently irrational rites, many of them involving prowling around trees, rejuvenate himself and the world. Stanley Hyman (1959: 429) – though his universalism will give any anthropologist pause – says it well:

> *The Golden Bough* is not primarily anthropology, if it ever was, but a great imaginative vision of the human condition. Frazer had a genuine

sense of the bloodshed and horror behind the gaiety of a maypole or a London-bridge-is-falling-down game, akin to Darwin's sense of the war to the death behind the face of nature bright with gladness, or Marx's apocalyptic vision of capital reeking from every pore with blood and dirt, or Freud's consciousness of the murderer and the incestuous wish. The key image of *The Golden Bough*, the king who slays the slayer, and must himself be slain, corresponds to some universal principle we recognize in life.

That comes pretty close to the taproot of my argument. For it seems to me that the best ethnography is an ethnography of the role of the imagination in culture. It is an ethnography attuned to the imaginative visions of the human condition present in those we work among. And it is attuned to those images that are central and recurrent, as in meditation, speculation and argument cultures ponder their conditions and their ultimate circumstances. It is attuned to a culture's sustained analogies that give order to and account for disorder in condition and circumstance. It is an ethnography that seeks to know and account for the power certain images have to capture the imagination in a particular culture at a particular time . . . say the force of self-aggrandizing images of individualist combat and entrepreneurial survival, the Social Darwinism, found among privatised Western Euro-Americans living under late nineteenth- and early twentieth-century industrial capitalism and commodity fetishism.

In any event, the ethnography of the imagination is an ethnography sympathetic to the attractive, sym-pathic lines of force produced by central images. As the Scottish Enlightenment, to whom Frazer was no stranger, might tell us, there is all of a 'moral philosophy' – the rubric under which the fledgling social sciences first trafficked, we recall – in the study of such lines of force. And the imagination, in so far as it is powerful, is always a 'moral imagination', capturing other imaginations by some vision or other and evoking associations in the interest of a certain state of things, certain forms of society and states of personal character . . . prowling around up to no good, or up to some good. Here is Hyman (1959: x) again introducing the artfulness and imaginative power of the great nineteenth-century and turn-of-the-century social thinkers, Darwin, Marx, Freud and Frazer:

I believe their books to be art, but I believe art itself to have an ethical as well as an aesthetic dimension, in that it is the work of the moral imagination, imposing order and form on disorderly and anarchic experience. That this vision of order and form is primarily metaphoric makes it no less real, since lines of force then radiate out from the work of art to order and re-order the world around.

So, thus, we are brought closer to the issue and essence of Enlighten-ment. And we are brought to the seed at the very centre of powerful imaginations; pithy metaphors of power! To give us more comparative and ethnographic perspective I invite the reader's company deeper into the forest . . . or rather into the particular forests of my fieldwork!

Treeing the Fugitive Moral Imagination – Trees of Civic Life and Death

The distance the modern human and social sciences have travelled from the 'moral philosophy' of the eighteenth-century Enlightenments, the Scottish and those associated with it, is debatable. It is clear that these Enlightenments were, like these modern sciences, intensely interested in the springs of human nature and, faced with the declining import-ance of the sacred and sacred sanctions, also intensely interested in what reason, substituting for dogma, might say about right conduct. But it is not clear that one can study these matters in any century independent of moral considerations. For example, in anthropological ethnography there are choices that must be made by the ethnographer that have moral implications, in so far as (1) one must inevitably select in one's own narrative what events and voices to represent, of which it can be asked are they right or wrong, beneficial or detrimental choices as regards local interests; and (2) the ethnography is never *sui generis*, but implied or suggested comparisons may always be present, which may imply moral judgement or animate the invidious. And there are local narratives, many if not all moral in tone and intention, of which the ethnographer must be aware and whose moral implications the ethnographer must assess. But let me root this discussion in fieldwork in Equatorial Africa (among Fang) and Northern Spain (among Asturians). I want to show in these ethnographic milieux how trees, by certain associative processes, can excite the moral imagination concerning the health or disease of corporate bodies, bodies corporeal and bodies politic as it were, and are thus powerful or power-associated imaginative devices.

If it may be thought, incidentally, that this ethnographic experience is of a very unique kind one might consider Gillian Feeley Harnick's (1991) *A Green Estate: Restoring Independence in Madagascar*, in which arboreal metaphors are organising to her argument, as they are organising to the Sakalava in their planting of themselves and their flourishing or root-starved genealogies in history and in the world.[3] Elsewhere, the focus in central Africa on slash-and-burn agriculture, *citemene*, where trees are sites of manly confirmation and cultural affirmation, has been a consistent theme in ethnography, from the pioneering 1930s work of Audrey Richards, for example, *Land, Labour and Diet in Northern Rhodesia* (Richards 1939), to the contemporary historical ethnography *Cutting Down Trees: Gender Nutrition and Agricultural Change in the Northern Province of Zambia, 1890–1990* (Moore and Vaughan 1994). Or one might consider, from a more practical point of view if one is desired, the long-term commitment to tree-planting, since the founding of the Arbor Day Movement in the 1870s, in the United States, in the Prairie and Great Plains States principally. There has been a recent upswing in this interest in tree-planting in the United States, Europe, indeed the world, as a counter to the destruction of the tropical rain-forests and the accumulation of greenhouse gases. Also plentiful is the literature on deforestation and reforestation, particularly in the Third World, in which the symbolism of trees and a culture's engagement with them is of focal consideration for the anthropologist as ethnographer (Feeley Harnick 1991; Sahlins 1994) or the anthropologist as developer (Murray 1987).

In any event, in both the cultural milieux I know best, Africa and Asturias, tree symbolism is of the greatest importance, and trees or parts of them are predicated upon individuals and upon groups to considerable, usually salutary, effect. Ecologically speaking, this is not surprising. Equatorial West Africa is one of the most richly forested parts of the earth; and the Cantabrian slope of Spain, in contrast to most of the Iberian Peninsula, was, until not too long ago, densely populated with oak and beech and ash forests . . . from which came the timbers of the Great Armada, just to evoke a symbolically powerful historical event in English-speaking lands.

A Tree Culture of the Equatorial Forest

Since I have written extensive ethnography on the place of trees in the religious imagination of Fang, I shall only summarise and point up those materials here. I shall have a little more to say about trees in Asturian culture. The index entries for 'trees' and for 'forest' in the ethnography of Bwiti run to easily several hundred items (Fernandez 1982: 701–2; 727–8), with particular attention paid to the way that the religion of Bwiti uses the many different tree varieties of the Equatorial forest to structure their Chapel and give it meaningful architectonic form. For the pillar of the Chapel, the *akon aba*, sometimes called 'the tree of heaven and earth', or 'the tree of life and death', is necessarily made of red *padouk* in order to symbolise the path of life and death that the Banzie, the adepts of Bwiti, travel during their initiation and during their subsequent life in Bwiti. But the supporting columns of the Chapel are made of different trees entirely, as are the beams, each with its particular symbolic weighting and particular contribution to the overarching architectonic. In the initiation into Bwiti, described extensively in Chapter 18, more than a dozen different trees are exploited for their sap, their bark, and particularly their leaves in order to minister in powerful potions, salves and unguents, and burnt offerings to the initiate, and thereby, by association, transform his or her bad body (*nyol abe*) and bring him or her as a new and purified, 'a goodbodied', member into the religion.

As far as direct religious doctrine is concerned, the Saviour figure, 'He Who Sees God' (*Eyene zame*), is conceived as having been crucified upon the *otunga* tree . . . a tree particularly strong in associations for Fang (Figure 4.1).[4] It is not surprising that with this dependence upon tree symbolism (in truth, of course, the Fang themselves are highly dependent economically *as well as symbolically* upon the equatorial forest in which they live) that the Bwiti religion calls itself and is called by other Fang a 'Religion of the Forest' or a 'Religion of Trees' (Fernandez 1982: 472). No ethnography of the Fang religious imagination – a powerful imagination, as I tried to demonstrate in too many pages – can be adequately written without giving careful consideration to the precise Fang knowledge of the rich diversity and great variety of uses of the Equatorial forest, and the potential ways that diversity can be both good to think with and a good by which to order behaviour.

Asturias: The Moral Agency of the Oak

Let me move on to present ethnographic work in Asturias, a heavily forested Celtic landscape where an ethnographer can spend hours with countrymen talking about trees. Let me focus on the oak (*Quercus hispanica*, or *Quercus robur*) and speak to the imaginative power of the oak in Asturian culture. I will single out this tree because it is the emblem of identity of the provincial capital and its residents, who are nicknamed *carbayon* (Great Oaks). For more than a century, as can be detailed, the oak has been a periodic symbolic focus of the identity

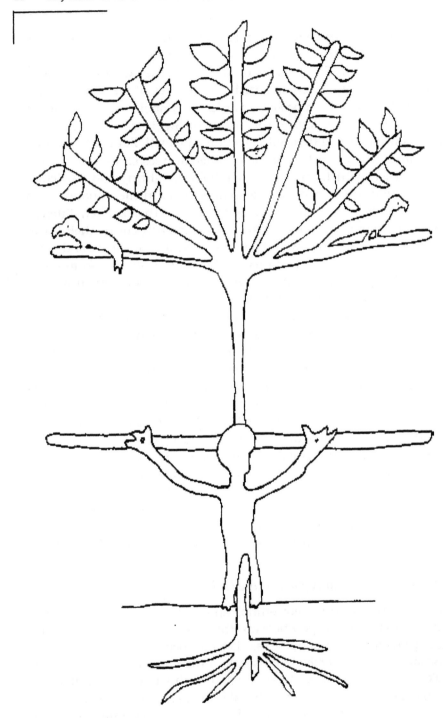

Figure 4.1 The 'Otunga Tree' of Bwiti on Which 'He Who Sees God' was Hung.

preoccupations of the inhabitants. It is also a tree imaginatively provocative in a general way to Asturians as both a tree of corporate Life and
a vehicle of corporate Death.[5] It might be expressed analogically, as in
fact it *is* expressed in the neighbouring region of Galicia, that both
men and trees derive their sustenance and character from being
'planted' in local geography.[6]

In any event, no more than in the case of the African work can I
give in this place a full ethnographic account of how trees and forest
are imaginatively provocative in the province. But one can suggest what
an adequate ethnographic account of these powerful local images would
involve. It would involve some prehistorical and historical references,
the place of the Oak among the ancient Indo-Europeans, for example,
whose 'arboreal orientation' has been clearly shown.[7] It would include
references in Strabo's geography to the surprising dependence, from
the classical view, of the pre-romanised Asturian tribes on the oak and
other nut trees and upon their dry fruits that gave nuts, acorn and
beech nut flour, and walnut oil. It would include the place of the oak
among other northern Iberian tribes such as the Basques, where it
continues to be the central symbolic tree of the Basque nation at
Guernika.

There is an instructive identifying contrast here to the rest of Iberia,
where the olive and the vine and their oils and fermentations predom-
inate, in contrast to the Asturian acorn and apple and the nutmeals,
nut oils and, of course, local cider; this is to say nothing of the symbolic
geography dividing butter-users and olive oil-users in Iberia! Such an
ethnography would involve a review of all the Asturian place-names
in which trees are referenced, particularly the oak.[8] It would involve
the many proverbs and maxims and tales, in which trees of various
kinds constitute the metaphoric expression, the objective correlatives,
of the proverbial wisdom conveyed.[9] It would involve, once again by
reference to folk and religious lore, an examination of the sacrosanct
place of beech, oak and chestnut groves, and tree and forest spirits, in
Asturian folklore. It would involve an account of the powerful place in
the local parochial imagination of the parish forests, as a source of
arboreal fruits of all kinds, dry and fleshy, and the struggle, since time
immemorial, over the local proprietorial rights over the forest (or at
least over specific trees), as between the individual family and the
community, and since the re-organisation of the Spanish State in the
early nineteenth century, between the village and parish community,
on the one hand, and the municipality, on the other.[10] All these
historical and cultural associations are potentially at work in variable

ways in the provincial imaginations where trees and forests are concerned, imparting a special quality, for example, to the arguments and actions of the contemporary ecological movement and its strenuous defence of the few remaining oak and beech forests in the Province.[11]

So the ethnography of the imaginative power of the Asturian oak, the *Carbayo*, which would be an ethnography of its *potent*-ial associations, is no easy descriptive task, but involves a complex prehistorical, botanical, folkloric, socio-cultural and political economic consultation. In the case of the Great Oak of Oviedo (Figure 4.2) for well over a hundred years now the replacement of that ancient tree, which had stood for centuries along the main thoroughfare of the town, the Calle Uria, has been a recurrent issue in civic life. After long debate, and singular and continuous public protest, the Municipal Council of Oviedo in 1879, in view of the evident increasingly decrepit state of the tree and of the need to widen out the main street, agreed to cut the old tree down. This caused much lamentation and an outpouring of reactive prose and verse in the local press.[12] It was an act very provocative to the moral imagination. But the memory of the tree did not die, nor the offence at its removal. Finally in 1949 the Municipal Government, in an act of unusual corporate memory and of civic time-binding, and in recognition of the original offence to the citizen's identity, placed a commemorative plaque at the spot: 'Here stood for centuries the Great Oak (*Carbayon*), cut down on the 11th of October of 1879, symbolic tree of this city. The Municipal Government agreed on the 14th of March of 1949 to place this plaque to perpetuate its memory.'

But the plaque still did not yet suffice, and the next year a new young oak was planted nearby in a side yard of the Opera House. In the increasing pollution of Oviedo's inner city this tree and several successors never really flourished, which occasioned comment in the press and the usual banter by taxi drivers and residents about the weakness, by association, of the municipal character and municipal economic health, the moral stature and well-being of the town and its citizens being read reflectively in the declining well-being of the local oak. The present planting seems to be flourishing, incidentally, in contrast to the diminished prospects that Oviedo and Asturias, along with the other north-western Coastal Provinces of Spain, have of entering robustly into European-wide competition in the EEC in the 1990s.

That the character and, in some way, the fate of a European city should be read in the vicissitudes of a succession of oak trees is nothing

Figure 4.2 The 'Great Oak' (*Carbayon*) of Oviedo (from *Gran Enciclopedia Asturiana*, Vol. 4, p. 67).

new to our knowledge or to our imaginations. If it is not enough to recall Strabo's observations on the dependency of the ancient pre-Roman Asturians on the oak and upon acorn flour, we know from Frazer (1958, Chapters 9 and 10), and Hubert (1932) the place of the oak in the European religious imagination. As Frazer (1958: 127) says, 'the oak-worship of the Celtic Druids is familiar to every one, and their old word for sanctuary seems to be identical in origin and meaning with the Latin *nemus*, a grove or wooded glade which still survives in the name of Nemi'. The tree around which the fated priest prowled was an oak, after all. But it was not only the Celts. Oak worship was especially powerful among the Germans. And Frazer (1958: 127), as so frequently in *The Golden Bough*, provokes our imagination, in this case our imaginative comprehension, of the identification between tree and humans, with the following item:

> How serious the worship was in former times may be gathered from the ferocious penalty appointed by the old German laws for such as dared to peel the bark of a standing tree. The culprit's navel was to be cut out and nailed to a part of the tree which he had peeled and he was to be driven round and round the tree until all his guts were wound around its trunk. The intention of the punishment clearly was to was to replace the dead bark by a living substitute; it was a life for a life, the life of a man for the life of a tree.

In relation to this particular instance of tree–city identification I report from Asturias, Frazer gives us the Roman example of the sacred 'fig tree of Romulus'.[13] As regards Hubert's (1932) work on the Celts, though he questions the frequent derivation of the priestly name 'druids' from the Celtic name of the oak (thus 'priests of the Oak'), he argues that they are closely attached to the cult of the oak 'from which they collect mistletoe and eat acorns to acquire divinatory powers' (Hubert 1932: 276, my translation).

It would be useful, perhaps, to exercise Frazerian powers of comparison between these two cases, African and Asturian, concerning the imaginative presence of trees. I would contrast the corporeal efficacy of tree *product* in the first case, the African, and the social efficacy of the tree *presence* in the second, the Asturian. For the product of trees, saps, the powder of wood or leaves, is used efficaciously to bring about changes of state and vital flow, to encourage more adequate growth or inhibit excessive, in afflicted living bodies in the first instance; while in the second the vitality and character of the tree itself is taken as a sign of social identity, that is, of social character and vitality. Asturians do not now use the laying on or imbibing of oak products for sustenance or healing, though they once did. Indeed in ancient Asturian times the acorn was a principal food stuff. And here, of course, we recognise the inevitable change over historical time of the meaning of these images as a consequence of changing polities and changing economies. In any event, Fang at the time of research did not primarily think of trees as symbols of the body social, though certain trees were thought to stand for what their various religious societies were all about. And Asturians did not regard the oak as a source of food or of medicinal products. The comparison is thus not a perfect parallel. Indeed, while the Asturians no longer use tree products to treat affliction symbolically, the healthy or afflicted nature of trees can register health and affliction, order and disorder, in the body social.

The Great Tree of Being: Humankind's Place in the Natural Order Imagined

One main thing the Scottish moral philosophers were interested in understanding, beside human understanding itself, was, as the titles of some of their works indicate, 'man's place in nature', and how human understanding worked in its natural and social context to effect that 'placement'. For the most part, these 'moral philosophers' were convinced that man was a social creature and a creature whose under-standing was fundamentally influenced by the sentiments and passions of his life in society. This is to say, by virtue of man's social nature and the social context of its operation, they doubted that there was any understanding that was not, in some respects, an exercise, covert or overt, in the passionate processes, processes of categorical inclusion or exclusion of groups. Which is to say that reason is an exercise always influenced by the virtuous or invidious placement of oneself or one's group in relationship to others. Indeed for Hume the efficacy of reason, the original influence and conviction it obtains, rests on the imagin-ation, that is upon the 'passionate imaginings' and 'passionate placements' which undergird it. 'Reason', as he says in *The Treatise*, his youthful and most emphatic work on the subject, 'is and ought to be the slave of the passions and can never pretend to any other office than to serve and obey them'.[14]

But beyond the problem of placement within a given society was the problem of 'placement' of the varieties of humankind and the varieties of cultures that Western explorations (since the time of

Herodotus perhaps, but much enlarged by the Renaissance and the Age of Exploration) had revealed. The problem of placement as it exaggerated, by an excitement of the imagination, the awareness of strikingly diverse kinds of human beings required some kind of image or 'speculative instrument' of placement. The image or model of choice for the ordering of the various orders of creation of the period was the 'Great Chain of Being' or 'The Great Tree of Being', two related but different notions, as we shall indicate. This was a chain or tree in which the orders of creation were arranged in ever more refined essences approaching the final refinement of divine essence itself. As Margaret Hodgen (1964) has shown in *Early Anthropology of the Sixteenth and Seventeenth Century*, the growing awareness of the variety of uncivilised tribes created 'the problem of savagery', which was the problem of the static or dynamic and the hierarchical or collateral placement of the newly discovered varieties of men (largely imagined from either meagre or inflated explorer's accounts) in relation to each other. The tendency in the earlier centuries had been toward hierarchical and static placement both of the orders of being and of the varieties of savage, barbarous and civilised men. In the nineteenth century, and particularly after Darwin, the tendency, under the influence of the evolutionary idea *and* that of the psychic unity of mankind, was toward dynamic and collateral placement.

For our purposes here, the models by which this orderly placement was achieved are of special interest. For there was a tendency to move from, first, fixed spheres or levels or monads of being – confinement of essence, that is, to its own sphere or level – to, subsequently, ladders or stairways of being, which envisioned progressive refinement or transformation of essence and thus ascent of being, and then to, finally, evolutionary trees, which were quite dynamic and collateral and which linked the kinds of being in their placement in an evolutionary flow of a common sap-like essence from its deposition in the elemental roots to its final disjunctive and radiating fruition out upon the furthest boughs. Logical and natural 'Trees of Being' had occurred quite early in the Renaissance (Figure 4.3); but the truly dynamic, collateral, transformative evolutionary trees, such as the well-known one from Haeckel (Figure 4.4),[15] were mid-to-late nineteenth-century and post-Darwinian in appearance.

These struggles to order nature, and, particularly, to place the varieties of humankind and their cultures (and the appeal to a variety of models and metaphors to obtain that order) must inevitably be of considerable interest to anthropologists, whose work is, one might argue, always at

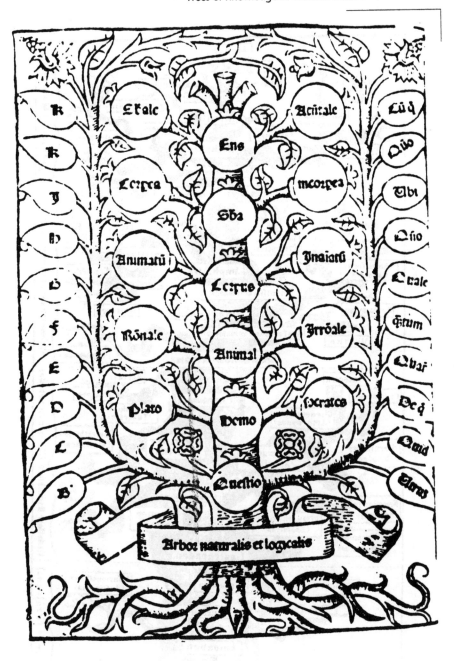

Figure 4.3 Tree Diagram of the Hierarchy of Being (from Raymond Lull, *De nova logica* (1512)). Reprinted in Margaret Hodgen: *Early Anthropology of the Sixteenth and Seventeenth Century*, Philadelphia, 1964, p. 399.

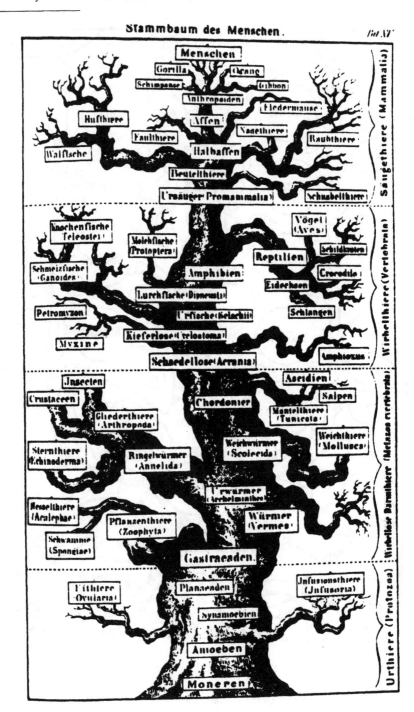

Figure 4.4 Haeckel's Evolutionary Tree (from Haeckel, 1874).

risk of being implicitly or inadvertently an ordering, and probably, as the eighteenth-century Moral Philosophers would argue, explicitly and necessarily a moral, that is passionate and approbative (or invidious), ordering of human natures. If we are inclined to believe that these ordering devices as ordering devices (without making specific reference to the problem of placement) and the service they offer to our understanding of the order of nature are all passions of the nineteenth century or earlier and, thus, obsolete to our present understanding, we may wish to consider the dependence on tree diagrams in modern transformational linguistics and the metaphor of the deep or root or kernel structure of language, which is transformed by the operational rules of linguistic branching into the abundant crown of the surface structure of language. Of course, much before this transformational model – indeed, since the discovery of the vast Indo-European family of languages of the nineteenth century, in fact – historical linguistics has employed language trees to model the relationships between languages in language families. Indeed, linguists will quickly realise how fundamental the presence of tree metaphors is in their work. As Paul Friedrich (1970: 11) remarks in a footnote to his study of Indo-European tree names, 'the stylistic problems in discussing PIE trees make one aware of the plethora of arboreal metaphors (mainly dead ones) in the literature of linguistics – stems, offshoots, roots, genealogical trees, branching diagrams, derivational trees etc'.

When we speak of genealogical trees (and language families arranged on genealogical trees) in linguistics, we are directly reminded of the presence of the arboreal model, the genealogical tree, in our understanding of the ordering of kin in family structures, whether we are referring to stem families or family stocks (or, in French, *souche*). Radcliffe-Brown and Forde (1950: 15–16) remind us, in reviewing the use of the body and body-appendage metaphor as 'one method of arranging sib-ship', that another way of reckoning degrees of kinship was by such 'stocks', 'a term derived figuratively from the Old German term for stump or trunk' . . . an arboreal reference in short. Of course, though all of these arboreal usages are mostly moribund and conventional and powerless, that is not to say they cannot be revived. The sense of the analogy employed is no longer very active in analytic usage either in linguistics or anthropology. Yet it can be demonstrated that contemporary analysis is not entirely freed up from the power and utility of these old analogies, and, in fact, that they are ever-present and potential in thinking.

This has been demonstrated by Lakoff and Turner (1989) for the organisation of categorical being in terms of 'The Great Chain of Being', an analysis relevant to the antique, once and future image of 'The Tree of Knowledge'. Lakoff and Turner point out that, though the Great Chain is taught in the history of literature as an idea important to the understanding of classical, medieval and renaissance authors and their worldviews (a conceit most prominently resurrected in the eighteenth century), it is by no means of purely historical interest; rather, 'on the contrary, a highly articulated version of it still exists as a contemporary unconscious *cultural model* indispensable to our understanding of ourselves, our world and our language' (Lakoff and Turner 1989: 167). And they show its hierarchical presence in the predicative process by which the more complex appeals to the less complex, the generic appeals to the specific, and the more prestigious appeals to the less for definition. These authors, however, want to do more than argue a pervasive cognitive vector of predication, i.e. of how our understanding makes use of the specific to understand the generic, and the less complex to understand the more. They want to call our attention also to the powerful implications of this commonplace metaphor, that is its implications for not only the dominant–subordinate relationship of being as between inanimate and animate, or merely sensate being on the one hand, and rational/self-conscious being on the other, but also its implications for hierarchical ordering of classes of human beings, the power that one class of humans is able to exert over another. 'The cultural model of the Great Chain concerns not merely attributes and behaviour but also dominance. In this cultural model, higher forms of being dominate lower forms of being by virtue of their higher, that is to say more refined or evolved natures' (Lakoff and Turner 1989: 208). Humans dominate animals and within their category dominate each other, a domination justified by reference to differences in essential being on some Great Chain. Lakoff and Turner note the many consequences for human history and social-political life of a cultural model based on the notion that a hierarchy of increasingly complex and increasingly refined, increasingly dominating essences is of the nature of the cosmos and of its inevitable and correct, if not its happy, order.

Anthropologists may question the universality of these tools of reasoning, these cultural models, but, at least within the Western tradition, we can easily recognise the profound ethical implications (in so far as the question of distributive justice is fundamental to ethics) contained in this metaphor. Had the Moral Philosophers contemplated 'The Great Chain' more intently (it was more explicit in argument in their century than in ours), they might have found that there was a whole moral philosophy in it. But, of course, our arboreal orientation here reminds us that there are other metaphors of hierarchical human placement and, as we have been suggesting, the tree metaphor, or what might be called, following the Great Chain analogy, the Great Tree of Being, is one of these. Of course there are important differences between a chain or ladder or stairway metaphor and a tree metaphor, whatever hierarchical commonalities they may possess. There is continuity of progression or progressive refinement in the former and disjunctivity, or radial differentiation, in the latter.[16] But in respect to the commonalities, we see that anthropologists are sensitive to the hierachising implications of the Great Tree version of the Great Chain metaphor. This is evidenced in Ralph Linton's (1959: v) clarification of what kind of a tree he specifically meant in choosing *The Tree of Culture* for the title of his compendium of world cultures:

> The title of the book refers not to the familiar evolutionary tree with a single trunk and spreading branches, but to the banyan tree of the tropics. The branches of the banyan tree cross and fuse and send down adventitious roots, which turn into supporting trunks. Although the banyan tree spreads and grows until it becomes a miniature jungle, it remains a single plant and its various branches are traceable to the parent trunk. So, cultural evolution, in spite of diffusion and borrowing and divergent development, can be traced to its prehistoric origins [. . .] the first part of [this study of cultural evolution] corresponds to the first growth of the banyan tree when it sends forth trunk and branches from its original roots. The second half of the book deals with the growth of civilizations, and the comparison here is with the branches which send down roots which find favorable ground and turn into sturdy independent trunks.

The adventitious re-rootings of the banyan branches evidently suggest a different and, perhaps, for an anthropologist, a more accurate and compelling metaphor than the common tree metaphor with the unidirectionality, hierarchy and finality of its spreading and diversifying fruitions. The banyan tree suggests a circularity, if not a tensile netlike interconnectedness of parts, in human affairs, both as regards cultural evolution and the evolution of understanding, that the normal tree metaphor either conceals or cannot manage to convey. The circular intertwined metaphor of the banyan tree, indeed, offers a different imaginative vision of the human condition, a different order of 'necessary connections' between human variety, than the tree metaphor pure and simple. The web metaphor, which is another powerful metaphor of the intellectual as well as the moral imagination and one that has been specifically proposed as much preferable to the tree metaphor for social science thinking (Kress 1969) also compensates for the discreteness and saliency and hierarchy of the tree metaphor. It was, incidentally, the metaphor that Frazer himself employed in the concluding parts of his argument with respect to the evolutionary reweaving of the intertwining threads of magic, science and religion.[17]

Another modern alternative to the hierarchical Great Chain or Great Tree of Being, is 'The Tree of Knowledge' itself as employed by Maturana and Varela (1988) in their book of the same name. These authors, contributors to the science of neuropsychology, seek to root human understanding in its cellular base. They wish us to understand the autogenesis or autonomy, or as they call it, autopoiesis, of both the life process itself and of human understanding. To summarise in the very briefest terms, they argue that life is a self-constituting system, and so, by necessity, is our understanding of it. There is, in their argument, a Humean scepticism about the possibility of any absolute certainty beyond what has been temporally constituted as comunally believable. But here we only wish to make clear that their choice of the tree metaphor expresses, for them, both the inter-nurturant unity of all forms of life (in contrast to the Great Ladder or Chain metaphor) and also the final circularity, which is to say self-constitution, of know-ledge and understanding. For as the leaves do not fall far from the tree of knowledge, so it, in effect, feeds and renourishes itself. This circularity of self-nurturance is seen in the drawing they choose for their leitmotif (Figure 4.5), as in the 'human is plant' or tree/mind/visual metaphor they have chosen for their cover (Figure 4.6, an adaptation of a painting by Salvador Dalí).

On the Passing Powers of the Imagination and the Landscapes of its Passage

> In Potebjna's examples from Slavic folklore, the willow under which a girl passes serves at the same time as her image: the tree and the girl are both co-present in the same verbal simulacrum of the willow.
>
> Roman Jakobson (1960: 371)

I want now to enter into the pithy final section of my argument, the heartwood, lest the argument become over-lush and spreading, banyan-like, in form. Of course, I have tried to preserve some ordering structure by depending on the sustained arboreal analogy, and something,

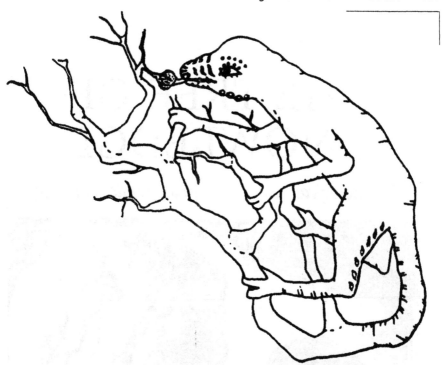

Figure 4.5 The Circularity of Self-Constitution of the Tree of Knowledge (from Maturana and Varela, *The Tree of Knowledge*, 1988, p. 240).

perhaps, of a tree-like structure in respect to the relationship between its roots in moral philosophy and its crown of ethnographic data. But it is time to put the argument in a nutshell. And since an anthropologist treating philosophy or cognitive psychology is in any event jumping 'out of his tree', I might better, indeed, do this by returning to the good earth of ethnography, which is to say the landscapes, in the broadest sense of the term, of ethnographic inquiry. For, of course, trees cannot flourish in academic soil ('bare ruined choirs' they will be), unless we can do more than stir our imaginations with the social resonance of these images. In fact we have hoped to do something more here. We have hoped not only to evoke the importance of these images in the dialogues and enactments of fieldwork but have also sought to explore something of the place of arboreality in human understanding itself. If arboreal interests are ethnographically demonstrable over and over again in my fieldwork (and surely not mine alone), something else is demonstrable as well. If trees in the African and Iberian work have been constellations of cultural meaning that are potent *points de repère*, either foci of activity or repositories of special

THE TREE OF KNOWLEDGE

The Biological Roots of Human Understanding

Humberto R. Maturana & Francisco J. Varela

FOREWORD BY J. Z. YOUNG

Figure 4.6 The Tree of Knowledge (Cover Drawing from S. Dalí in Maturana and Varela, 1988).

social signification, or both; they are also *points de repère* that give us
insight into the connectedness of culture, which is to say the play of
relations of proximity (contiguity) and similarity.

For we have pretended to more in this chapter than simply to have
explored a set of images widely and evocatively used in many cultures,
though in variable ways.[18] We have wanted also to think about the
way such images, which are found in nature, have been used to give
order to nature, and especially to give moral order to the nature of
human relationships, that is to give insight into the ordering of human
understanding of the *connectivities* of culture. Since the scepticism of
Hume, to be sure, confidence in *connectivity* has been posed as a
problem. It may be true that it has become less of a problem, at least
as far as the human sciences are concerned, for the problem of the
direct connection of cause and effect has been largely converted to a
problem of probabilistic calculation of co-occurrence. And the problem
of belief by frequency of associations, while not surplanted, has been
displaced sideways towards the peripheries by the study of the role of
imageless thought and innate mental schema in action. Nevertheless,
all is not imageless, and associations continue to play their role and,
indeed, the play of images in mind and culture is something that
continues to give vitality – corporeality – to the structures of lives as it
gives power to the imagination.

Here let us take advantage of an opportune quotation from Roman
Jakobson, which we use as an epigraph to this final section. Jakobson
treats of a subtle but constant transformation in experience: the way
that things contiguous to each can come to seem similar and to stand
for each other, can come to provide understanding of some essential
features of a passing subject of interest, say the kind of understanding
we obtain when we speak of the willowiness of young women. These
kinds of connections, the discovery of possible parallelisms of likeness
and unlikeness in our experience, are constant in culture and are one
way that cultures obtain a certain coherence of perceptually separated
parts. And they are one way that order (or at least the conviction of
order) is obtained in the affairs of culture. There is, of course, a whole
dynamic poetic theory, the dynamic relations and transformations of
things similar and things contiguous into each other, that treats of
this phenomenon. The play of tropes is what it is really about. To this
theory Roman Jakobson, the author of our epigraph, was a major
contributor.[19]

I do not propose to treat of that theory in any extended way here;
but I do wish to highlight the fact that it is such play, in this context

the imposition of similarity upon contiguity, that has long been going on with the tree imagery we review. It is a play that is popular and imaginatively active among these forest-dwelling or forest margin-dwelling cultures I have treated. For, in their passings to and fro in their contiguous forests, they have become connected to their trees, and out of this connection has come a sense of similarity between trees and themselves and trees and their body social and body politic. Trees are powerful in their imaginations, and powerful imaginations among them make use of that fact. An ethnography of these powerful imaginations, among many other attentions and atunements, is enriched by attention and atunement to the weight of these images. We might say that this atunement is necessarily attentive to the landscape that is contiguous to a particular culture, through which that particular people pass in their activities and parts (or the whole) of which it is in their power to convert to clarifying and ordering similarities. It is of more than passing interest, then, to note the way that this argument is relevant to that landscape school of local ethnography (*paisajismo*) aimed at understanding provincial and 'national character' that was once popular in Europe – certainly in the Spanish provinces where our own ethnography was conducted – in the late nineteenth and early twentieth centuries (Rodriguez Campos 1991: 99–111). Reflecting a much broader geographic determinism of the period, this romanticised if not pantheistic conception of culture sought to explain local and provincial character as a consequence of the impact of the particular natural characteristics of particular provinces or regions. One has to recognise a certain mystical element (pantheism) in this argument, a relation of *pathos* between men and the earth from which they spring, or a 'direct relation between a given landscape and the spiritual inclinations (the souls) and the characterological tendencies of its inhabitants' (Rodriguez Campos 1991: 107–10).

But despite the deterministic excesses of this argument it is, in interesting part, compatible with the argument being put forth here in so far as it recognises that the landscape offers, among other contiguous experiences of human life, primary images out of which or on the basis of which men and women, turning contiguities into similarities, can construct their senses of themselves, of their social relations and of the world – of their moral obligations, in short, in the widest sense of the term.[20] One does not pass through the lights and shadows of a landscape heedlessly and fruitlessly. Just as one constructs the differentiations of the social world, so one can use the entities, such as trees and forests, of the larger world to act as *points de repère* and embodiments of categorical obligation to that differentiated social order. One can use such sign-images to make connections.

In any event, the imaginative 'power' pointed up by Jakobson that men and women have to take contiguities and make them into similarities is the kind of 'power of connectedness' that the eighteenth-century 'moral philosophers', particularly Hume, denied to reason but discovered in imagination. And though it is not the kind of political-economic power we mainly have in mind in reasonable social science argument, it is, it might be argued, a mimetic power that lies behind and is crucial to the convictions, or power to convince, with which these more obvious and reasonable worldly powers operate.[21] To have eaten of the fruit of the tree of knowledge is more than to have discovered human wilfulness and the will to power. It is to have become enlightened as to how that wilfulness becomes convincing to itself and others!

Acknowledgements

This paper is a much-reduced version of a lecture, 'The Ethnography of Powerful Imaginations: Trees as Moral Models', given as a Monroe Lecture at Edinburgh University in October 1991. This, in part, accounts for its focus on the Scottish Enlightenment and the Scottish 'moral philosophers'. I would like to acknowledge the kind hospitality of the Department of Social Anthropology at the University and of its Professor A. P. Cohen. I am grateful to various colleagues for their collegiality and sylvanity in commenting on the original version of this paper: Gillian Feeley Harnick, Paul Friedrich, James Redfield, Peter Sahlins, Milton Singer, George Stocking.

Notes

1. An originating occurrence which becomes an organising metaphor for Nur Yalman's (1967) ethnographic study *Under the Bo Tree: Studies in Caste, Kinship and Marriage in the Interior of Ceylon.*

2. See Chapter 1 ('Symbols in Ndembu Ritual') of *The Forest of Symbols* by Victor Turner (1967: 19–47).

3. See particularly Chapter 9 ('Rooting Ancestors') of *A Green Estate: Restoring Independence in Madagascar*, and page 464: 'this book is about growing, grafting

and chopping ancestries to seize the land in which they are rooted [. . .] In organising my account of these movements around trees [. . .] I have followed the local idiom. These trees do not represent the diverse common grounds where masters of the land and strangers articulate their differences about growing and dying, they *are* the common grounds' (Feeley Harnick 1991). For Europe we may anticipate the forthcoming work of Peter Sahlins on the Demoiselle movement in nineteenth-century France, deeply exploitative, in their protest, of forest symbology.

4. It is of interest that in the Western tradition the cross of the crucifixion was known as 'The Tree': a Tree of Death to interact contrastively with the Tree of Life of the Garden, as a structuralist might point out.

5. One could expatiate almost as well upon the beech or the chestnut or the hazel, for these nut trees too are richly meaningful and widely distributed in Asturias.

6. See Xaquin Rodriguez Campos (1994: 41–8), who discusses the particular sense of 'rootedness' in the landscape experienced by Galician nationalists. The particular analogy that interests us is expressed in the following: 'Efectivamente o galego expresa frecuentemente unha ligazon desproporcionada co seu lugar de nacemento "como se fora un arbre", en palabras de V. Risco (Risco 1920: 6). Imaxe que fora expresada poeticamente por E. Ponmdal moitas veces, vendose por exemplo nos seguintes versos:

> Castazos de Dormea
> Os de corpos ben comprido,
> de graciosa estatura,
> dobrados e ben erguidos:
> Ouh! castazos, semellantes
> os celtas nosos antigos;
>
> ————
>
> Por fin na nosa vellez, despois do bo tempo ido,
> xuntos volvemos a vernos
> mais con diferente destino
> (Queixumes dos pinos, 1895)'.

7. See Paul Friedrich (1970), and, in particular Chapter 2 ('Botanical ordering', pp. 13–26) for a discussion of the 'arboreal orientation' of the proto-Indo-Europeans.

8. As, for example, in the reference book of Asturian nomenclature by Xose Lluis Garcia Arias (1977), *Pueblos Asturianos: El Porque de Sus Nombres,* especially Chapter 7 ('La Fitotoponomia o Las Plantas').

9. To be consulted here would be Luciano Castanon's (1973) collection of Asturian proverbs, *Refranero Asturiano,* and also the collection edited by Xuan

Xose Sanchez Vicente and Jesus Cavedo Valle (1986), *Mitoloxia: Refraneru Asturianu (Ordenau por temes),* in which these proverbs are thematically organised.

10. See here the developing work of Peter Sahlins, already mentioned, on this struggle over the rights to the forest in the Ariège of Pyrenean France.

11. Of interest in connection with the oak forest of Muniellos in central south-western Asturias, is, for example, the long and intense campaign, reported periodically over the years in the local press, to defend it against various kinds of exploitative development.

12. As, for example, this poem of bitter protest at the felling of the oak referenced in *La Gran Enciclopedia Asturiana,* Gijón 1970, Vol. 4, p. 67:

> Mi nombre al pueblo di, bajo mi copa
> que pomposa las ramas extendia,
> el pueblo su solaz aqui tenia
> y abrigo el estudiante de la sopa.
>
> Mi tronco fue un altar; y a él se atropa
> la noble indignación que se encendía
> y retaba con ruda valentia
> al invencible usurpador de Europa.
>
> Hoy de mis hijos el menguado aliento,
> con desdén indecible me maldice
> y sin piedad me arranca de mi asiento!
>
> Oh triunfo sin igual! Con voz entera
> de su silla cruel ingrato dice:
> Dar muerte al Carbayon antes que muera!

13. 'The withering of the trunk was enough to spread consternation throughout the city [. . .] Whenever the tree appeared to a passerby to be drooping, he set up a hew and cry which was echoed by the people in the street, and soon a crowd might be seen running helter skelter from all sides with buckets of water, as if (says Plutarch) they were hastening to put out a fire' (Frazer 1952: 111). See also the place of the ancient olive on the Acropolis of Athens as symbolic of the city's fate. See also in Herodotus, Book VIII. 55, the story of this olive tree, which sprang back to life immediately after it and the Acropolis were razed by the Persian invasion under Xerxes . . . a harbinger of the eventual Greek victory. Finally, see also Sophocles' *Oedipus at Colonus* (98–103).

14. David Hume (1898 (Vol. II): 95), *A Treatise of Human Nature*, as excerpted and commented upon in Louis Schnider (1967: 7–8). Hume frequently remarked that *The Treatise* was too 'youthful' and 'impetuous' a work, even though it was the groundwork for all his later efforts.

15. Discussed at length in Part I, Chapter 5 of Stephen J. Gould's (1977) *Ontogeny and Phylogeny*.

16. Steven J. Gould, the evolutionary biologist, has written repeatedly and as perceptively as anyone about the models and metaphors that have guided and misguided evolutionary thinking. In his 1991 collection *Bully for Brontosaurus: Reflections in Natural History*, he offers a sharp critique, relevant to present discussion, of the 'distortions imposed by converting tortuous paths through bushes into directed ladders'. Evolutionary continuity, he points out, 'comes in many more potential modes than the lock step of the ladder. Evolutionary genealogies are copiously branching bushes – and the history of horses is more lush and labyrinthine than most' (Gould 1991: 175). Thanks to David Sutton for this reference.

17. 'We may illustrate the course that thought has hitherto run by likening it to a web woven of three different threads, the black thread of magic, the red thread of religion and the white thread of science, if under science we may include those simple truths drawn from observation of nature of which men in all ages have possessed a store' (Frazer 1952: 826).

18. These complex images, such as the tree images, may well qualify as what Rodney Needham (1978) has called synthetic images. These images are constituted of bundles or constellations of primary qualities widely present in human experience (Needham teases us with the Jungian term archetype), though variably constellated and made meaningful only in partial ways in particular cultures. This makes them widely evocative and apt subjects for inter-cultural communication.

19. That is to say the figurative interplay of metaphor, metonym, synecdoche and irony (see Fernandez 1991). But see the pioneering statements by Roman Jakobson here, not only in the article from which the epigraph is taken (Jakobson 1960), but also in Jakobson and Halle (1956). In the instance of the epigraph quoted, Jakobson (1960: 371) goes on to say, quoting Goethe's 'Alles Vergängliche ist nur ein Gleichnis' (Anything transient is but a likeness), that 'in poetry where similarity is superinduced upon contiguity, any metonymy is slightly metaphorical and any metaphor has a metonymical tint'. At the root of these tropic transformations is a basic ambiguity, also insisted upon by Jakobson, as to the direction of connectivity that has a certain Humean ring to it.

20. See Rodriguez Campos' (1991: 108) discussion of the ethnography of the Galician regionalist Vicente M. Risco and his tendency to take for granted

that 'the landscape acted directly upon the soul of its inhabitant', although as a close reader of the folk psychology (*Volkseele* or *Volkgeist*) of Wilhelm Wundt, Rodriguez Campos remarks, Risco understood that 'direct action' consisted in the fact that the landscape offered primary images with which humans could construct their conception of the world.

21. In this regard see the discussion of the mimetic power of transformation and conversion in Michael Taussig (1993). Though not framed in Prague School terms, what Taussig discusses is the possibility of the dynamic – 'magical' is his term – transformation in the developing contact situation between Euro-Americans and the coloured 'races' from mere contiguity to the recognition of similarity . . . or what amounts to the same thing, the shift from a sense of contagion to a sense of sympathy!

References

Castanon, L., *Refranero Asturiano*, Oviedo: IDEA, 1973

Feeley Harnick, G., *A Green Estate: Restoring Independence in Madagascar*, Washington, DC: Smithsonian Institution Press, 1991

Fernandez, J. W. (ed.), *Beyond Metaphor: The Theory of Tropes in Anthropology*, Stanford: Stanford University Press, 1991

Frazer, J. G., *The Golden Bough: A Study of Magic and Religion*, 6th edn. Abridged 1 vol., New York: MacMillan, 1958 [1922]

Friedrich, P., *Proto-European Trees*, Chicago: Chicago University Press, 1970

Garcia Arias, X. L., *Pueblos Asturianos: El Porque de Sus Nombres*, Salinas: Ayalga, 1977

Gould, S. J., *Ontogeny and Phylogeny*, Cambridge: Cambridge University Press, 1977

—— *Bully for Brontosaurus: Reflections in Natural History*, New York: Norton, 1991

Hodgen, M., *Early Anthropology of the 16th and 17th Century*, Philadelphia: University of Pennsylvania Press, 1964

Hubert, H., *Les Celtes depuis l'époque de la Tène et la civilisation celtique*, Paris: Renaissance du Livre, 1932

Hume, D., *A Treatise of Human Nature*, ed. T. Greene and T. Grosse, London: Longman Green, 1898

Jakobson, R., 'Closing Statement: Language and Poetics in Theory', in E. Sebeok (ed.), *Style in Language*, Cambridge: Cambridge University Press, 1960

Jakobson, R. and M. Halle, *Fundamentals of Language*, The Hague: Mouton, 1956

Kress, P. F., 'The Web and the Tree: Metaphors of Reason and Value', *Midwest Journal of Political Science*, 13, 1969, pp. 395–414

Lakoff, G. and M. Turner, *More Than Cool Reason: A Field Guide to Poetic Metaphor*, Chicago: Chicago University Press, 1989

Linton, R., *The Tree of Culture*, New York: Knopf, 1959

Maturana, H. and F. Varela, *The Tree of Knowledge: The Biological Roots of Human Understanding*, Boston: Shambhala, 1988

Moore, H. L. and M. Vaughan, *Cutting Down Trees: Gender, Nutrition and Agricultural Change in the Northern Province of Nigeria – 1890–1990*, Portsmouth: Heinemann, 1994

Murray, G., 'The Domestication of Wood in Haiti: A Case Study in Applied Anthropology', in R. Wulff and S. Fiske (eds), *Anthropological Praxis: Translating Knowledge into Action*, Boulder, Col.: Westview Press, 1987

Needham, R., *Primordial Characters*, Charlottesville: University Press of Virginia, 1978

Radcliffe-Brown, A. R. and D. Forde (eds), *African Systems of Kinship and Marriage*, London: KPI & Routledge Kegan Paul, 1950

Richards, A., *Land, Labour and Diet in Northern Rhodesia: An Economic Study of the Bemba Tribe*, London: Routledge, 1939

Rodriguez Campos, J., 'La Etnografía Clásica de Galicia: Ideas y proyectos', in J. Prat, U. Martinez, J. Contreras and I. Moreno (eds), *Antropología de los Pueblos de España*, Madrid: Tecnos, 1991

—— 'Cultura e Experiencia Humana Na Antropoloxia Romantica de Galicia', in *Actas do Simposio internacional de Antropoloxia en Memorial Fermin Bouza Brey. Consello da Cultura Galega, Santiago de Compostela*, 1994, pp. 41–8

Sahlins, P., *Forest Rites: The War of the Demoiselles in Nineteenth Century France*, Cambridge, Mass.: Harvard University Press, 1994

Sanchez Vicente, X. X. and J. Cavedo Valle, *Mitoloxia: Refraneru Asturianu (Ordenau por temes)*, Xixón, 1986

Schnider, L. (ed.), *The Scottish Moralists: On Human Nature and Society*, Chicago: Chicago University Press, 1967

Sebeok, T. E. (ed.), *Style in Language*, Cambridge: Cambridge University Press, 1960

Taussig, M., *Mimesis and Alterity: A Particular History of the Senses*, New York: Routledge, 1993

Turner, V., *The Forest of Symbols*, Ithaca: Cornell University Press, 1967

Yalman, N., *Under the Bo Tree: Studies in Caste, Kinship and Marriage in the Interior of Ceylon*, Berkeley: University of California Press, 1967

Part II

Trees, Human Life and the Continuity of Communities

Trees and People: Some Vital Links. Tree Products and Other Agents in the Life Cycle of the Ankave-Anga of Papua New Guinea

Pascale Bonnemère

The Ankave are a group of some one thousand forest horticulturists living in three closed valleys of the Gulf Province of Papua New Guinea. Their territory has roughly the shape of a thirty-kilometre-wide square. A minimum of one-and-a-half day's walk is necessary to cover the distance separating Ankave land from the nearest road, airstrip, school, shop, or health centre. The altitude of Ankave land, which is entirely covered with forests, except for patches of permanent grassland where hamlets have been established for many generations, varies between 600 and 2,300 metres.

The vegetal world is of key importance in Ankave daily life. It provides the bulk of their food, and most of the raw materials they need for technical activities. The gardens produce mainly tubers, bananas and sugar cane. An important complement to the diet comes from the seasonal fruits and nuts of trees grown spontaneously, or deliberately maintained and planted, in particular the red pandanus and the *Pangium edule*. As these two species mature one after the other, their fruit are available all year round. Despite the proximity of Ankave settlements to forests and rivers, and despite the importance of wild pigs, marsupials, cassowaries and eels in ceremonial exchanges between affines, hunting and fishing are secondary, irregular activities (Lemon-

113

nier 1993). And although a few pigs are raised (0.5 per capita), Ankave diet is primarily based on plant food (Bonnemère 1993).

Since access to manufactured goods is minimal, many basic objects are made from trees or other plants. For example, the Ankave beat tree bark (mainly *Ficus* bark) to make capes, loincloths, netbags, and leashes for piglets. Wood is also a major raw material used to build houses, fences and bridges, and to manufacture bows and arrow-heads, shields and hourglass-shaped drums. In the absence of clay pots, bamboo tubes are used as vessels for drinking water and for cooking small quantities of tubers and leafy vegetables. Trees are clearly the main vegetal material used by the Ankave, who make all kinds of objects with them. In fact, only a very small number of tools (needles and awls) are made from cassowary or pig bone.

Besides being used for their material quality or by-products, several woody plants classified as 'trees'[1] also pervade Ankave ritual life: the red pandanus (*Pandanus conoideus*), several varieties of the *Ficus* species, the areca-nut palm (*Areca catechu*), the reddish-purple-leafed cordylines (*Cordyline fruticosa*), and secondarily the ɔru'wə ' (*Syzygium* spp.) and the ʃaoxə' (*Elaeocarpus sphaericus*) trees. Investigating the meanings assigned to trees and tree-products in life-cycle ceremonies, the main collective events of Ankave social life, is thus highly relevant to the understanding of the relations the Ankave establish between people and trees. As we shall see, such an undertaking leads the researcher to study representations of human growth and maturation.

Who are the Ankave-Anga?

The Ankave belong to a set of some 70,000 people known collectively as Angans. Divided into forty or fifty tribes or local groups speaking twelve related languages, the Angans share many cultural features, such as patrilineal descent, absence of large-scale ceremonial exchanges, and the paramount importance accorded to war and male initiations, which underpin and express asymmetrical relationships between men and women. Nevertheless, there are notable differences between Anga groups. Amongst the Ankave, unlike such northern Angans as the Baruya and the Sambia, about whom Maurice Godelier and Gilbert Herdt respectively have written extensively, the marriage system is governed by negative rules supplemented with small bridewealth payments;[2] young girls are not initiated; menstruating women are not secluded; and male initiations have never involved boy-inseminating practices (formerly called ritualised homosexuality). In contrast to those

Anga groups who stress the role of semen in making boys grow and mature (Mimica 1991), Ankave male rituals emphasise the role of the young boys' mothers and sisters, and make use of various products (plant, mineral and animal) related to femininity (Bonnemère 1996).

The promotion of bodily growth is the main purpose of most of the rites the Ankave hold for small children of both sexes and for young boys in particular. Girls are said to mature almost exclusively on their own and do not need to undergo physical treatments of the same intensity as those considered necessary for boys. Initiation rituals[3] are the place where male maturation takes place. These sets of rites can be divided into three main periods: the first stage when boys aged from eight to twelve have their septum pierced; the second stage, taking place from several weeks to a year afterwards, named after the main rite involved, that is the (violent) smearing of boys with red pandanus seeds (the boys then become ʃəmaʐinə', from ʃəmaʒə', red pandanus tree); and the third and last stage, organized when a man's first child is born. But, as the whole period of pregnancy is surrounded by specific behaviours it might also be considered as part of the third-stage rituals. With the exception of the *Ficus*, whose bark is used to make the capes and breech cloths of male initiates, as well as the capes of their fathers and mothers, a common feature of the trees appearing in male rituals is the colour red, whether it applies to the fruits, the leaves, the bark, or the mixture of an areca nut and a betel leaf after chewing. And, as I am going to show, it is precisely for this reason that they are considered good candidates for ritual use, for the main purpose of initiation rituals is to make boys grow and mature.

Trees in Life-cycle Rituals

The Red Pandanus

Pandanus conoideus is a planted tree that grows to a height of between three and five metres. Botanists describe the genus *Pandanus* as 'woody palm-like plants',[4] with a grey-coloured trunk and, commonly, propping roots. Red pandanus, like some other species of the same genus, is believed to be parthenogenic (Hyndman 1984: 287). The Ankave call it ʃəmaʒə', a subdivision of their life-form taxon i'kə'a', which, as noted earlier, corresponds to our own 'tree' concept. They distinguish and name fifteen varieties of ʃəmaʒə', among which one produces yellow fruit instead of red; these varieties bear fruit at different times throughout the rainiest season, which extends from August to April. Trees are

found at altitudes ranging from 700 to 1,300 metres. They are prop-
agated from cuttings and take about four years to mature and come
into fruit (Sillitoe 1983: 112). The fruit can be described as a long seed
cluster, 'tapering to a blunt rounded point, and almost cylindrical with
a somewhat triangular cross section' (Sillitoe 1983: 112). 'The edible
portion is the hard red (or yellow) waxy mesocarp and pericarp between
the hard, inedible seeds' (Hyndman 1984: 295). As is the case in most
New Guinea societies, red pandanus trees are planted and maintained,
and their fruit is collected and prepared exclusively by adult men. To
prepare the oily juice to be spread over tubers, the fruit are first split in
half and cored with a cassowary femur bone. They are then cooked in
bamboo tubes, or in stone ovens, depending on the quantity. After
cooking, the red oil is squeezed by hand from the softened seeds. The
operation is repeated three or four times; the juice obtained each time,
which has a slightly different aspect, is known under different and
specific names.

Lexical analysis confirms the Ankave analogy between human blood
– and more specifically maternal blood – and red pandanus juice.
ʃəmaʒə' is like female blood, it is said. It is not considered a hot
substance (a feature which would associate it with femaleness as well),
and it contributes to increase the amount of blood in the body, and
make the skin shiny. Blood is called taʒə', a word entirely inappropriate
with reference to red pandanus juice processing, and hence one that
no one ever uses in this particular context. But the word for the oiliest
and reddest juice that comes from the first pressing is referred to by a
paronym of the word for blood, tanə'[5] (for more details, see Bonnemère
1994a: 25). The tanə' is in fact obtained by mixing the thin red layer
which covers the seed (called kə'ka'a') with water.[6] A blood clot is also
designated by the term kə'ka'a'. It is said that, when ingested, only the
tanə' goes directly into the veins; the kə'ka'a' and the less oily juices
obtained after the first squeezing become faeces. The analogical
relationship between blood and red pandanus underlies a series of
practices related to growth, health and procreation. When a woman is
pregnant, for example, she must not restrain her consumption of red
pandanus juice, because the foetus feeds on it. It is this red juice that
makes it grow and provides its blood. Her husband, on the other hand,
cannot eat this particular food, because it is feared that there will be
too much blood, causing haemorrhage during childbirth. The same
thinking applies when a young girl menstruates for the first time: her
future husband abstains from eating red pandanus for several days.

Because the main purpose of initiations is to promote the growth and maturation of young boys, and because blood is regarded as the main agent of bodily growth, its vegetal substitute occupies a prominent place in these ceremonies. The second-stage rituals, as we have already said, are even designated by the name for red pandanus. Both men and women know that young boys undergo smearing with red pand- anus *seeds* immediately before being decorated with specific ornaments such as the forehead band, made of beaten bark dyed with red pandanus juice. The modalities of this knowledge, however, differ considerably depending on whether you are a man or a woman, that is, on whether or not you are allowed to witness the rituals held in the forest (Bonnemère 1994b). The ingestion of red pandanus *juice* by the initiates during the first stage of the ceremonies is one rite strictly concealed from women.[7] Red pandanus fruits are used here in two separate ways, which are gender specific. Whereas the oral ingestion of red pandanus juice is considered a maternal kind of nourishment (it is for instance a recommended and prized food for pregnant women), pandanus seed smearing is an action performed eclusively by men.

Ankave male initiations symbolically re-enact most of the events that pertain to the process of procreation, from sexuality to mother gestures just after childbirth. I use the ethnographic material briefly presented, and restricted here to the red pandanus (but see Bonnemère 1996: 345– 52 and in press for further details), to interpret the consumption of red pandanus juice during the first stage of the rituals under discussion as an imitation of what pregnant women do to make the foetus grow. This analysis is consistent with the fact that the mothers of initiates, who are secluded during the rituals, endure many of the restrictions they also respect during pregnancy. My interpretation of male initiation as 'rebirth' also guides the way I analyse the evident similarity between the initiates' smeared bodies (particularly their shoulders and faces) and the reddish appearance of newborn babies covered in their mothers' blood (Bonnemère 1996: 349–50). The question that immediately arises is why Ankave men splash the initiates' heads with the oily pigments of red pandanus seeds rather than with the juice. Previous analyses of sexual asymmetry in northern Anga groups (Godelier 1982; Herdt 1981, 1987) point to an answer. They have shown that, during initiations, the main purpose of men is to sever boys from their mothers in order to turn them into adults through the ingestion of semen. At the same time, men constantly deny the role of women in the procreation process, attributing the power of making the foetus grow to the seminal substance. But the Ankave attribute this power to the mother's blood, the substance that makes the foetus' blood. Notwithstanding, Ankave initiation rituals illustrate a similar attempt by men to override the role of women in procreation by using a vegetal substitute for female blood in their own way. Eating red pandanus juice in great secret and smearing the seeds rather than the juice are two examples of such an attempt.

Two myths that focus on red pandanus also illustrate the male endeavour to defeminise a substance associated with females. The main events of the story (the origin myth of the red pandanus tree) are as follows:

> Somewhere near Menyamya (the centre of present-day Anga land), a man emerged from the earth. This man gave all those who followed him a clan name. He was the only one who had none. Then some people killed him. Each clan received a part of his body. The Ankave were given the blood and several bones. From a clot, a reddish purple-leafed cordyline (*oxemǝxǝ'*) appeared; from the blood itself, a red pandanus emerged. They didn't know anything about this tree. When it bore fruit, they tried it, and found it sweet. They kept the tree and its fruit well out of the women's sight, and planted many cuttings.
>
> The men soon decided that they would forbid the consumption of red pandanus juice during the nose-piercing ceremony, which they performed with a bone from the man-who-had-no-name's body. One day, the initiation master, who had ingested some red pandanus juice, had a dream: the spirit of the man-who-had-no-name was telling him to smear the faces and shoulders of the initiates with red pandanus to make them grow because the red pandanus juice was his blood.

The second myth relates how a woman discovered the existence of the red pandanus tree:

> A long time ago, women did not eat red pandanus juice. Men blocked the way to the trees so women did not know that they bore fruit. At that time, only adult men and boys who had already undergone the 'smearing-red-pandanus' ceremony could eat it. One day an old woman followed her husband and saw the men squeezing red pandanus. Soon afterwards, she fell sick. A woman shaman examined her and, after hearing her story, wanted to see what the men were doing in secret. Both women went to the spot and saw red pandanus seeds on the ground. They wrapped some up and took them home. The old woman died. The woman shaman went back to the spot, and saw the tree which bore a great amount of red fruit. She returned home and told her discovery to her husband. He told all the men, who then proposed to the women to eat the red juice. Ever since, red pandanus is processed and consumed in the village.

In these myths, red pandanus juice, closely associated for both men and women with maternal aliments, becomes a substance exclusively associated with men. Finally, the first red pandanus tree grew where the blood of a male 'ancestor' was spilled, and, since then,[8] only men have prepared and consumed the 'vegetal blood'.

To summarise, among the Ankave, as in northern Anga groups, a correspondence exists between the representations of intra-uterine growth and the ways in which boys are made to mature. However, both the substances involved and the ritual operations undertaken are different: semen and boy-inseminating practices (fellatio) among the Baruya and the Sambia; red pandanus, either eaten or smeared, among the Ankave. In the Ankave case, although men imitate a process connected with women (men believe that it is maternal blood which feeds the foetus), they reappropriate what they consider its substitute – the red pandanus – in two different ways: by using the seeds instead of the juice, and by imagining that a male body is at the tree's origin. In any case, it is clear that male domination and sexual asymmetry, articulated through ideas and actions connected with procreative substances and their vegetal substitutes, are common to all the Anga groups. As for tree symbolism, the link between red pandanus and blood – the most vital body substance – is clearly strong, as is evidenced by the terms used for naming the different stages of juice preparation. Additional lexical homologies between the human body and the pandanus tree can be cited. The trunk, for example, is called *eʒə'*, 'bones'; the fruit is called *na'*, i.e. 'body', and the leaves surrounding the fruit *Səmazinə'*, the term used for the breech cloth made of beaten *Ficus* bark (see below).

The Cordylines

Cordylines are woody plants with long leaves of various colours widely found throughout the Pacific region. In New Guinea, where they are mainly ornamental, cordylines are planted in gardens or near houses; their leaves are cut and used in body decorations. Cordylines, with their remarkable ability to reproduce from cuttings severed from the solid stalk and simply stuck back into the ground, are potent symbols of growth and productivity. The Ankave call the cordylines *warəba'*, which, like the term used for red pandanus, is a subdivision of the life-form taxon *i'kə'a'*. Fifteen cultivars of *warəba'* are distinguished and named. Those with green leaves are planted as living fences for domestic enclosures, where they continue to grow long after the first dwellers have moved away. Parents place the newly cut hair of their children[9] at the base of the green cordylines surrounding their houses. In a similar fashion, and to mark the end of the mourning period, which lasts at least one year, the relatives of a deceased who had stopped cutting their hair during mourning deposit their cut hair in the green cordylines of the closest domestic enclosure. But rather than green cordylines, two reddish-purple-leafed varieties (*oxemǝxǝ'*[10] regarded as male, and *ǝ'irǝ'* regarded as female) are prominently used in initiation rituals. As mentioned earlier, the same myth relates the origin of both the red pandanus and the *oxemǝxǝ'* cordyline, which comes from a blood clot of the man-who-had-no-name. As for the *ǝ'irǝ'* cordylines, one version of another myth tells that they originated from the body of an old woman who killed and ate four men who were brothers, before being killed by the fifth (see below).

During male rituals, the *oxemǝxǝ'* cordylines are used in two ways: as fences for marking out a ritual space, notably in the third stage of the ceremonies; and, during the second stage, as decorations held by the initiates who come back to the village after having been smeared with red pandanus seeds. It is noteworthy that each of these cordylines has been taken by older men from their own domestic plots and secretly brought to the bush. When the initiates arrive at the village, their mothers also wave cordylines with rapid up and down movements, but, unlike their sons, they use *ǝ'irǝ'* cordylines. Finally, during the third stage of the rituals, the body decorations received by new fathers are placed on a platform surrounded with *oxemǝ xǝ'* cordylines. After the ceremony, each man takes a cutting to plant back home. This is how red cordylines 'circulate' continuously from one ritual stage to another, and from one generation to the next.

The Areca-nut Palm

As in many other South-east Asian and Pacific societies, the Ankave make generous use of the *Areca catechu* fruit. Again, the term designating the eleven varieties of this palm, *nǝngijǝ'*, is a subdivision of the life-form taxon for tree, *i'kǝ'a'*. Most of these varieties grow spontaneously and bear fruit several times a year. People consume the inner nut of the fruit with betel leaves (and/or vines) and lime, which they make by burning the bark of certain species of trees. The mixture, chewed, gradually turns into a bright red runny paste which is spat out after ten minutes or so, leaving the mouth feeling intensely dry, mainly because of the lime. Although the areca-nut palm is not directly used during initiation rituals, I mention it here because it is explicitly prohibited at specific times during ritual performances. More generally, the Ankave refrain from chewing betel whenever blood is flowing or likely to flow, either naturally (i.e. in menstruation and child delivery), or at times of internal conflict or inter-tribal fighting, or during ritual events such as initiations. Moreover, those mourning the death of a close relative do not consume areca nuts, imposing this restriction on themselves out of sympathy for the deceased, who is no longer able to partake in this convivial pleasure.

Earlier analyses have shown that areca nuts are associated with corpses, the fluids of decomposition, and dried-up, lifeless blood. Apart from being the instrument of conviviality *par excellence*, betel chewing enhances physical beauty, strengthens the teeth, and sweetens the breath. Those who have not consumed enough areca nuts during their lifetime loose their fluids too rapidly upon death, thus exhaling a particularly pungent smell. These ideas and beliefs, the reasons given for using – or not using – areca nuts during rituals, and the prohibitions surrounding their consumption all relate to the power they exert on one vital substance, blood.

Formerly, in times of war, specialists would work magic with an areca nut, the spirit of which literally 'sucked up' the blood of enemies, and their strength along with it. Warriors chewed areca nuts before and after battle, but never during, for the nuts were full of enemy blood. After adultery, the cuckolded husband may use areca nuts to cast a spell on the lovers and make them bleed to death (Lemonnier 1992: 92–3). Finally, the only magical procedure used by women to achieve temporary or permanent sterility requires the manipulation of areca nuts, which affect the female procreative substance, blood, by drying it up. All these examples make it clear that the Ankave assign to areca nuts the function of retaining and absorbing blood, and bodily substances in general. They associate the mixture obtained by chewing the nuts with blood, albeit a particular type of blood, the blood that flows out of the body, the blood of a corpse. It seems to me, then, that red pandanus and areca-nut palm represent two opposite states of the same substance, blood, according to whether the individual is alive or dead. Whereas red pandanus juice is a substitute for the blood that circulates inside the body and nourishes it, betel quid is associated with lifeless, dried-up blood. Furthermore, betel quid acts upon blood only when the latter leaves the body. It is worth noting that the relationship between areca nuts, death and the drying process of bodily fluids precludes contact between these nuts and red *oxemɔxɔ'* cordylines. The myth mentioned earlier, according to which these cordylines and red pandanus have grown out of the blood of the same primordial being, further confirms the difference between the red pandanus and the areca-nut palm. This situation comes close to being one of total paradox. The fruits of red pandanus and areca-nut palm seem alike when consumed, and they are – on the whole – prohibited during the same occasions. But there is also a relation of profound incompatibility between them, since one is on the side of growth and maternity, while the other belongs to the domain of sterility and death. What these two trees really share in Ankave thought is a strong affinity with the human body. This assertion has already found confirmation in the myths and the vocabulary discussed earlier. It is further supported by the myth on the origin of the areca-nut palm, of which I collected only one version:

An old man planned to kill five brothers who had taken refuge at the top of a tree. Each brother in turn threw down a liana, starting with the oldest. Only the vine of the youngest brother reached the ground. The old man then tried to climb up. The boys cut the liana, so the old man fell to the ground, but without hurting himself too seriously. The third time the youngest brother threw down a liana, the old man was killed. The five brothers chopped his corpse into pieces. The oldest took one arm, the second took the other arm, the third took one leg, the fourth took the other leg, and, before leaving, they told the youngest to take the head. But as he soon found his burden too heavy, the youngest brother put the head down, not coming back to the spot where he had left the old man's head until some time later. There he saw palm sprouts. He went back several times to watch the different species of palms grow. Several years on, he remarked that the palms the wood of which is used for bows had grown tall. Later, he saw fruit. Several months later, he saw that the fruit were ripe, and chose one to offer to his brothers to taste. After they had eaten, the youngest brother went back to the spot and picked many fruit to plant them.

According to this myth, then, the first areca-nut palm comes from the decomposed head of an old man. This origin is somewhat confirmed by the vocabulary used to designate the different characteristics of an areca nut. It is described as having veins – or blood vessels – a nose and an eye.[11] Interestingly, the red quid itself (i.e. not the runny paste finally spat out, but the solid part), is called kə'ka'a', or blood clot. As in the case of the red pandanus tree and its fruit, here too the Ankave have established a close link between the human body and the areca-nut.

The *Ficus*

If the varieties of cordylines used in male initiations have red leaves, if the fruit of the red pandanus and the food obtained from it are bright red, and if the betel quid is also red,[12] nothing of the sort can be said of the *Ficus*. As already mentioned, every Ankave wears a bark cape called *jɔ'o'*, a term also used to name the *Ficus*, itself a subdivision of the tree taxon *i'kə'a'*. The bark cape is a piece of beaten bark almost wide enough to wrap the entire body; its length varies from just above the knee to just below it. Men and women wear it, especially when it is cold or rainy. But only fully initiated boys and adult men wear the breech cloth, *iʒiara'*, which, once looped around the neck, covers the lower back and buttocks. It is given to boys at the same time as their first grass skirt made of reeds, which they receive at the end of the two first sets of initiation rituals. These two pieces of clothing are some of the distinctive marks that represent the transformative process the initiates are undergoing, and the effectiveness of the rites.

When initiation rituals are planned, a great number of new bark capes (*jɔ'o'*) are made, not only for the boys, but also for their parents. Whereas every father receives one cape, mothers receive one cape if they have only one son undergoing initiation, and two if they have more. This fact leads me to interpret the bark cape as symbolising both the boys themselves, and their relationship to their mothers. This interpretation is confirmed by the fact that, for the whole duration of the initiations (they last several weeks), mothers and sons go every day at dawn to soak their capes in different streams, and must keep the wet cloth on their shoulders all day long. In short, the pieces of cloth the Ankave make by beating *Ficus* bark express a particular state of the person, as well as a certain type of relationship between mothers and sons. A closer examination of the various meanings of the word *iʒiara'* brings further insight. This term has three different meanings: the men's breech cloth, the wings of an insect chrysalis emerging from the larva, and the leaves surrounding the red pandanus fruit. The semantic field of this term, and the practical contexts in which these items are used or evoked, allow us to understand the ways in which boy maturation is conceptualised during initiation rituals.

Metaphors of Male Growth and Maturation

For the Ankave, growth is materialised as the increased quantity of blood in the body. This is particularly true for foetuses and babies. The mother, through her own blood during pregnancy and her milk after birth (it is believed that breast milk is transformed into blood in children's bodies) is the main provider of blood. As soon as individuals are able to eat on their own and thereafter throughout their life, red pandanus becomes the main food capable of producing blood. As already discussed, *tanə'*, the oily red substance that men squeeze out from cooked red pandanus fruit, is thought to pass directly into the veins.

The main purpose of male initiations is to make boys grow and become strong men. The model the Ankave have adopted to achieve this goal is that of human procreation, in particular intra-uterine growth and birth. This explains why many of the material elements used in ritual are also used during pregnancy and delivery. For example, the vegetal cane *məʒi'* is used to cut the umbilical cord *and* is inserted into the boy's pierced septum; a sugar cane cultivar is given to the parents of a first-born child soon after birth *and* to initiates; a number of edible plants are prohibited during pregnancy *and* during initiation. The model of human procreation is also discernible in several of the actions performed during male initiation rituals. For instance, the – secret – consumption of red pandanus juice by initiates recalls the diet of expecting mothers. Or the difficult progress of initiates pushed by their mother's brothers through a bushy corridor, and splashed on their heads and shoulders at the exit, is an obvious re-enactment of the birthing process. Finally, the commentaries made by the mothers of initiates, who draw explicit parallels between what is imposed on them during pregnancy, delivery and the ritual ordeals undergone by their sons, leave no doubts on the fact that Ankave male maturation is modelled after human gestation and birth.

The matter is, however, not so simple. The term *iʒiara'*, which applies equally to the chrysalis and to the breech cloth made of beaten *Ficus* bark – the main material support of male initiation – puts in parallel the metamorphosis of larvae into winged insects and the transform-ation of boys into men. Given that the leaves enclosing a red pandanus fruit are also called *iʒiara'*, the analogy seems to link the breech cloth and the leaves. I would like to suggest, therefore, that the breech cloth enveloping the initiate whose body, full of blood, has grown and developed (as a result of his secret ingestion of red pandanus juice) plays a role identical to that of the leaves surrounding a red pandanus fruit (called *na'* or 'body'), potentially filled with red juice. I would say that, while the fruit of a tree (pandanus) is a metaphor for the boy's body, a tree part (Ficus bark) serves as a metaphor for a process (maturation) thought of and enacted as a human physiological process (gestation and birth). The image of an animal metamorphosis, with blood/red pandanus juice acting as the operating agent of this process, forms the basis of this metaphor.

A story that can be viewed as the myth explaining the origin of initiation rituals offers additional support to this analysis. Here again, the transformation of boys into men is expressed through an animal metaphor:

An old woman lived alone near the headwaters of a river. One day, a man came to this spot looking for his dog. But the woman said she had not seen the animal and asked the man to climb a breadfruit tree and pick the fruit. When he came down, she beat him to death with a stone axe, before eating his body. Later on, each of the man's brothers came in turn, looking for him. Each time, the old woman asked the brother to pick her some breadfruit. Just as he was about to climb the tree, the last brother noticed some blood and earth on the trunk. He asked the woman to step back from the tree, saying that it would be dangerous for her to stand too close when he threw the fruit down. She backed up a short distance, and the young man threw a big fruit directly into her eyes. She died immediately. He then went into the woman's house and saw a bamboo tube full of human bones. He took it out and cut the woman's corpse into pieces, which he hid in the ground nearby. Then, he went to the river and poured his brothers' bones into the water before going back home. Several years later, he went back to the spot: first where he had put the woman's body and then to the river. In the water, he saw tadpoles; but there was nothing on the grave. He went back home and stayed there for several seasons. When he looked at the water again, the tadpoles had become frogs with four legs. Later on, he saw human legs and arms; on the grave, a small *ə'irə'* cordyline had begun to grow. Later still, he saw boys playing together in the river and, beside the grave, he noticed several red-leafed plants.

The man then decided to prepare clothes and ornaments for the boys. He asked the women to make those while he was making bows and arrows. There were many boys, as each bone had turned into a new person. When everything was ready, the man went to the river and began to dress the boys with the clothes and ornaments. He also pierced their septa. Then they all went down to the hamlet, holding *oxemɔxə'* cordylines. In the village, the women were shaking ə'irə' cordylines.

In this story, the animal metaphor used to express the boys' maturation is the tadpole developing into a frog.[13] The similarity between the tadpole and the chrysalis[14] is obvious; in both cases, the adult animal is quite different from its initial and intermediary states. This is certainly the reason why the Ankave have chosen them to conceptualise the radical transformation undergone by male initiates. For, in their view, as well as in that of other Angans, to become a man implies the severing of the mode of relation that existed in childhood between the male child and his parents, and, most especially, between him and his mother. Male maturation is supposed to bring about a drastic change in the physical – and mental – state of initiates. Ankave men and women insist that boys who have gone through the initiation rituals are completely different from what they were before – so different, in fact, that their own mothers do not recognise them. To conclude this point, if the growth and maturation of boys during initiation parallels the process of human gestation and birth, it also implies a process of radical transformation comparable to animal metamorphosis. Tree products identified with nurturing substances from the human body are crucial to this process of transformation. Consequently, to understand Ankave conceptualisations of male growth, one must envisage a symbolic world where animal and plant metaphors are closely intertwined, without emphasising the latter to the expense of the former, for that would amount to telling only half the story. Moreover, one should not forget that the processes expressed through such metaphors are conceived in a way that is specifically human.

Human Beings and Trees

If we consider the vocabulary used for different parts of the ritually most important trees or woody plants, a common feature appears. The Ankave terms used for these particular tree parts and plants also refer to the human body. For example, while the normal word for tree trunk is *mə'kə'*, the word used to refer to the red pandanus trunk, *eʒə'*, also means 'bone'. Similarly, most tree fruits are called *Songwə'*, but the red pandanus and the areca-nut palm fruits are *na'*, that is, 'body'. And, as discussed earlier, several body-like features are associated with the areca nut. Lexical data provide the analyst with evidence supporting the view that Ankave people draw close connections between trees and humans. And so does the use of trees in both ritual and everyday contexts. I have documented in some detail the use of plant materials in initiation rites, and, as I hope to have shown, most trees and tree products used in ritual share a common feature: the colour red. They also have in common the ability to regenerate vegetatively.

Furthermore, red pandanus trees, areca-nut palms and red and green cordylines are all widely used as territory markers (Bonnemère and Lemonnier 1992: 150–3). Ankave people walking in old gardens or villages with the ethnographer explain the land rights of their parents and grandparents, as well as theirs, by pointing to a red pandanus, an areca-nut palm, or a fence of cordylines. Red pandanus trees are often planted in gardens which are no longer producing. If a man gives a piece of land to someone else, instead of saying just this, he will say that he has given a red pandanus tree away. As for the red cordyline *oxemэxэ'*, it expresses the continuity between generations of men. This is precisely the reason why the Ankave use the red cordyline in the initiation ritual, and it is this use which gives them their specificity; they are otherwise similar to the initiation rituals performed by their Anga neighbours. There is therefore more to red pandanus trees, areca-nut palms and cordylines than their quality as providers of bodily substances, or as beautifying agents. They are also, and perhaps above all, symbols of generational continuity; they, in fact, symbolise the clan territories themselves (Bonnemère and Lemonnier 1992: 153–4). I mentioned earlier that, generation after generation, red cordylines pass from ritual locations in the bush to domestic enclosures in the village, and back to sacred areas. Domestic fences of green cordylines serve as repositories of mourners' and children's hair. People say that this will secure child body growth, for these plants grow fast and tall. Among the Melpa, a cordyline or a banana tree is planted on the spot where 'the child's navel-string and the mother's placenta are buried together' (Strathern 1982: 119), a variation on the theme: 'As the plant grows, so the child will grow' (Strathern 1982: 120).

Whereas in some societies it is wood that provides metaphorical models to conceptualise society, particularly the notions of growth and maturation (Bloch 1992; Rival and Bloch 1995), the plants selected by the Ankave as suitable items to think about and act upon contexts in which human growth and maturation are the main focus are chosen on the basis of their mode of reproduction, as well as for their physical characteristics. This difference may imply a contrast in the conceptualisation of time. The Ankave do not regard tree longevity as an appropriate basis for a metaphor expressing the succession of generations and the reproduction of society through time. Rather, their conception of duration stresses the link with a primordial human male, in the blood of whom the red pandanus and the red cordyline originated. This link is metaphorically re-activated in every initiation rite, when red cordyline cuttings are gathered, and then replanted in the house garden plots of each initiate. Men simultaneously establish a strong sense of solidarity amongst themselves by enduring physical and psychological ordeals together, and share the same diachronic relationship to the primordial male being in whom these trees take their origin.

Acknowledgements

I would like to thank the Maison des Sciences de l'Homme, the Ministère des Affaires Etrangères, the National Geographic Society, the Fondation Fyssen and the CNRS-GDR 116, which have all enabled me to carry out fieldwork among the Ankave-Anga since 1987. This research would not have been possible without the warm welcome and collaboration of the Papua New Guinea Institute of Medical Research.

Notes

1. As far as I know, the Ankave system of classification of the vegetal realm contrasts the life-form taxa *i'kə'a'* (trees or plants with a hard trunk), *wi'wə'* (plants with a watery or juicy trunk such as banana trees and sugar canes), *ara'* (herbaceous plants), *ngwə'* (lianas), and *səxə'* (bamboos). Each of these categories comprises one or more levels of subdivision. When asked, people say that pandanus, cordylines, *Ficus*, areca palms and the other trees discussed here can all be considered subdivisions of the taxon *i'kə'a'*.

2. Whereas marriages with bridewealth payments are now, and since the mid-1970s, found among the Sambia (Herdt 1987: 33), the Baruya continue to marry as they did in the past.

3. I have been doing fieldwork among the Ankave since 1987 in collaboration with Pierre Lemonnier. A great proportion of the data presented here on male initiation rituals has been collected by him, as no woman is allowed to witness what men do during their reclusion in the bush.

4. Writing about classifications, Herdt (1981: 118) says that the 'Sambia distinguish two types of trees (...) *Iku* is generic for tree (...). The only other major category encompasses both palms and pandanus trees. It lacks a single categorical gloss, however (...).' This does not seem to be the case among the Ankave, since areca-palms, palms with aerial roots – a category that comprises the Highland pandanus – other palms, and red pandanus are each designated by a specific taxon included in the taxon for tree, *i'kə'a'*.

5. Such lexical phenomena are also attested among the Sambia. Herdt wonders whether 'the lexical term *kùnaalu* (for pandanus trees and nuts) is not linguistically "motivated" by a very close referential pronoun, *kànaalu*, denoting a "mother and child" pair', for the Sambia 'invariably select human procreative metaphors and analogies in depicting the growth of a [Highland pandanus] seedpod' (Herdt 1981: 119).

6. Note that the yellow fruit of one *Pandanus conoideus* cultivar do not produce *tanə'*.

7. If I have chosen to reveal secret practices rather than conceal them, it is mainly because of the oldest Ankave's concern that their culture be described as precisely and exhaustively as possible in these times of great changes. This being said, I would like the reader to be aware of the secrecy that surrounds some of the ritual actions analysed here and to respect it.

8. For the Ankave, the stories we may call origin myths refer to a real past and are called upon when people seek to explain their present-day actions.

9. Except in one case: when a mother cuts the hair of her children for the first time, she places it in different plants according to the child's sex (Bonnemère 1996: 271).

10. This term juxtaposes two separate terms, *oxə'*, 'man' and *məxə'*, 'fight' and also 'anger'.

11. Similarly, to name a pandanus nutpod and the parts attached to it, the Sambia use a lexical set that refers to human physiology: stomach, umbilical cord, mouth, head (Herdt 1981: 119).

12. Here I have only treated the major trees appearing in the male rituals; but, as mentioned earlier, two more trees are present, though quite secondarily. They too are selected on the basis of their colour. The *ɔru'wə'* (*Syzygium* spp.) is a huge forest tree with a bright orange trunk; the *Saoxə'* (*Elaeocarpus sphaericus*) is a deciduous tree with leaves that turn red before falling. The terms by which both trees are designated are subdivisions of the taxon *i'kə'a'*.

13. Note that a metaphor taken from the vegetal world is superimposed on this animal metaphor, since the myth depicts the growth of *ə'irə'* cordylines and the transformation of frogs into boys as rigorously simultaneous events.

14. As far as I know, frogs and winged insects that develop from a chrysalis have no particular classificatory position in the Ankave taxonomic system of animals.

References

Bloch, M., 'What goes without saying: the conceptualization of Zafimaniry society', in A. Kuper (ed.), *Conceptualizing society*, London: Routledge, 1992

Bonnemère, P., '*Pangium edule*: a food for the social body among the Ankave-Anga of Papua New Guinea', in C.-M. Hladik *et al.* (eds), *Tropical Forests, People and Food. Biocultural Interactions and Applications to Development*, Man and the Biosphere Series, vol. 13, Paris and New York: UNESCO, The Parthenon Publishing Group, 1993

—— 'Le Pandanus rouge dans tous ses états. L'Univers social et symbolique d'un arbre fruitier chez les Ankave-Anga (Papouasie-Nouvelle-Guinée)', *Annales Fyssen* 9, 1994a, pp. 21–32

—— 'The secret of the red seeds. Notes on some life-cycle rituals among the Ankave-Anga of Papua New Guinea', paper presented at the 2nd ESO conference, Basle, 15–17 December, 1994b

—— *Le Pandanus Rouge. Corps, Différence des Sexes et Parenté chez les Ankave-Anga (Papouasie-Nouvelle-Guinée)*, Paris: CNRS Editions, Editions de la Maison des Sciences de l'Homme (coll. Chemins de l'Ethnologie), 1996

—— 'Quand les hommes répliquent une gestation. Une analyse des représentations et des rites de la croissance et de la maturation des garçons chez les Ankave-Anga (Papouasie-Nouvelle-Guinée)', in M. Godelier and M. Panoff (eds), *La Production du corps*, Paris: Editions des Archives contemporaines, in press

Bonnemère, P. and P. Lemonnier, 'Terre et échanges chez les Anga (Papouasie Nouvelle-Guinée)', *Etudes rurales* (Special Issue 'La Terre et le Pacifique) 127–8, 1992, pp. 133–8

Godelier, M., *La Production des Grands Hommes*, Paris: Fayard, 1982

Herdt, G. H., *Guardians of the Flutes: Idioms of Masculinity*, New York: McGraw-Hill, 1981

—— *The Sambia. Ritual and Gender in New Guinea*. New York: Holt, Rinehart and Winston, 1987

Hyndman, D. C., 'Ethnobotany of Wopkaimin *Pandanus*: Significant Papua New Guinea plant resource', *Economic Botany* 38(3), 1984, pp. 287–303

Lemonnier, P., 'Couper-coller. Attaques corporelles et cannibalisme chez les Anga de Nouvelle-Guinée', *Terrain* 18, 1992, pp. 87–94

—— 'The eel and the Ankave-Anga of Papua New Guinea: material and symbolic aspects of trapping', in C.-M. Hladik *et al.* (eds), *Tropical Forests, People and Food. Biocultural Interactions and Applications to*

Development, Man and the Biosphere Series, vol. 13, Paris and New York: UNESCO, The Parthenon Publishing Group, 1993

Mimica, J., 'The incest passions: An outline of the logic of the Iqwaye social organization, Part 2', *Oceania* 62(2), 1991, pp. 81–113

Rival, L. and M. Bloch, 'Call for Papers for the Conference "Trees and wood as social symbols"', 1995

Sillitoe, P., *Roots of the Earth. Crops in the Highlands of Papua New Guinea*, Kensington, Australia: New South Wales University Press, 1983

Strathern, A., 'Witchcraft, greed, cannibalism and death: some related themes from the New Guinea Highlands', in M. Bloch and J. Parry (eds), *Death and Regeneration of Life*, New York: Pergamon, 1982

The Coconut, the Body and the Human Being. Metaphors of Life and Growth in Nusa Penida and Bali

Rodolfo A. Giambelli

Introduction

The importance of tree symbolism in Asia has been acknowledged in the early writings of Majumdar (1927) and Viennot (1954), and its significance in South-east Asia has been recognised in Bosch's (1960) seminal work. However, with the exception of James Fox's (1977) study of the borassus palm, there have been very few anthropological analyses of South-east Asian people's pragmatic interest in, and symbolic attention to, specific trees. The coconut palm (*Cocos nucifera*),[1] which occupies a special place in the life of all South-east Asian people, is particularly important for the inhabitants of the islands of Nusa Penida and Bali, who extensively use it for practical as well as ritual purposes. Nusa Penida, where the material presented in this chapter has been collected, is a limestone island located between Bali and Lombok.[2] Nusa Penida forms part of the Klungkung regency, and, as such, is historically regarded a part of Bali. Its 45,000 or so inhabitants consider themselves Balinese. Farming is the main economic activity, with maize being the most important cereal grown on the island. Although Nusa Penida social organisation is modelled on Bali's, the influence of Balinese caste estate groups (*brahmana*, *ksatria* and *wésia*), whose presence in the island is far from being sizeable, is less significant than in Bali itself. However, the hierarchical division between *jero* and *jaba*, which reflects the

133

division between landowners – who claim former links with Balinese estate groups – and land labourers – with no such claims – appears to be more consequential.

In this chapter, I discuss the practical and cultural meanings attributed to the coconut, a ubiquitous symbol extensively used in Nusa Penida and Balinese society. I also analyse the metaphors relating the coconut palm and its fruit to different aspects of the culture of these Indonesian islands within the broader context of botanic idioms widely spread throughout Austronesia. The first part of the chapter examines the significance of the coconut palm in relation to forest trees, the economic and cultural importance of its by-products, and the customary laws regulating the ownership of – and access to – coconut trees. The second part considers the relationship between the palm and the person, the meaning attributed to coconut planting, the analogies drawn between the palm and the human body, and, finally, the set of contrasts drawn between the coconut palm and the banyan tree. My main argument is that the coconut palm and its fruit mark people's lives from birth to death. The coconut, prototype of all domesticated and fruit-bearing trees, stands symbolically between the undifferentiated and dangerous forest trees and the conspicuous and socially positive banyan tree. The stream of symbolic associations that links human beings with the coconut, while evoking a constant flow of images principally associated with life-bringing circumstances, characterises crucial aspects of the Balinese and Nusa Penida cultures, in which botanical metaphors play a central role in local conceptions of growth and of the relationship between humans and the natural world.

Tree and Palm Classification

While domesticates and wild plants belong to the same general category, *kayu,* they are contrasted both practically and symbolically. The cultural significance of the coconut palm as a domestic plant can be measured in relation to the status of forest plants. In Nusa Penida all plants with hard stems, whether grown wild or planted, are classified as *kayu.* This term, which means both 'tree' and 'wood', is polysemic. Moreover, its semantic field comprises two functional and partially overlapping classes: *kayu* and *punyan.* In fact, if *kayu* refers to all hard-stem plants, its meaning is more restricted in practice, as the word *punyan* is used to refer to live, domesticated fruit-producing plants such as the coconut palm (*punyan nyuh*) or the mango tree (*punyan poh*). But once cut down, most plants classified as *punyan* become *kayu.* For example, a mango tree (*punyan poh*) becomes *kayu poh* after felling. But the coconut palm, once felled, becomes *séséh nyuh*, due perhaps to its special status and fibrous wood – a characteristic it however shares with other palms. Shifts in classifiers are further illustrated in Table 6.1:

Table 6.1 Differences between classificatory terms associated with living and cut trees

The live tree (Balinese name and botanical name):	Once cut becomes (Balinese name):
punyan poh (*Mangifera indica* Linn.)	*kayu poh*
punyan nangka (*Apotrocarpus integra* Merr.)	*kayu ketéwél*
punyan ntal (*Borassus flabellifer* Linn.)	*séséh ntal*
punyan nyuh (*Cocos nucifera* Linn.)	*séséh nyuh*
punyan buah (*Areca catechu*)	*séséh buah*
punyan biu (*Musa paradisiaca* Linn.)	*gedebong; batang* [NP]

The shift from *punyan* to *kayu* or *séséh* is not the only feature that characterises domesticated trees. Classification terminology for particularly important plants is affected by their status as live or dead (with a shift from *punyan nangka* to *kayu ketéwél*), and also by their developmental cycle. A coconut palm, for example, is known under different terms, according to its stages of growth. Finally, domesticated plants – especially the coconut palm – become symbolically charged in comparison with forest trees. Whereas the coconut palm is associated with attributes pertaining to the social sphere, forest trees stand for the wild. This opposition is manifest during the thanksgiving ritual for all fruit-bearing trees known as *Tumpek Pangatag*. In this ritual, celebrated every six Balinese months, coconut palms are dressed like people and treated like ancestors. Forest trees are never treated in this way, nor are they directly associated with positive ancestors. On the contrary, they are believed to be inhabited by all kinds of spirits, including evil ones. The salience of this contrast may be better appreciated if presented as below:

coconut palm	forest trees
domesticated / humanly planted	wild
planned growth / planted in a planned landscape	naturally grown
tended	not tended
fruit-bearing	not necessarily fruit-bearing
detailed knowledge of the tree and its fruit	lack of in-depth knowledge
treated as ancestors	inhabited by all sorts of spirits, among them evil spirits.

Importance of the Coconut Tree and its Products

People of Nusa Penida and Bali, whose knowledge of the various types of coconut grown in the islands and of their different uses is highly developed, have a range of specific terms covering all tree parts with great precision. *Punyan nyuh* is the common term for a fully grown coconut palm. While *punyan* indicates that the tree has been planted by a human and is productive, *nyuh* signals the presence of fruit. Different terms are used to refer to the young non-productive plant, whereas only one term, *séséh nyuh*,[3] is used for a felled coconut tree. A coconut tree can reach the age of sixty or sixty-five, however its productivity generally declines sharply after forty (it starts producing nuts between its sixth and tenth year). Six growth stages[4] are recognised, from the germinating nut to the mature plant. The nut's rate of growth and degree of maturation are also closely monitored, with each stage corresponding to a specific use receiving a different name. In the village of Sakti, for example, five basic stages of fruit development, from pollination to maturity, are differentiated; the first four terms correspond to growth stages in the immature nut, the last one to the ripe coconut.[5]

Every part of the coconut palm is used daily in all sorts of traditional activities. Coconut water, the prime ingredient of the lustral water used in blessing, is extremely important in all ritual contexts. Decorations, offerings, mats, and the walls and roofing of non-permanent shelters are made with the palm's leaves. The pulp of young and tender nuts is eaten; when ripe, the kernel is processed into copra or cooking oil. Oil is also used as hair or skin ointment. Freshly grated coconut pulp produces coconut milk (*santen*), as well as the basic ingredient for numerous culinary preparations, ranging from sweets to *saté* (a mixture of pounded raw meat mixed with coconut milk, grated coconut and spices skewered on thin pieces of bamboo and grilled). In some areas of Nusa Penida, old dry leaves and spathes are still the main source of fuel, while coconut shells are still made into bowls. Finally, coconut wood is still the main timber for the construction of traditional Balinese houses. The economic value of coconut palms as a cash crop is not negligible either.[6] Whereas nuts and young leaves are directly sold for cash in urban areas, they are bartered or exchanged as ritual prestations in rural areas, where it is copra and coconut oil that make up the bulk of market transactions. In any case, the coconut is so central to the whole utilitarian and symbolic complex that no part of the tree is wasted. Quite clearly, people's real material dependence on the coconut palm in Nusa Penida and Bali is reflected in the palm's cultural importance as well.

Coconut Distribution and Ownership

Access to coconut products, particularly to young immature leaves (*busung*) and nuts, is absolutely crucial for participating in the islands' religious life. As all important rituals make use of coconut products, no ritual can be performed without coconut fruit or leaves. In certain areas of Nusa Penida, *jeroan* (houses that claimed higher status within the community), the traditional owners of all coconut plantations, have had a monopoly over the production and distribution of coconut produce; to a certain extent, this is still the case today. *Jaba* (outsiders, those who do not belong to the *jeroan*, and hence occupy an inferior position) were either given farmland already containing coconut plantations (whose produce they could lawfully use), or reduced to asking *jeroan* for coconut fruit and leaves each time they needed them. To this day, *jaba* from the South of Nusa Penida travel to the island's northern villages before important religious festivals (such as *galungan* and *kuningan*) to ask members of the local *jeroan* for coconuts. They sometimes bring small gifts along to disguise the request as reciprocal exchange. In Sakti (a north-western village), coconut produce is commonly passed from *jero* to *jaba* as part of their patron–client relationship. *Jaba* do not pay for the coconuts, but lend their labour or help whenever asked to in exchange. A few figures will help the reader gauge the level of nut consumption. A very common ritual such as *tutug kambuhan*, performed forty-two days after the birth of a child, requires no fewer than two hundred nuts (this includes the nuts needed for prescribed offerings, and those that go in preparing a meal for twenty-five people). This example illustrates how *jero* status is reinforced by coconut tree ownership, and is tied to the power of bestowing or withholding coconut produce.

Botanic Idiom

In his study of kinship metaphors in one eastern Indonesian society, Fox (1971) documents the existence of a 'botanic idiom' in Rotinese language, by which he explains the fact that kinship relations are expressed in terms of botanical analogies, as well as the nature of ritual chanting, which consists in elaborating an already well-developed plant semiology. As Fox (1992) shows, the linguistic recurrence of this botanic idiom is probably due to the fact that Austronesian discourse has for centuries expressed characteristic Austronesian origin structures and systems of precedence in terms of botanical categories of growth.

The concept of a 'botanic idiom' is best expressed as a set of analogies that associate flora and human beings, but cannot be fully accounted for by using a classificatory approach. Nusa Penida society, like all other Austronesian societies, shows a great awareness of plants. Categories central to Balinese life are formed with reference to trees and plants, and it is from this perspective that I propose to analyse the relationship between the coconut palm and human beings. Although my approach to coconut symbolism is semiotic, I do not limit my examination of the coconut botanic idiom particular to Nusa Penida to its linguistic manifestations, but discuss all the aspects of plant semiology in Balinese life. In particular, I consider: (1) the rituals associated with the plant; (2) the analogies between the coconut and the human body; and (3) the ritual use of coconut in some of the most significant Balinese life crisis ceremonies.

Planting a Coconut, the Symbol of Life

People adopt a respectful, polite behaviour whenever they deal with the coconut palm. In particular, a coconut tree is never fully harvested, for it is known that constant and exhaustive depletion of fruit or young leaves causes the tree to stop producing and wilt. The ideal relationship between the owner and the tree is one of balanced and equal sharing of its produce. This is why part of the fruit (especially the young fruit)

and the unfurled leaves should always be left on the tree. The other
reason, of course, is that cutting the unfurled leaves, which contain
the terminal bud, causes the palm's premature death. The majority of
the coconut palms grown in Nusa Penida are of a tall variety that may
take some time before it produces its first fruit.[7] However, tree-owners
long for their trees to grow and bear fruit fast, as the symbolism
associated with tree planting illustrates. Planting a coconut palm, a
traditionally male activity, requires that a special procedure be followed.
The landowner, the future beneficiary of the tree and its produce, is
responsible for the planting. He first chooses a suitable sprouting nut,
digs a hole, and then asks one of his sons (or his male heir) to sit astride
his shoulders (*ngandong anak cenik*), while he squats by the hole, in
which he places the nest of a small bird. If unavailable, the nest may
be replaced by a layer of short grass, over which the shooting coconut
is placed. The hole is then carefully filled up with earth, and the
planting ceremony concluded.

The key to understanding this procedure rests on a pun and a form
of mimicry that is obvious to any local. Coconut planters are said to
wish to obtain a small, easy to climb and very fruitful tree. A mature
plant with such characteristics is called *punyan puuh*; it is generally
very difficult to obtain. The small bird (possibly a quail) whose nest is
used in the planting ritual is called *kedis puuh*, and the short grass variety
padang puuh. As *puuh* in both terms means something small, by
induction the lexical and physical association of the nest of a small
bird or short grass inside the planting hole with the growing plant
characterises small size as a positive quality.[8] The inductive reasoning
behind the man's unusual posture is similar. The other main quality
desired from a tree is its fruitfulness. The man who does the planting
is himself an example of fertile fruitfulness, as exemplified by the
presence of his son sitting astride his shoulders. In Nusa Penida, all
men – and women – are expected to be fecund and productive. In a
way very similar to the coconut, which is the fruit (*buah*) of the coconut
palm tree, the child is the 'fruit' of his father's belly (*niki panak buah
basang tiange*). With this analogy, the productive power symbolised by
the man and his offspring, passed over to the seed through the action
of planting, becomes the model for the tree's productivity. Here too
we find the belief (and hope) that the positive qualities found in one
domain (human, animal or botanic) get transferred by way of physical
and semantic collusion to the other (botanic).

Coconut planting also refers to the need for securing genealogical
continuity, so greatly felt in Balinese society. Planting a coconut is

mamula nyuh. *Mula*, the root on which this verb is formed, refers to the planting of a seed that shows manifest signs of roots at the moment of its sowing. *Mula* is derived from *kamulan* or *kemulan*, which, in the Balinese context, indicates the place where a descent group originates, and where it, just like a growing and fruitful tree, has its roots.[9] Coconut planting, with its associated images of future productivity and growth, represents, therefore, a botanical event used to refer to the source of an origin group.

The events surrounding exhumation and the *Tumpek Pengatag* festival constitute further references to coconut planting as a desire to establish firmly in the ground a lasting symbol of life and productivity. During exhumation (*ngebét*), a ritual preceding cremation, a shooting coconut (*pujer*) is exchanged for the head of the deceased, and placed in the grave in its stead. The coconut, which is retrieved from its temporary location by someone who is not a relative of the deceased before the grave is filled, is replanted elsewhere. The nut will grow into a – seemingly – everlasting palm, symbol of the life-potential of the deceased, and, more generally, of life originating within the ancestors. As such, it symbolises the continuity of successive generations, a constant theme in Balinese culture. The same association is particularly explicit during the *Tumpek Pangatag* annual festival (also known as *Tumpek Bubuh* or *Tumpek Wariga*). The link between ancestors and fruit-bearing trees is renewed during the festival, which consists in the ritual dressing of a coconut palm by a married couple. The coconut palm, covered with human clothes, addressed as 'grandmother' (*dadong*), and presented with offerings and food, symbolises all fruit-bearing trees. The purpose of the ritual is to request of the ancestor-tree a bountiful harvest for the next season. The ancestor-tree, in a reciprocal gesture, is offered porridge to eat. In both instances, the coconut palm is *twice* the bearer of life: it leads the ancestors to a new life, and provides food for the living. Last but not least, a shooting coconut (*pujer*) is given by the groom's family to the bride's family during marriage (*ngantén*) ceremonies, as a symbolic exchange for the new wife. The coconut, the living symbol of the daughter who leaves the family's house, is planted in the bride's family's garden. The high-yield plant is offered as a compensation for the new life potential (offspring) that has been given away.

The Coconut and the Human Body

The similarity between the coconut and a person rests upon their analogous life cycles. The time a coconut needs to develop from flower to harvestable fruit roughly equals the length of time needed for human gestation; the length of time between planting and the first harvest (i.e. from six to ten years) approximates to the time needed for a child to become an adolescent; and above all, the plant's life-span is almost the same as the life-span of a man or woman. These parallels are especially marked at the time when a first-born child cuts his or her first teeth, an occasion celebrated with the planting of a coconut in a ritual called *ngempugin* (from *empug* 'to rise', 'to sprout' or 'to appear'). The child is then given the hard kernel of an old coconut to taste for the first time, chew on, and strengthen his or her teeth. From then on, it is said, the parallel lives of the child and the coconut palm progress in a similar fashion. The palm becomes a kind of living *alter ego* for the person it is linked to. If fruitful, it becomes a positive model of development for the human being.[10]

Terms That Apply to Both a Coconut and a Human Being

A series of terms that apply equally to the coconut palm and the human body[11] further evidences the cultural significance of the relationship between this tree and the Balinese person. As Table 6.2 (which charts the correspondence between plant and body parts, and the Balinese terms used to refer to them) shows, these terms cover almost all the important botanical parts of the tree:

Table 6.2 Correspondences between parts of the coconut plant and body parts and Balinese terms used to refer to both

Correspondences Between Plant and Body Parts			
Coconut Tree and Fruit	*Common Balinese Terms*		*Human Being*
sap / lymph	*getah*	*getih*	blood
sap / lymph	*tuak (nyuh)*		breast milk
leaf canopy	*bok*		hair
kernel / endosperm	*isi*		flesh
nut	*nyuh*	*nyonyo*	breast
coconut water	*yéh nyuh*	*yéh nyonyo*	breast milk
coconut shell	*kau, cangkok*	*kaun sirah, cangkok sirah*	skull

The lexical rendering of some of the terms in Table 6.2 is identical for both plants and body parts; others (i.e. *nyuh* and *nyonyo*) are clearly cognates and, as we shall see, closely related. Looking briefly at the first of these terms, for example, we discover that while the lymph of any tree is *engket*, that of the coconut may also be referred to as *getah*, which is similar to *getih*, the term used for human and animal blood. On the basis of Table 6.2, let us now investigate in greater detail some aspects of the analogy between parts of the coconut palm and parts of the human body. I first discuss the relationship between female breasts and milk and nuts and *tuak*, and then the links between the coconut palm, the wooden pillar of a traditional Balinese *balé*, and the self.

Breasts, Nuts and Tuak

A clear equivalence is drawn in Nusa Penida between the coconut fruit and the female breast; both provide food for humans and, in some circumstances, both are thought to have a similar shape. As already mentioned, a mature nut is *nyuh*, and the water it contains *yéh nyuh*. The term for female (and male) breasts is *nyonyo*, and for breast milk *yéh nyonyo*. *Nyonyo* is a reduplication of *nyo*; the pronunciation of *nyuh* and *nyo* is almost identical. The analogy between coconut and female breast as food providers is taken further during the first three or four days of the newborn's life, when the mother feeds her baby with the watery, gelatinous pulp of a young coconut (*kuud mara ngerépé*). Balinese women believe that the first breast milk (colostrum) to appear after childbirth is too dense and raw to be fed to infants. In the period preceding the production of fluid, white milk, mothers anoint their breasts with a local balm (*boréh*) and wrap them tightly with a sash. According to local belief, the combined action of balm and sash produces the heat that matures and fluidifies the milk.[12] To nurse is *manyonyo*, and a child asking for breast-milk is *ngidih yéh nyonyo*. This analogical reference focuses on a double equivalence, that between coconuts and nursing mothers' breasts, and that between coconut water and breast milk. In sum, the correspondence between coconuts and breasts is (1) visual (the shapes of breasts and young nuts are explicitly compared); (2) material (coconut pulp and water are used as substitutes for breast milk); and (3) lexical (the pronunciation of the terms *nyuh* and *nyo* is almost identical). This far-reaching symmetry once more demonstrates the depth of the connection between the coconut palms and the people of Bali.

An additional parallel is drawn between mothers and coconuts as life-providers. If a nursing mother needs to leave her child behind for a while, she may ask another woman to breast-feed her baby during her absence, a request known as *ngidih tuak*, literally 'to ask for *tuak*'; this special breast-feeding is called *nuakin* (from *tuak*). In both instances, while the milk is directly referred to with the word for coconut sap (*tuak*), the feeding is referred to as 'tapping the sap from the coconut inflorescence' (*nuakin*). Furthermore, women's breasts are sometimes called *tuak* in Nusa Penida. Finally, it should be stressed that the *tuak* analogy (coconut sap = mother's milk) shifts the reference from the nut to the tree, which, from this perspective, virtually becomes equivalent to a nursing mother who provides the 'flow of life' for her children.[13]

On Saka, Tiang, Tapis *and* Kamben Adegan

The relationship between coconut *tapis*, a pavilion's wooden pillars (*balê*), and the notion of self further illustrates the ways in which humans and coconuts are culturally linked. In some villages of central Nusa Penida, pavilion pillars in a compound or public hall are sometimes wrapped in bast fibre, a fabric-like tissue called *tapis* that connects the stalk of a coconut palm leaf to its stem. A dressed pillar is perceived to be analogous to a person. Such a perception coalesces a number of relations that are worth examining more closely.

Pavilion and house pillars are lodged in special pedestals made of marble, coralstone or other stone-like materials. These pedestals (*sendi*) are treated with respect; they should never be damaged or given away. A niche is opened on the pedestal's vertical axis for holding the pillar. The post must not touch the hard base of the niche, on which old Chinese coins (*pipis bolong*) and white thread – signs of purity and value – covered with a section of coconut skin (*sambuk*) are placed to avoid all contact between the two. The pillar, fashioned in a way that preserves the grain of the wood, is then fitted. Pillars are closely associated with the owners of the particular buildings in which they are found. For instance, the strong unity between a house and its inhabitants is emphasised by the fact that the body measurements of the building's owners are used to determine the dimensions of pillars. All house pillars (*saka*, *tiang* or *adegan*) have a square base whose length and width are multiples of *rai*, a finger measurement.[14] In cremation rites *adegan* refers to a small piece of wood on which the image of the person to be cremated is drawn. The piece of wood stands for the person it represents. The pillar is sometimes referred to as *tiang*, a Balinese term also used

Figure 6.1 *Tapis* of a young coconut tree (Pikat, Nusa Penida 1991)

with reference to the self. Upon completion, buildings (including pillars
and other structural components) are purified and inaugurated in a
ritual called *mlaspas*, by which they are brought to life (*urip*), and
endowed with strength (*pasupati*). A section of the ritual called *pangurip
miwah pasupatian* includes the anointment of a building's pillars with
chicken blood (*getih*), coconut shell charcoal (*areng*) and lime (*pamor,
apuh*). The respective colours of these elements, red, black and white,
are commonly understood as representing the pillar's blood, flesh and
bones.[15]

I found in Nusa Penida several pillars dressed with coconut *tapis*.
Wrapped around the post's central section, the *tapis* is kept in place
with a tightly woven bamboo frame. Once in place, it receives the name
of *kamben* (*i.e. kamben adegan*), that is, of the long piece of fabric (the
Balinese equivalent of the Javanese *sarong*) which men and women
traditionally wrap around their body to cover it from waist to ankles.
In former days, women used to wear a black (or dark) woven fabric
called *tapih*[16] under their *kamben*. The women of Nusa Penida
traditionally wove both *kamben* and *tapih*. To summarise, house pillars
are brought to life and dressed as carefully as humans. And just as *tapih*,
woven with different colours and worn as outer clothing becomes
kamben, coconut *tapis*, wrapped on a bamboo frame on the pillar, marks
the pillar's change of status from lifeless to living *kamben adegan*.

Ritual Significance of the Coconut

Coconuts are extensively used in offerings (*banten*). Whole nuts make
one of the components employed in fashioning the symbolic
accompaniments presented in all major rituals. Coconut is also used
as an ingredient (for example shredded kernel) in the making of
offerings. The use of coconut is so widespread in Balinese rituals that
it would be impossible to list all the preparations that are found. I
focus instead on the use of coconut as a ritual vessel containing parts
of the human body, before outlining the symbolic structure that seems
to govern the ritual use of coconuts in Bali.

Coconuts, Body Matters and Balinese Life Rituals

In a significant number of Balinese life-crisis rituals, a coconut becomes
the vessel for parts of the human body. During such rituals, a coconut
is opened, the water thrown away, and the cavity is filled with body
remains, after which it is sealed, and, finally, buried or thrown into

Figure 6.2 A married couple clothing a coconut palm during the *Tumpek Pengatag* festival (Sakti, Nusa Penida 1990)

the sea. Coconuts become the containers of human body substances, for they are considered efficient protecting devices against ill-intentioned (human) predators such as *léak*, who, if in possession of such remains, would harm their owners. I briefly refer to four rituals making use of coconuts as vessels of human substances.

Just after childbirth, the placenta and the afterbirth (*ari-ari*) are washed and placed in a large coconut buried in front of the kitchen, where births normally take place. The coconut, which is believed to contain the 'four siblings' of the child (*kanda pat*), and whose content is considered 'polluting', is buried in the compound's most defiled area – the *kelod* side. This brief ceremony is known as 'to bury the afterbirth' (*nanem ari-ari*), and the coconut simply as the 'afterbirth vessel' (*wadah ari-ari*). To secure a person's growth and prosperity, offerings are placed where the *kanda pat* were buried throughout his or her life.

Then comes the teeth-filing ritual (*matatah, mapandes*) which marks the transition from adolescence to maturity. During *matatah* the saliva and any leftovers from the filing are carefully collected in a coconut vessel (*wadah pees*), which is then buried at the base of the *sanggah* inside the house compound. As – according to local belief – a man or woman originates from the *sanggah* (*kemulan*), all his or her parts must be returned there.[17] In contrast to what occurs in the first ritual, the *wadah pees* vessel is buried in the sacred ground of the auspicious (*kaja*) part of the compound.

During the death rituals, a young coconut (*bungkak*) is filled with the ashes of the deceased in two different instances, first during the cremation ritual (*ngabén*), and then during a post-cremation ceremony (*ngrorasin*) held twelve days after. The ancestor's icon is referred to as *sekah tunggal* during *ngabén*, and as *sekah kurung* during *ngrorasin*.[18] Both icons are thrown into the sea to allow for the full purification of the deceased body. They are adorned with flowers and other ritual objects, and wrapped in a white cloth on which propitiating formulae are inscribed. The term *sekah* is similar to *seka*; it is related to the old Javanese word **seka**, which means 'one' or 'together', and effectively it refers to the process of 'being one', by which both *sekah* come to stand for the deceased at different times during these rituals, and to symbolise the unity of humans with their environment.

In the deification ritual (*nganteng linggih*), new divine ancestors, although not directly represented by a coconut, are embodied in coconut water. The material realisation of their blessing sprinkled over believers on all ritual occasions is simply the water of a young coconut. Therefore a young coconut becomes indexical of the god-ancestors, for its water (the water of life) is considered to embody their very essence. It is as such that coconut water becomes the prerequisite of any Balinese ritual.

On the basis of these four rituals, it is possible to say that coconuts in Nusa Penida and Bali mark the progress of a person's life from defilement at birth, to post-cremation purification after death. Whereas a coconut filled with 'polluting' afterbirth is buried in front of the kitchen, the water of a young coconut, the purest fluid of life, is used after cremation and subsequent deification rituals as the material manifestation of the blessing bestowed by god-ancestors on their living descendants. The movement from *kelod*, the cardinal point of the Balinese compass associated with impurity and the sea, to *kaja*, the cardinal point associated with ancestral purity and the Gunung Agung, the highest volcano of Bali, parallels this transition. Table 6.3 summarises these movements and transitions:

Table 6.3 Use of the coconut as container of human body parts or as representative of the human body and soul to mark the progress of human life from birth to death and deification

Progress from childhood	>		*to ancestry status*
Progress from defilement	>		*to purification*
Progress from kelod	>		*to* kaja

Birth:	**Maturity:**	**Death:**	**Deification:**
(*lekad*)	teeth filing (*matatah*) >	cremation (*ngabén*) and post-cremation (*ngrorasin*) rituals >	(*nganteng linggih*)
A coconut filled with the afterbirth is buried in the area in front of the kitchen	A coconut filled with the saliva and teeth waste is buried below the house *sanggah*.	A coconut filled with the ashes of a cremated body or its icon (in *ngrorasin*) is sunk into the sea.	No coconut is used in the iconic representation of ancestors. An ancestor's deified body is represented by a stylised human form called *prarai*, which is placed inside the *sanggah* in elevated position.
The icon is called: *Wadah ari-ari*	The icon is called: *Wadah pees*	The coconut used (*kelapa gading*) is referred to as *kasturi*, from the name of a flower (*bunga kasturi*) associated with it.	However, the blessing of the ancestor-gods, which is materially sprinkled over believers on all ritual occasions, is composed of the water of a young coconut. Thus, a young coconut is indexical of the god-ancestors, as its water, the water of life, embodies their essence.
		During cremation (*ngabén*) the icon is called *Sekah tungga* or *sekah kurung*.	
		During *ngrorasin* the icon is called *sekah kurung*.	

Seeds

The Balinese custom of burying coconuts containing parts of the human body in the ground or sinking coconuts containing human ashes at sea is directly connected to the fact that the coconut – the fruit – is, above all else, the coconut's – the palm's – seed. On a number of occasions, people in Nusa Penida told me that a coconut is like a sibling, for in it are buried the four components of the afterbirth, which, to a Balinese, represent a person's elder brothers. The way in which the afterbirth is disposed of and buried within a coconut, the importance of the burial location, and the continued influence these remains are supposed to exercise on a person's life, are best understood in the context of Balinese beliefs about living beings, *including* trees and buildings. Central to these beliefs is the notion that all living beings are 'founded' on a seed, which represents their origin. In the same way as a coconut tree is brought to life by the nut that is its seed, so the life of a human being is connected to, and depends on the 'seed' (*wadah ari-ari*) represented by the coconut containing the afterbirth, which is buried right after delivery. Like trees, human beings need well-rooted foundations in the earth – the earth that, for any agricultural society, is the basis of all life.

The same is true of the foundations of all major buildings and shrines. In Nusa Penida and Bali, an offering called *pejati* is buried in the ideal centre of a building before it is used for the first time. Interestingly enough, a *pejati* (*pajati*), one of the commonest ritual offerings, is composed of a cylindrical container made of coconut palm leaves, in which are placed: raw rice, Chinese coins (*pipis bolong*), a piece of white cotton thread, a huskless coconut (*nyuh gundul*), an egg, and the seeds of cereals, legumes and vegetables grown by local farmers. Corn, sorghum seeds, red beans, long beans, and soya beans, as well as a small onion and a small red chilli pepper, may also be added. *Pejati* (from *jati*, 'true' or 'genuine') is an offering confirming that the intentions of those who sponsor the ritual are sincere. Placing this offering at the foundation of a building reiterates the fundamental idea that the most significant forms of life in a farming society are the seeds that make life possible. Seeds are paradigmatic of life and growth, and tree growth (i.e. a tree grown from its seed) is the developmental model *par excellence* for both humans and buildings. Thus, a *pejati* contributes to the development of the building, just as a seed represents the origin of a tree, or just as the vessel containing the afterbirth (*kanda pat*) relates to a human being's origin and subsequent growth.

The Coconut and the Banyan

The role of the coconut as a polariser of metaphors associated with individual human beings is better understood when contrasted with the symbolic role played by the banyan. These two morphologically distinctive trees become the focuses of very different symbolic representations; the coconut as representative of the individual, and the banyan of the village collectivity. All villages in Nusa Penida have trees that do not produce edible fruits, and have neither utilitarian nor botanical use, but are nonetheless greatly significant to the locals. This is particularly the case for the banyan tree (*Ficus benjamina* Linn.), commonly known as (*punyan*) *bingin*.

Throughout Nusa Penida and Bali, the banyan tree marks the *banjar* landscape.[19] Most villages have a banyan at their centre, which, if old (i.e. over a hundred years), grows very large and tall. An old banyan's massive trunk is never composed of a single stem, but of a congeries of buttressing stalks, its former aerial roots. Its surface roots spread out in every direction, and its branches form a curtain of thin aerial strands descending to the ground. A dome of green leaves covers the massive structure. Viewed from afar, its appearance is one of outstanding unity. Banyans do not grow in village central spaces by chance; they are in fact planted in chosen spots by village priests (*pamangku*) who perform a special ritual sanctioning the tree–village association. While all banyans are generally known as *kroya*, the name *bingin* is reserved for ritually purified mature trees. A young tree still identified as *kroya* is planted within the village precinct, possibly in an area close to the cockfight pavilion (*wantilan*), or the village meeting hall (*balé banjar*). In this early phase, the banyan is not yet considered sacred. Later on, when the tree assumes its more definite shape and features, that is, when its aerial roots begin to appear and when its foliage takes on its characteristic shape, a cleansing rite (*meras bingin*) is performed. The banyan is then compared to a human being who has reached sexual maturity, and the cleansing ceremony, during which offerings are made to the tree, to a rite of passage. Once purified, the tree is for ever called *bingin*. From that point on, its leaves can be used in any of the community rituals.[20] The cleansing ceremony is justified on the ground that sacred banyan leaves may be used in the post-cremation ritual (*ngroras*) to make effigies (*sekah*) of the cremated dead, which are then dispatched to the sea for further purification. Sakti people say that all – and only – those belonging to the village have their *sekah* made from the communal *bingin*. The sacred banyan leaves are collected by the relatives of the deceased in a ritual called *ngangget*, in which the men cut the leaves with their long knives, while the women, who hold sheets or mats above their heads underneath the tree canopy, gather the falling ones. Only leaves that do not touch the ground are considered unpolluted, and hence suitable for ritual use.

A banyan tree is generally endowed with spiritual strength (*tenget*), and, as it grows, it becomes one of the focal points of village life. Informal meetings, children's games, cockfights and ritual processions take place in the shade of its extended branches. The tree, considered sacred, cannot be climbed by children or adults. Dried parts are cut out to preserve the tree's longevity. In Sakti, a small shrine (*pasimpangan Ratu Gedê*) is placed under the branches of the sacred banyan to receive the mask of Rangda when the goddess visits the tree for the ritual performance of the Calon Arang play. During such visits, the goddess, who is addressed as 'the great lord' (*Ratu Gedê*), changes from life-threatening to protective deity. Because of its age and the particular use of its leaves, the banyan provides a link between the community of the living and its ancestors. Moreover, its association with the Hindu god Wisnu, the preserver of the universe, further emphasises the tree's role as a continuity marker in village life. Its longevity, the religious practices of which it is a focus, and its botanical peculiarities (i.e. its longlasting stem made up of single–multiple parts that form a coherent unit) have all joined in making the *bingin* a unique symbol of the *banjar* community.

When the coconut palm and the banyan are considered together, the contrast between them appears clearly. It is expressed on two interconnected levels, one physical and visual, the other symbolic. As the following chart illustrates, physical differences underlie tree symbolism:

coconut palm: physical ground	**banyan: physical ground**
single stem	congeries of stems and aerial roots
fronds	small leaves
clearly defined canopy	large and extended canopy
non-visible roots	external visible roots
producing edible fruit	producing non-edible fruit
short-lived; its life spans the individual human life	long-lived; it extends the life of a human being and spans the life of further generations

coconut palm: symbolic ground	banyan: symbolic ground
privately owned	public
planted on private ground	planted on public ground
object of ritual planting made on behalf of the owner	object of ritual planting and life crisis rituals made on behalf of the whole village
associated with the individual	associated with the collectivity, it stands for the village and its inhabitants
associated with the owner's ancestors	associated with higher gods
not endowed with spiritual strength	*tenget* (endowed with spiritual strength)
symbolises all fruit-bearing trees	symbolises the unity of the community

In the light of the ethnographic evidence discussed throughout this chapter, it is possible to say that the coconut palm is generally conceived as the prototype of all fruit-bearing trees (as it is in the *Tumpek Pangatag* ritual), but not of *all* trees. The coconut palm occupies in fact an intermediary position between, on the one hand, the undifferentiated, non-domesticated and negatively charged forest trees, and, on the other, the great, long-lasting and positively valued banyan tree. This is not surprising, given that a coconut palm is not as vast or enduring as a forest, and that it lacks the banyan's longevity and composite arch- itecture. If the forest is the realm of undifferentiated negative spirits, the coconut symbolises the complexity of an individual's life from birth to death, and the banyan enshrines the virtues and unity of the *banjar* collectivity.

Conclusion

I have, in this chapter, sought to outline the cultural importance of the coconut in one South-east Asian society, thereby contributing to asserting the overall significance of trees in traditional societies, and the place they deserve in anthropological studies concerned with the natural environment and the ways in which it is perceived in traditional societies.

For economic and symbolic reasons, the coconut stands out as one of the most important plants in Nusa Penida and Bali. My intention has been to reflect on its significance through concrete empirical and symbolic examples. I have argued that the cultural importance of the coconut demonstrates, on the one hand, the place and role of the flora in the lives of Balinese and Nusa Penida people, and reflects, on the other, the pervasive character of the botanic idiom throughout Austronesia. The high symbolic importance of the coconut tree in these islands derives from the fact that it is imbued with life. The coconut palm, with its botanical characteristics, is considered akin to humans and its productivity and root foundation, the model of a successful existence, that perpetuates itself from generation to generation. Nuts are generally associated with female breasts, while coconut water is believed to have nutritional properties analogous to those of breast milk. Leaves are regularly used for ritual offerings and decorations. As lustral water, coconut water is the prime ceremonial ingredient. Coconuts become ritual vessels for human remains and body parts. The palm's life cycle develops in parallel to the human life cycle. In this agricultural society, the coconut, an essential component of rites of passage, is doubly implicated in people's well-being: it provides food for consumption, and metaphors for life. However, far from representing the archetype of all trees, the coconut palm is the exemplar of all domesticated and fruit-producing trees associated with human ancestors. As such, it is prized for its productivity and its extensive association with the human person, in contrast to both the wild undifferentiated forest, and the long-lasting, collective banyan.

Notes

1. Spelling in the present article conforms to the following conventions: all the Balinese words in the text have been written in italics (e.g. *banten*); terms peculiar to the Balinese spoken in Nusa Penida are characterized by the code [NP] (e.g. *lenger* [NP]); local floral terminology is glossed parenthetically in the text with botanical terms in italics, e.g. *ambengan* (*imperata cylindrica*); occasional Indonesian terms such as Pancasila or Camat have been simply underlined; old Javanese words have been printed in bold (e.g. **dahana**).

2. I conducted fieldwork in Nusa Penida and Bali between September 1989 and January 1992 under the sponsorship of L.I.P.I. (Lembaga Ilmu Pengetahuan Indonesia) and the local supervision of Udayana University. During the whole period I benefited from an ANU RSPAS Ph.D. scholarship. My special thanks

go to the people of Nusa Penida. I owe a particular debt of gratitude to the members of *banjar* and *desa* Sakti who hosted me during my stay in Nusa Penida.

3. Only felled palms become *séséh*; this reflects their relevance in Balinese culture. The term *séh*, which means 'to change', commonly refers to the changing of clothes. In a Balinese temple festival the gods are always cleansed and their clothes changed before the opening of the festival; the new set of clothes given to the gods is made into a specific offering called *séh.*

4. The growth of the coconut tree is defined in six stages as follows:

I – *Pujer* indicates a germinating coconut.

II – *Mapungkil* refers to a 4/5-year-old plant in which the start of the formation of the stem above the ground can be observed.

III – *Nyuh tubuh* applies to a well-developed palm whose first flowering has not occurred yet.

IV – *Matlaktak* is a 6/7-year-old plant.

V – *Punyan nyuh* is a mature tree.

VI – *Nyuh tua* is an old coconut.

On the ethnobotany of the coconut palm and the specific attributes of these stages of growth, see Giambelli (1995, Chapter X).

5. The dimensions of a nut, the consistency of its kernel, and the quantity of water contained in it are all related to the age of the fruit. Nuts are very closely defined, and in Sakti the development of a nut is pictured as follows:

I – *Bungsil* is the first stage of growth in the fruit.

II – *Bungkak* refers to a nut 10 to 13 cm long, almost entirely filled with water.

III – *Klungah* indicates that the nut shows the first signs of endosperm formation.

IV – *Kuud* designates a nut with a fully formed endosperm.

V – *Nyuh* refers to a mature nut.

On the specificities of these stages, see Giambelli (1995, Chapter X).

6. According to FAO (1992: 10) sources, Bali produced in 1988 59,816 metric tons of coconuts, equivalent to 2.82 per cent of Indonesia's total production. During the 1978–88 decade, Indonesia was the second largest producer of coconuts and coconut by-products after the Philippines. However, during the same period, Indonesia's internal market grew appreciably, and the nation also became the largest coconut consumer. This has influenced Indonesia's ability to export coconut products, so that its share of the world market has been relatively low compared to its productive potential.

7. Different varieties of coconut are grown in Nusa Penida. Local varieties are distinguished by a specific name and recognised by the external traits of the plant and of its fruit, that is, by differences in plant dimensions, leaf colour,

and fruit size, shape and colour. The coconut varieties found in Nusa Penida are known locally as: *Nyuh Barak, Nyuh Beruk, Nyuh Bulan, Nyuh Enggalan, Nyuh Gadang, Nyuh Gading, Nyuh Jemulung, Nyuh Julit, Nyuh Puuh, Nyuh Sudamala, Nyuh Tabah, Nyuh Udang.* On the distinctive features of these varieties see Giambelli (1995, Chapter X).

8. On the one hand, the nest stands for the bird; but as it is placed on the floor of the hole, it also on the other hand comes to host the seed as if the seed were a small bird.

9. On *kemulan* as 'origin point' of an 'origin group' see also Geertz and Geertz (1975: 64), Guermonprez (1990: 64), Boon (1977: 65–6) and Fox (1992). On *mula* and *mamula* as planting see Giambelli (1995: 108). See also Giambelli (1995: 222) for the analogy between coconut and banana planting.

10. In Europe trees were also planted – and still are – to commemorate important events such as birth (Thomas 1984).

11. The general equivalence between human body and plant is not a theme confined to Balinese culture; it is also present in ancient Hindu Indian treaties and tradition. In his attempt to formalise these similarities, Madjumdar (1927: 27) writes:

A more elaborate attempt [to formalise plant internal morphology] is seen in Vrihat Aranyaka Upanishad, where the inner structure of plants is described after the analogy of the human anatomy [. . .] The body of the plant is exactly like the body of man; the *hairs* of man corresponding to the *leaves* of plants and his *skin* corresponding to the *dry exterior bark* of the plants (234-28-1).

The flesh of the human body answers to the *sakara* (soft tissue next to the skin) of plants: his nerves standing for the *kinhata* (fibrous tissue in sakara as in jute, etc.) of plants, both being equally strong. Just as the bones of man lie behind his flesh, also wood, *daru*, lies behind the sakara (and occupying the centre) of plants and the marrow (pith) is alike in both (236-30-3).

12. Due to its density and yellow colour, the colostrum is held to be an inferior type of breast milk and is generally disposed of; the white fluid milk that follows it is preferred.

13. For a birth ritual in Eastern Indonesia that involves the washing of the child in coconut water, see Jensen (1963: 197).

14. A *rai* is the index finger's length taken from the knuckle to the tip. The term *adegan* is related to *adeg* ('the shape of' or a 'body figure'), and *ngadeg* ('to stand').

15. The three colours are also associated with the Hindu gods Brahma, Wisnu and Siva. Howe (1983: 154) indicates a set of associations relating the elements anointed on the post (blood, charcoal and lime) with specific parts of a living tree:

Table 6.4 Summary of the characteristic elements used to perform *pangurip miwah pasupatian* and their referents according to Howe and Nusa Penida people

elements	according to Howe these elements stand for:	colour	in Nusa Penida these elements are thought of as:
chicken blood (*getih*)	the sap of a tree (*getah*)	red	blood. In Nusa Penida only coconut trees are credited with *getah*. The sap of any other tree is known as *engket*.
charcoal (*areng*)	the hardwood (duramen) of a tree. In Balinese it is called *les*.	black	flesh
lime (*pamor, apuh*)	the new wood (alburnum) which is placed between the cortex and the duramen. In Balinese it is called *kubal* and has a clearer colour than the inner hardwood.	white	bones

16. Fraser-Lu (1986:21) indicates that in Java the kain panjang, a longer version of the sarong used to be worn on more formal occasions, when worn by a woman is referred to as *tapih*.

17. This also applies to the forelocks cut on this occasion. The hair is placed in a small container made of coconut leaves (*tipat blayag*) and then buried under the *sanggah*.

18. It may also be called *sekah asti*, for it contains the ashes taken from the bones (*asti*) of the deceased.

19. *Banjar* may refer to a hamlet, to a group of residential units, or, as in Nusa Penida, to a whole village. The term, which is generally associated with administrative (*banjar dinas*) and customary (*banjar adat*) functions, also refers to the inhabitants of such a community, as well as their specific institutions.

20. The banyan tree is widespread throughout Java, Bali and Indonesia. Its symbolical importance has been recognised and used by the Indonesian government, for which it is one of the five emblems composing the national Pancasila icon. The tree, which traditionally symbolises the ideal *banjar* unity, has thus become the symbol of national unity under the slogan 'Persatuan Indonesia' (One United Indonesia). At *desa* level, banyan trees are not only planted as community religious symbols; they are also planted in public

inaugurations at crossroads and other places by state subdistrict and district officers (Camat) to mark the unity of the state. Last but not least, the banyan tree is the symbol of the largest Indonesian party, the Golkar political party, to which all civil servants belong.

References

Boon, J., *The anthropological romance of Bali*, Cambridge: Cambridge University Press, 1977

Bosch, F. D. K., *The Golden Germ*, 'S-Gravenhage: Mouton, 1960

FAO, *Coconut Oil and Copra Production, Marketing and Trade*, Bangkok: FAO Regional Office for Asia and the Pacific, 1992

Fox, J. J., 'Sister's child as plant: metaphors in an idiom of consang-uinity', in R. Needham (ed.), *Rethinking Kinship and Marriage*, London: Tavistock, 1971

—— *Harvest of the Palm*, Cambridge, Mass.: Harvard University Press, 1977

—— 'Origin Structures and Systems of Precedence in the Comparative Study of Austronesian Societies', paper presented at the 1992 Symposium on Austronesian Studies, Taiwan; published in P. J. K. Li, Dah-an Ho, Cheng-hwa Tsang and Ying-Kuei Huang (eds), *Austronesian Studies Relating to Taiwan*, Taipei: Academica Sinica, 1992

Fraser-Lu, S., *Indonesian Batik*, Singapore: Oxford University Press, 1986

Geertz, H. and C. Geertz, *Kinship in Bali*, Chicago: University of Chicago Press, 1975

Giambelli, R. A., Reciprocating with Ibu Pretiwi. Social Organisation and the Importance of Plants, Land and the Ancestors in Nusa Penida, unpublished Ph. D. Thesis, dept. of Anthropology, R.S.P.A.S., Australian National University, Canberra, 1995

Guermonprez, J.-F., 'On the Elusive Balinese Village: Hierarchy and Values versus Political Models', *Review of Indonesian and Malaysian Affairs*, 24, 1990, pp. 55–89

Howe, L., 'An introduction to the cultural study of traditional Balinese architecture', in *Archipel* 25, 1983, pp. 137–58

Jensen, A. E., *Myth and Cult among Primitive Peoples*, Chicago and London: The University of Chicago Press, 1963

Majumdar, G. P., *Vanaspati. Plants and Plant-Life as in Indian Treatises and Traditions*, Calcutta: University of Calcutta, 1927

Thomas, K., *Man and the Natural World: Changing Attitudes in England 1500–1800*, Harmondsworth: Penguin, 1984

Viennot, O., *Le Culte de l'Arbre dans l'Inde Ancienne*, Paris: Presses Universitaires de France, 1954

'May Blessings Come, May Mischiefs Go!' Living Kinds as Agents of Transitions and Transformation in an Eastern Indonesian Setting

Signe Howell

On the third day of the elaborate nine-day annual pre-planting ceremonies performed by the northern Lio on the island of Flores in Indonesia, the priest-leaders of the ceremonial houses of a core village initiate one sequence to be completed on the following day.[1] This is the sequence that replaces last year's bundle of areca nuts (*ke'o*) and betel-pepper leaves (*sirê*), wrapped in a sugar-palm leaf (*mokê*). The new bundle will be kept for the year to come in the most holy part of the ceremonial house, suspended above the ancestral offering place. This sequence temporally encloses, as it were, another sequence, the most sacred of the planting ceremony as a whole, and the one that gives it its name, namely, the cooking and symbolic eating of a specially cultivated tuber (*uwi*). The whole cycle is called 'the ceremony of eating the tuber' (*nggua ka uwi*). These two sequences constitute the dominant reference point for the numerous other prescribed sequences of the ceremony. The replacement of the areca/sugar-palm bundle is called 'the trunk old is exchanged with the new' (*pu'u olo sore walu e'o muri*). This paper will explore the significance of these two palm trees.

In the chapter on religion in his introductory book entitled *Anthropology*, published in 1912, Marett[2] explores the meaning and function of religion in human society. He maintains that religion is congregational and traditional; that its methods and doctrines are standardised; and that its performance is ritualised (1912: 212). In a beautiful turn of phrase, Marett sums up the general aim of religious practice as: 'May blessings come, may mischiefs go' (Marett 1912: 233) and suggests that the employment of 'wonder-working things' is integral to its achievement. He wonders what is so special about these objects, to make them suitable media for magic. He refuses to speculate about mystical or pre-logical reasoning, because such an approach not only exoticises so-called primitive peoples and their ways of life, but also radically distinguishes them from supposedly less primitive peoples. Instead, Marett (1912: 232) suggests that everywhere human religious striving leads to perceive some things as 'wonder-working', a property which turns them into eminently suited vehicles for avoiding dangers and achieving the good life.

I wish to examine here the use and significance of the areca and sugar palms by viewing them as 'wonder-working things'. More specifically, I seek some understanding of why they feature so prominently in the pre-planting agricultural ceremony just described, despite their being unrelated to the agricultural cycle as such. What is it that makes these two palm species so significant? By identifying their distinctive features, I will argue that these are of a special quality (narcotic) which makes them particularly appealing to the human imagination. In other words, it may not be accidental that the products of the areca and arenga palms have infiltrated the confines of Lio meaning-making processes. My argument will be that two related processes may be observed: a transformation of natural kinds into cultural kinds, and a transformation of living kinds into artefacts (cf. Bloch 1993). Having established the basis of my argument, I now turn to symbolising processes, tropes, metaphors and analogies.

If we, at least as a minimal definition, agree with Lakoff and Johnson (1980: 5) that, '[T]he essence of metaphor is understanding and experiencing one kind of thing in terms of another' then, in the present context, the task is to identify the properties and qualities that make the areca and sugar palms potent vehicles for metaphoric evocations. However, such an approach can only account for part of the story, for symbols do not only pertain to intellectual endeavours; they also pertain to the emotional side of human existence. They are made meaningful through experience and action.

Several anthropologists have recently argued that it is analytically illegitimate to search for commonalities in perceptions and values about the world (Borofsky 1994; Keesing 1989). I do not fully agree with such propositions, but do think that the debate has forced us to rethink the anthropological project. The ritual context, which has tended to be the sole source for anthropological symbolic interpretations, has perhaps blinded us to the semantic varieties of other, more mundane, but not necessarily less significant, arenas of symbolising in social life. The aim, in my view, should be to maintain the theoretical gains obtained in the pursuit of a kind of cultural grammar, while at the same time exploring the contextualised and processual organisation of knowledge. Symbolic usage is not only constantly evolving, it is also conservative, and, in many cases, multivocal. Marilyn Strathern (1991: xx) has made the important point that '[T]he relativising effect of multiple perspectives will make everything seem partial; the recurrence of similar propositions and bits of information will make everything seem connected.' Such 'partial connections', I suggest, are inherent to symbolic usage. An awareness of this allows one to abandon an exclusive theoretical reliance on core or dominant symbols, and move instead to an examination of symbols in action in different contexts.

While broadly agreeing with the critiques of the anthropological tendency to concentrate the study of forms of social life on the ritual context (de Boeck 1994), I nevertheless consider ritual contexts to be particularly dense with symbolic constructions (see Turner, in particular Turner 1974). As such, they provide the anthropologist with useful *entrées* into, and clues to, principles of social organisation, as well as cultural thinking and values. However, rituals are only one source; social interactions of all kinds must be examined. The aim should be to seek to identify the partial connections, both between related and seemingly unrelated elements in the same context, and between the same elements in related and seemingly unrelated contexts, in order to give proper allowance for differences in meanings, while at the same time eliciting the connections.

Confining myself to one fairly delineated social world, one village domain amongst the northern Lio, I wish to consider some aspects of the employment of areca and arenga (more commonly known as sugar) palms, and their respective products, betel and palm wine, in a series of both ritual and mundane contexts. I explore them in terms of both conjuncture and disjuncture of elements and meanings. To be aware that identical objects are employed in different situations with different purposes and meanings does not mean abandoning the idea of a constitutive association that would provoke *some kind* of similar imaging in people's minds whenever they are confronted with these objects. To get at these, one needs to consider the perceived and attributed qualities of the items in question, and the different uses they are being put to, as well as the history of their meanings and use.

Metaphors need not have goals, but they are infected with past meanings. Turner's (1967: 21) proposal that the Ndembu milk-tree is a dominant symbol in the sense that such symbols are 'regarded as not merely means to fulfilment of the avowed purposes of a given ritual but also, and more importantly, refer to values which are regarded as ends in themselves' is still a helpful way to think about the issue, although it takes one only part of the way. The force of dominant symbols may be their multivocality. I wish to argue that past significances, as well as explicit and implicit meanings of symbolic objects or actions, adhere to objects and actions, and are evoked, however diffusely, on subsequent occasions of their employment. Semantically, each object and action used symbolically may be thought of as being constantly on the move, incorporating into them those elements and meanings from past employments and contexts that somehow resonated with the observers and participants. Despite informants' insistence to the contrary, no ritual is identically performed every time it is carried out. For all sorts of reasons, additions and omissions occur. This is reflected in participants' understandings, as well as in future performances. If the same objects or actions appear in many different contexts, it seems reasonable to assume that they are particularly dense with meanings; that they are well suited for making a variety of partial connections and for creating new semantic constellations. It is from these perspectives that I examine the northern Lio's symbolic use of areca (*Areca catechu*) and arenga (*Arenga pinnata*).

From Living Kinds to Human Artefacts

Bloch (1993: 114) has argued recently that much religious symbolism is concerned with passages between living kinds and artefacts. He suggests that this process may be a replication of processes of cognitive development. In other words, the suggestion is that there is a human proclivity to use living kinds symbolically. Although using a different perspective, Needham (1978) has explored a similar line of thought. I will not debate Bloch's or Needham's ideas here, but declare an agreement in principle, and give an example of how certain properties of living kinds can become symbolically highly significant. I will then argue that it is these properties that make the transformation of living kinds into artefacts relevant. Trees and plants are eminently suitable as metaphoric vehicles for growth and maturation, or for degeneration and regeneration (Bloch 1993; de Boek 1994; Fernandez, this volume, Chapter 4). Such symbolic potentials of trees are noted by the Lio, who take full advantage of them in many contexts. I wish to suggest, however, that while these aspects of trees may also be of some relevance in the case of the areca and arenga palms, it is the *transformative* qualities of their main products – betel and palm wine – that are exploited in Lio usage. The process by which betel and palm wine effect and transform bodily and mental states is used analogically in ritualised action. This will be my focus in what follows.

Northern Lio interaction with living kinds is frequently predicated upon regulative sets of ideas and values. Some trees, particularly those that humans regularly use and thus make into artefacts, have (or are inhabited by) spiritual beings (*nitu*). Tree spirits may be both helpful and dangerous, depending on the quality of their relationship with humans. The banyan tree so central in Buddhism is also sacred among the Lio, where it features in many ritualised contexts. According to myth, the original banyan is linked to the human (male) body and blood. A brother and sister were eating chicken. A bone got stuck in the boy's throat. The sister cut a hole in it and pulled the bone out. She licked the blood and put her finger on the wound. It healed and the bone became gold. She planted the gold and the banyan tree grew out of it. It bore golden fruit and henceforth was the source of all gold. Ever since, gold has been the main item of exchange in binding relationships of all kinds, but particularly those of marriage and alliance. Gold has been associated with maleness. I shall return to the significance of this below.

Effecting Sociality

Betel and palm wine represent good examples of the transformation of living kinds into human artefacts, which, moreover, become vehicles for a multiplicity of symbolic activities. I say this not just because betel and palm wine are significant in so many different contexts, but also because they may be said to express metaphorically human sociality, human fertility, and human vulnerability. Just as nuts and sugary liquid (living kinds) are transformed into betel quid and wine or arak (artefacts), the mental and bodily states of those who ingest these artefactual products are transformed under the effect of intoxication. I suggest that the fact that betel and palm wine are transformative in a physiological sense, and that they affect human consciousness and bodily states, may be a contributing factor to their being employed as 'wonder-making things' in so many different contexts. There is an analogical relation between the transforming effect on humans and the transformation of social situations.

Betel quid (prepared with areca nuts, the leaf or long pod of the betel-pepper vine, and lime) makes the chewer pleasurably dizzy. Palm wine intoxicates, especially when it has been further distilled into arak. In moderation, these effects are regarded as desirable, but excess is negatively sanctioned. More to the point, the ingestion of these intoxicants is an inherently social act. Betel, and to a lesser extent palm wine, is the medium that transforms people, ancestors and spirits from bounded separate outsiders into interacting interlocutors. What we observe here is a passage from living kinds to tools which can effect human communication and make relationships.

The Importance of Betel

Betel-chewing is endemic to south-east Asia. Both the areca palm and the betel vine are native to the Indonesian Archipelago (Rooney 1993). The habit of chewing the quid was reported by the first European travellers, who made it clear that no one would leave the house without taking the ingredients necessary for making the quid. It was noted that '[C]hewing betel [. . .] was not a matter of personal preference [. . .] It was a social necessity for every adult in society' (Reid 1985: 530).

The northern Lio say that betel keeps hunger at bay. Perhaps this is a contributing factor to its formalised use in agricultural rituals, but not, I suggest, the prime one. Both betel and palm wine may be characterised as multivocal symbols, but their transformative quality is a stable feature discernible across context (see also Ellen 1991). Betel marks beginnings and initiates social events. Betel is always offered before the real business of any occasion may begin. People told me that 'it opens the path for talking' as when, for example, a relative or friend enters one's house casually, when potential wife-takers first arrive on matrimonial business, or when spirits and ancestors are addressed during the whole gamut of rituals. Other moments of transition also require areca and betel, such as birth, death, exchanges of all kinds, transfer of rights, or installations of priest-leaders. They are also used magically during healing and strengthening rituals.

Among the Lio, as in most other parts of the Malay and Indonesian worlds, betel is associated with marriage – primarily so on the man's side – and, as such, has strong male connotations. The Indonesian word for the nut (*pinang*) is incorporated into various words concerning engagement. For example, *pempinangan* means 'applicant, suitor, betel-nut box' (Echols and Shadily 1990). According to northern Lio mythology, the wife-receivers in the early days of humanity would present their wife-givers with a bamboo section filled with gold from the banyan tree mentioned above. After the banyan was cut down, the bamboo was filled with areca-nut juice, and presented together with some gold pieces. Today, areca nuts and betel pods, while offered by either party when entertaining the other, and placed on top of all items of exchange, still have wife-receiving – hence male – connotations in matters of marriage and alliance. On other occasions, areca and betel may carry female connotations; and on yet others, they are not gendered.

Northern Lio people practice swidden agriculture. Rice is the most prestigious staple, but it is not abundant, and its regular procurement requires co-operation with spirits and ancestors. Its origins are traced mythically to the body of a girl who, upon discovering by accident that some hitherto unknown plant (rice) grew out of the blood from a wound, asked her brother to cut her up and scatter her blood so people need not go hungry. Various parts of her body turned into rice, tubers, yams and vegetables. This was the birth of agriculture; the girl is referred to as Rice Mother. According to some versions, her eyes became areca nuts.

Places of origin have religious significance in northern Lio life. For example, priest-leaders from long established virtually independent villages must return to the origin village from time to time to request saplings from areca and betel vine to plant back home. When the village of origin rebuilds its temple, priest-leaders from satellite villages must arrive with cuttings from the same trees to plant in the central village area. These acts represent the 'recognition of ancient ties'. In other words, the manifestations of living relationships are expressed through the continuous replacement of seedlings from these particular trees, whose narcotic products, according to my argument, denote relationship and communication *par excellence*.

The Importance of the Sugar (Arenga) Palm

The arenga palm was 'among man's first sources of sugar, used before the sugar-cane was harnessed for his service' (Burkill 1966: 232). When cut, the palm (Lio: *moké*) releases a milky sweet liquid (*moké*) which may be drunk immediately after tapping, when it is only slightly alcoholic. It can be distilled into a clear, powerful alcohol known as arak. Arak is a necessary part of many rituals, especially those including food offerings. In ritual contexts, food-offerings and meals are preceded by areca, and accompanied with palm wine. The Lio tell a myth about the origin of palm wine. Following the self-sacrifice of Rice Mother, people ate themselves replete. They became thirsty, but had nothing to drink. A young girl went to urinate. Her urine turned into palm wine. In some versions, the girl then turned into a sugar palm whose sap could be tapped.

Unlike the areca palm, which grows from planted seeds, the arenga palm self-germinates. The first time either palm is harvested, the harvest unfolds according to prescribed ritual actions that evoke the mythical past. Moreover, the spirits of the two palms are invited to engage in a friendly relationship with their human harvesters. In preparation for the first tapping, a chicken is sacrificed, and an egg broken over the inflorescence to be tapped. The whole process is accompanied by several invocations, including one which orders the tree to 'lift up its *sarung* and urinate', in direct reference to the myth of the young girl who did just that. Palm wine has strong female connotations, and is, together with rice and woven cloth, a prescribed wife-givers' gift. However, some people say that the liquid is the semen of the male supreme deity Sun–Moon. All Lio formal communication with ancestors or deities (male and female) are expressed through a meal offering, which, depending on the occasion, may be raw (untransformed) or cooked (transformed). Whichever, it is always preceded by areca nuts and betel leaves; the cooked meal also includes arak (transformed palm wine). The accompanying invocations invariably begin with 'we offer betel, food is coming' and 'eat rice, eat meat, drink palm wine'.

Potent (Actual and Symbolic) Qualities of Palm Wine and Betel Quid

I want briefly to examine some of the similarities and differences between the areca and arenga palms, and their products (betel and wine) which might possibly account for their centrality in Lio ritualisation, and for the fact of their joint presence in the central part of the pre-planting ceremonies.

Firstly, with regard to inherent qualities, both betel and palm wine have slight narcotic effects. They are the only agents for the transformation of mental, emotional and bodily states that the Lio employ, whether individually or collectively. Both their taste and effect (readily experienced by all, regardless of sex and status) are thought pleasant.

As artefacts, their inherently transformative quality is used symbolically in situations where transition and transformation of categories, status and relationships are wanted, as well as on occasions of temporal and spatial transitions. They are therefore good both to eat and to think!

Secondly, both are living kinds thought to have originated out of the female human body. Amongst the other vegetal foods of similar origin, only rice is subjected to elaborate ritualised actions. However, only areca and wine are believed to have magical properties affecting fertility. Rice, the Lio's prime food, came from the blood of the first young girl, and palm wine from her urine (or from Sun–Moon's semen according to the alternative version), that is, from liquid substances that transcend body boundaries, and regulate transitions between the inside and the outside. Analogical relationships exist between various bodily substances and the perceived properties of their associated living kinds. The white milky juice of the sugar palm is likened to mother's milk, semen and urine. Blood, semen and milk are all transformative and life-promoting. Blood from a live sacrificial animal must be applied to significant persons and objects during many life-promoting rituals (Howell 1996b). Areca nuts, originating from the eyes of the first young girl in the origin myth, are conceptually different from bodily fluids; but the areca nut, chewed with its accompaniments, produces in profusion a bright red liquid to be spat out. The Lio make explicit associations between this liquid and blood. The red spittle, thought to be reminiscent of blood, is often spat on people and objects, in the same way as the blood of sacrificial animals is applied to them. Therefore, areca and sugar palms, transformed body parts and them-selves transformative agents, are brought into contact with rice (the most valued of the transformed foods) at the time when rice is to be regenerated for the next harvest. It is worth noting at this point that eyes, the medium for orientation and understanding, trigger a very different kind of transformative process.

Thirdly, and following on from the last point, betel and wine are, in the Lio context, bearers of both male and female characteristics. This androgyny (Howell 1995) allows them to stand forth in particular contexts gendered in either mode. One feature of the sugar palm, not lost on the Lio, is that it produces both male and female inflorescences, and that it is the male inflorescence that produces most sap. At the same time, palm wine evokes femaleness in many ritual contexts, a fact not unrelated to either its mythical origins or its role as a wife-giver's prescribed gift. While no such botanical feature is found for the areca, its female origins and male usage in early marriage transactions render it similarly apt to be gendered in either a male or female mode. I therefore wish to suggest that these are sufficient indications of the fact that the cultural importance of androgynous identity among the Lio motivates the particularly potent and multivocal metaphoric nature of both palms. I have argued elsewhere (Howell 1996a) that the possibility for an object, or category of person, to emerge constituted in either a male or female mode is an important aspect of Lio ideological constructs (Howell 1995 and 1996a). At first sight, it is tempting to argue that the areca palm may best be interpreted as metonymic maleness and palm wine as metonymic femaleness. In many contexts this would, indeed, be the correct interpretation. However, maleness and femaleness as ideas and values need context for any meaning to emerge. The meaning of gender and gendered meanings vary. Moreover, in some given contexts, maleness and femaleness are complementary values; in others they are hierarchial. If the relationship is hierarchical, then either gender quality encompasses the mode of sociality and constitutes it. The ability to change, to stand forth gendered in one or either way, or even to be gender-neutral, is characteristic of significant persons and objects among the northern Lio. Betel and palm wine both make partial connections which may or may not be gendered, and when gendered, may not be so consistently. They both change their meanings and are agents of change. This is what makes them so dynamic. If rice can never evoke anything but femaleness, and gold maleness, areca nuts and palm wine can transcend their gender specificity, thus allowing both analogical and historical evocations. These two artefacts, the products of living kinds, are not, however, central to Lio social and ritual life merely as abstract symbols; they are central as items used in social actions. The gendering of sociality occurs only in certain situations; by and large, in those specifically concerned with fertility and regeneration (human, agricultural, ancestral, or spiritual) and those concerned with life-taking activities such as sacrificial killing and warfare, in which the offering of areca nut is endemic at every stage.

Last, but by no means least, both artefacts are supremely social. Betel initiates all communication and accompanies all exchanges. It is ever-present as the symbol of sociality *par excellence* – regardless of context. Sociality, for the Lio, is not only what makes life meaningful, it is also what denotes communication and acknowledges mutuality. Correct social behaviour is a pre-requisite for fertility and the continuous flow of life. As transformative media, betel and palm wine both transform encounters into social relationships. I now turn to the *ka uwi* (eating the tuber) ceremony, with special emphasis on the re-placing of the areca/sugar palm sequence.

The *Ka Uwi* Ceremony

As most anthropologists know, it is difficult to conjure up anything like a clear picture of significant local events from the way people describe them beforehand. I gathered quite a lot of information about the annual 'Eating the tuber' ceremony before witnessing it, just by talking to people, and formed what I thought was a fairly complete picture of the ceremony. But, as it turned out, I was completely unprepared for much of what took place. In particular, I was astonished by the sequence of changing the bundle of areca nuts wrapped in sugar-palm leaves mentioned at the outset of this chapter. Although I had seen some wizened leaves standing in the corner next to the ancestral offering place inside ceremonial houses, I had never thought to enquire about them. For a long time, I was at a loss to grasp the bundle's significance.

As already stated, the day of the *uwi* ceremony is the most sacred of the various planting sequences. Northern Lio agricultural ceremonies, as well as other life-promoting rituals, all invoke the cosmogonic and the early social pasts, and seek to conjoin them with present-day activities. Again and again, details from these times are invoked during ritual sequences, including the one under discussion. Until Rice Mother offered her body, people had been eating rotten wood and wild tubers (*uwi*). This wild tuber is today procured only from the ritual ancestral fields, where they are cultivated by priest-leaders, and only for the purpose of the ceremony. It is in this sense more generally and conceptually linked up with cultivation.

The day starts when the male and female 'priest-leaders of the land' walk ceremoniously to the ritual field, where they dig up the tuber to be brought to the ceremonial house. The previous evening, the priest-leader couple went under the cover of darkness to the abandoned village of origin to collect areca nuts and betel vine. They wrapped the nuts together with the leaves inside the black fibres of sugar palm, enclosed the bundle inside the plaited leaves of a sugar palm, and left the parcel in a sacred banyan tree. Once the tuber is inside the ceremonial house, the bundle is ceremoniously retrieved from the tree, brought into the house, and placed on the floor next to the tuber. The male priest-leader sacrifices a chicken, whose blood he leaves dripping on to the bundle and tuber. The tuber is then cut into seven slices, which are baked by the female priest-leader. The two ends are kept and, together with the knife, put inside a small basket. The peel is examined; its shape indicates the number and sex of children to be born in the next year. The house priest-leader takes seven areca nuts from the bundle on the floor, and hands one to each of the seven priest-leaders who sit on the floor in a circle. After having invoked the ancestors, the chief priest-leader asks:

– *Tiko do ata fai?* 'Has everyone received the woman?'

A priest-leader replies:

– *Nata kita keu ana lo'o ata fai.* 'We eat areca nut [like] the small girl child.'

They all bring their areca nut to the mouth, carefully avoiding biting into it. The chief priest-leader subsequently hands out betel leaves to wrap up the areca nuts. After a brief invocation, he admonishes the other priest-leaders:

– *Nata ma'e sallah.* 'Eat betel, don't do it wrong' (i.e. don't put it into the mouth)

and each priest-leader pretends to bite the nut out. The seven priest-leaders are each given a slice of baked tuber to eat, and a glass of arak. The slices are put to the mouth but not eaten. The following dialogue ensues:

– [first speaker] *Tika do ata fai?* 'Has everyone received the woman?'

– [second speaker] *Ka kita uwi ana lo'o ata fai.* 'We eat *uwi* [like] a little girl.'

After the betel and the *uwi* have been bitten into but not eaten, they are placed on the ancestral offering place. The areca/palm-wine bundle from last year is replaced with the new one. The small basket containing the two tuber ends (which will be planted later in the ritual field for the following year), the areca nuts, and the betel leaves is hung inside the bundle. The seven priest-leaders are now given a meal of cooked rice from the ritual field, the cooked meat of the sacrificed chicken, and some vegetables. Each is then given a glass of arak.

One point to note here is that the areca, the betel and the tuber are likened to a woman and a little girl. In the context of promoting agricultural fertility, a context which, as I have argued elsewhere (Howell 1996b), must be understood as being constituted in a female mode, the symbolic vehicle employed – areca – evokes female fertility. The more common male associations of betel and marriage are here submerged. However, the role of areca as substitute for gold in the gifts made by wife-receivers is also latent in the sequence and the practice of offering betel to guests; and so is Rice Mother, whose eyes gave birth, as it were, to the nut. The tuber also evokes Rice Mother in the sense that the latter, by allowing her body to become the main source of vegetable foodstuff, has caused humans to end their dependency on the wild tuber. To centre the rice fertility ceremony on this tuber thus implies that it acts as a marker expressing the transformed conditions of social existence from hunting-gathering to agriculture. The areca and arenga palms are the two trees most intimately connected to human social existence. Their products, betel and palm wine, are agents for transformations signifying that a person, a significant object, and a relationship are fashioned, as well as born.

The remaining days of the pre-planting ceremony are dedicated to the first eating of the new rice, and to the preparation of rice for planting. Again, one may discern an endless concern with recycling and transforming the old into the new. Subsequent ritual events emphasise maleness and femaleness, directions (right and left), and temporal marking. Each new sequence is opened with the offering of areca and betel pods. Each ritualised meal (including offerings) includes palm wine. Each spatial and temporal transition is effected by these two palm products, which, ever-present, form links between the ceremony's various disparate sequences, and mark them off. The final ceremony consists in the 'Return of the Great Spirits' (*sumba nu'a polo ria*). The two palms are again in focus. At the outset of the ceremony, the spirits were invited to participate; now it is time they leave humans alone for the year to come. A rather elaborate meal is prepared for them, to which all villagers must contribute 'something humans eat, something humans don't eat, and some areca and betel'.[3] Five trays covered with sugar-palm leaves are carried round the village, on which each household must place its contribution.

The food collected is brought to the sacred space outside the temple, where five long sugar-palm branches with attached bundles of nuts have already been laid. Then, each of the four symbolic corners and the centre of the village are marked out with a tray containing a miniature pestle and mortar, areca nuts, and some of the collected food.

Each tray, covered with a sugar-palm branch, is carried to its destination. Once in position, the branch is erected above the tray, its stem pushed into the ground, its leaves providing shelter. In the sacred centre of the dance–burial place, tied to a long bamboo stick (*dodja*) suspended above the central offering stones, is a sugar-palm branch. Untouched since the previous year, it is now solemnly replaced. A small basket filled with new rice specially prepared from the ancestral field is attached to the sugar-palm branch, whose leaves are said to be the ships of the Great Spirits. The leaves are taken home by the spirits, who will bring them back in the following year.

Concluding Remarks

Extremely rich symbolic evocations punctuate these nine days of agricultural ceremonies. I have in this chapter concentrated on the significance of the ritualised replacing of the bundle made of areca, betel and sugar-palm inside the ceremonial houses. My interpretative quest has sought to accommodate the premiss that the two trees are natural living kinds, and explore how their natural attributes become tropes. Relationships between living kinds and humans may be expressed metaphorically, metonymically, and analogically as well as practically. My suggestion is that one way of interpreting such relationships is to unravel culturally attributed and actual pertinent qualities of the living kinds in each case, and then examine how these are used symbolically, or, in other words, to look for the creation of an analogical relation between the object used as symbol and the object being symbolised. Such relations are acted out again and again whenever the objects are used. Through practice, and through ingesting, and by offering betel and wine as significant markers at many social moments, the northern Lio infuse and recreate the meanings of their social universe. Who is to say where cause ends and effect begins?

Betel offering is ubiquitous in Lio social and ritual life, and the giving, receiving and chewing of betel is enmeshed in a range of meanings, only some of which I have had time to explore here. Although less a part of daily life (but enjoyed on many social occasions), the giving, receiving and drinking of palm wine is a necessary ingredient in ritualised transactions that include commensality. The very fact of their ordinariness, and the fact that their transformative effects are experienced daily by all, may be a contributing factor to the symbolic power of their transformative qualities. However, my argument has been that to seek wholly consistent meanings and one-to-one symbolic relationships in the numerous appearances of betel and wine would be misplaced. These two products are nevertheless employed with consistency. Betel and palm wine are both necessary ingredients in all social interactions, whether between humans or between humans and spirits. Their efficacy is social. They ignite, establish, reconfirm and transform relationships. Grounded in cosmology, they are ethical media *par excellence*, bringing the interlocutors into mutually binding relationships – a task for which they are eminently suited because their narcotic qualities explicitly effect transitions of states. At one level, analogic connections are, I suggest, made between the transformation of mental, emotional and physiological states, and, at another level, between social, temporal and spatial states. This partly accounts for the central role of areca and arenga palms in the annual agricultural ceremony that marks the end of the old, and the beginning of the new, agricultural year. All the sequences are, in their different ways, saying something about temporal processes, i.e. about endings, beginnings, transitions and continuity.

The 'exchanging old for new' sequence in the middle of this pre-planting ceremony, which celebrates links with the past as necessary pre-requisites for the continuous flow of life, when last year's wine and betel are replaced with this year's, draws together the many partial connections of betel and wine (the prime agents of transition) encountered in disparate contexts. The numerous meanings come together during this sequence, transcended, in what could be called a 'complete connection'. For a brief moment – the duration of the ritual sequences – there is a fusion of all the disparate meanings of the areca and arenga palms. Multivocality becomes condensed, not into one meaning, but into all the meanings being expressed simultaneously. All significant Lio relationships are evoked: marriage, alliance, birth, death, rebirth, healing, ancestors, deities, spirits, natural kinds and human kinds, friendships, rights and responsibilities. I would further suggest that the agents for communication and transformation must also be subjected to ritualised renewal processes. Living kinds must regularly be transformed by humans into artefacts for them to be used magically in transformations. This, I suggest, is why replacing the areca/sugar-palm bundle encloses the 'eating the *uwi*' ceremony. Palm wine and betel quid are indeed 'wonder-working things'; things that enable people to believe that they may, with impunity, request in their invocations to the spirit world: 'May blessings come, may mischiefs go!'

Notes

1. Fieldwork among the northern Lio was conducted in 1984, 1986, 1989 and 1993 under the auspices of the Indonesian Academy of Sciences (LIPI) and was sponsored by Universitas Nusa Cendana at Kupang. This particular ceremony was observed in Kanganara in July 1986.

2. The original manuscript prepared for the conference was subsequently used as a basis for the Marett Memorial lecture at Exeter College, Oxford. I have retained some of the references to Marett because I find that his discussion on 'wonder-working things' is pertinent to my main argument. I am grateful for the invitation issued jointly by the Institute of Social and Cultural Anthropology and Exeter College, both of the University of Oxford.

3. It is interesting to note that areca and betel are mentioned separately and not as part of that which humans do not eat. This emphasis on these items further enhances their significance.

References

Bloch, M., 'Living kinds and symbolism', in P. Boyer (ed.), *Cognitive Aspects of Religious Symbolism*, Cambridge: Cambridge University Press, 1993

Borofsky, R. (ed.), *Assessing Cultural Anthropology*, New York: McGraw-Hill, 1994

Burkill, I. H., *A Dictionary of the Economic Products of the Malay Peninsula*, Kuala Lumpur: Ministry of Agriculture, 1966, (First published 1935)

de Boeck, F., 'Of Trees and Kings: Politics and Metaphor among the Aluund of Southwestern Zaire', *American Ethnologist* 21(3), 1994, pp. 451–73

Echols, J.M. and H. Shadily, *An Indonesian-English Dictionary*, Ithaca: Cornell University Press, 1982.

Ellen, R., 'Nuaulu betel chewing: ethnobotany, techniques and cultural significance', *Cacalele* 2(2), 1991, pp. 97–122

Howell, S., 'Rethinking the mother's brother: gendered aspects of kinship and marriage among the northern Lio, Indonesia', *Indonesia Circle* 67, 1995, pp. 294–317

—— 'Many contexts, many meanings? Gendered values of the northern Lio of Flores, Indonesia', *Journal of the Royal Anthropological Institute* (NS) 2, 1996a, pp. 253–69

—— 'A life for life: blood and other life-promoting substances in Lio ethicality', in S. Howell (ed.), *For the Sake of our Future: Sacrificing in Eastern Indonesia*, Leiden: CNWS Monograph 42, 1996b

Keesing, R., 'Anthropology as interpretive quest', *Current Anthropology* 28(4), 1987, pp. 161–75.

Lakoff, G. and M. Johnson, *Metaphors We Live By*, Chicago: Chicago University Press, 1980

Marett, R.R., *Anthropology*, London: William Norgate, 1912.

Needham, R., *Primordial Characters*, Charlottesville: University Press of Virginia, 1978

Reid, A., 'From betel-chewing to tobacco-smoking in Indonesia', *The Journal of Asian Studies* XLIV (3), 1985, pp. 529–47

Rooney, D. F., *Betel Chewing Traditions in South-East Asia*, Oxford: Oxford University Press, 1993

Strathern, M., *Partial Connections*, Manchester: Rowman & Littlefield, 1991

Turner, V. W., 'Symbols in Ndembu Ritual', in *The Ritual Process*, Ithaca: Cornell University Press, 1967

—— *Drama, Fields and Metaphors*, Ithaca: Cornell University Press, 1974

'The Grove is our Temple.' Contested Representations of *Kaavu* in Kerala, South India

Yasushi Uchiyamada

Introduction

Strangers who come to Kerala find the landscape densely greened with trees and groves. The Reverend Samuel Mateer, who worked in the princely state of Travancore in South Kerala during the mid-nineteenth century as a missionary of the London Missionary Society, was no exception. He described the Travancorean landscape in his *Native Life in Travancore* as the land where '[T]he botanist will find much to interest and delight in the flora' (Mateer 1883: 1). The Travancorean landscape described by the colonial missionary-ethnographer is indeed rich in cash crops such as ginger, pepper and coconuts, but my purpose here is not to explore its botanical diversity; instead, I wish to take the reader to the social world of former 'soil slaves', for whom certain trees and groves embody the burning passions of spirits and deities. These trees and groves are polyvocal and polysemic social symbols, and the subjects of fierce but silent negotiations and contests.

The ethnography I am about to present documents the meaning of 'sacred groves' (*kaavu*) for Untouchables, who are regarded by their higher-caste neighbours as 'ignorants with no culture' and 'super-stitious'. During fieldwork, I became less and less interested in the tales of 'cultured' middle-class and middle-caste people, but increasingly fascinated by Untouchable narratives about trees, groves and ancestors. It is therefore the experience and the representations of these 'ignorants', for whom trees, groves, ancestors, soil and people are

177

intimately connected, that I attempt to convey here. I am aided in this task by the intersubjective space that daily encounters with my Untouchable neighbours created, allowing me to ask the 'right' questions about trees and groves. Their answers I then compared with those of the higher-caste people who lived in the same village.[1] My informants sometimes described certain trees and groves in terms of indigenous dyadic notions. To them, these trees were both 'sacred' (*sudham*) and 'fearful' (*bhayam*).[2] They also described their nature in terms of 'life-force' (*shakti*) and 'fault' (*doosham*). I shall in this chapter follow my informants in combining the notions of *shakti, doosham, sudham* and *bhayam* to describe the nature of these trees and groves. I shall also examine emic distinctions between soft and hard trees, as well as those between planted trees, and trees that grow naturally.

Funeral Coconut Trees

As the Reverend Mateer (1883) observes, Malayali house gardens are crowded with graceful coconut trees. But at a closer look, one may find a meagre and undernourished coconut tree – or two – on the south side of the house. These are the coconut trees of the deceased. With the exception of former Untouchables, all Hindus (those who cremate their dead as well as those who bury them) plant a coconut known as *chudala teengu* (literally 'cremation-pyre coconut') in the region immediately above the corpse's navel. Middle-caste Nayars plant a 'funeral coconut' in the cremation pit after having removed the bones. These they store in an earthen pot, which they bury under a jack-fruit tree, where they are left for a few years – until being taken to a 'crossing place'[3] on the coast for immersion. Lower-middle-caste artisans also plant a 'funeral coconut' on the grave of a deceased, more or less at the level of the navel. The funeral coconut tree that grows out of a cremation pit or a burial place inspires special feelings in the relatives of a deceased person. The tree is honoured as the 'mother's coconut tree', 'mother's brother's coconut tree', 'father's coconut tree', and so on. Its fruit are believed to be suitable for black magic. It is loved by family members, but feared (*bhayam*) by those who are unrelated to the deceased. Funeral coconut trees, which are never watered nor manured, rarely survive the dry Summer. In a sense, they represent the remaining life-force of a ghost, and its continuing power to grow in this world. This is why, while they are greatly loved by surviving relatives, nothing is done to keep them alive.

By contrast, jack-fruit trees, usually planted at the south-west corner of houses, are supposed to live long. They are associated, not with the ghost of an individual family member, but with all the ancestors of the house and the (past and present) family group it shelters. The house jack-fruit tree is therefore a metaphor or metonym for the longevity of the house-family group (*kudumbam*). It is 'sacred' (*sudham*), but not 'fearful' (*bhayam*). There are clear differences between the symbolic meanings of funeral coconut trees and house jack-fruit trees, but both are *planted* by the family members of deceased persons. As we shall see, trees and groves associated with powerful spirits are, on the contrary, believed to emerge *naturally*.

Paala Trees

As an introduction to the narrative universe of my informants (a world where trees and people merge into each other), I summarise a number of stories about two *paala* (*Alstonia scholaris*) trees that stand in the middle of *punja* (low-lying waterlogged land) in Nagarajanadu. *Paala* comes from *paal*, 'milk'. *Paala* trees (i.e. milk trees) are hardwood trees that produce a thick white sap, and are considered 'sacred' (*sudham*) and 'fearful' (*bhayam*). Untouchable Pulayas,[4] who live near the two milk trees of the story examined here, told me that tying a cow's afterbirth to a milk tree would cause the cow to produce milk in profusion. They also told me that a Syrian Christian farmer who had tied his cow's afterbirth to one of the milk trees in the *punja* found his cow dead upon returning home. Hindus and Syrian Christians believe in the superhuman 'life-force' (*shakti*) embodied in *paala* trees, and so do the Pulayas, for whom it is not only highly fertile, but also extremely dangerous. The dominant Nayars (warriors and landlords) and their Pulaya former 'soil slaves' tell the following story[5] about these two trees:

> A long time ago, this area was ruled by a Nayar family known as the Kollakayil family. The Kollakayil owned vast paddy-fields, and had the power to kill their subjects. On the morning (it was harvest time) this incident took place, the family head[6] went to the paddy-field in the *punja* to supervise his 'soil slaves' harvesting paddy. He saw a Pulaya measuring paddy with a bamboo measure. This angered him greatly, for he had ordered the slave to wait for his arrival before measuring the harvest. Suspecting the slave of pilferage, he threw his walking stick (the symbol of his authority and status) violently at him. The walking stick hit the bamboo measure with which the slave had protected his face, before bouncing back into the face of the Nayar, knocking his front teeth out.

He felt so ashamed and ridiculed that he ordered his men to execute the Pulaya slave.

The slave was taken to a scaffold located in a neighbouring village. Before the execution, he was allowed one last wish. The Pulaya said: 'Let seven generations in the Kollakayil family, seven sheds of buffaloes, and seven sheds of cows perish.' He was then beheaded, his head and body falling off the scaffold and rolling back to his *punja*. Two *paala* trees 'blazed up' (*paala kaalicchu*) from the spot where his head and body had rested. The once prosperous Kollakayil family suffered a series of misfortunes, until it was finally reduced to parting with its vast fields.

The two *paala* trees are still 'blazing' in the *punja*, where their eerie shapes serve as reminders of the *shakti* they embody, the superhuman anger, jealousy, and emotional attachment to this world of the ghost of the executed Pulaya slave. The passions such trees embody become manifest only when enacted by humans. It is through story-telling, ritual performance, and remembrance that the trees' 'life-force' (*shakti*) and 'fault' (*doosham*) are revealed. The 'life-force' and 'fault' of the two milk trees in question are revealed by the worshipping activities (*puja*) of the Pulaya lineage head (*muuppan*), who goes to the trees to pray for his executed ancestor, thus renewing the connectedness of the Pulayas to the land and soil, while reviving the fear the trees inspire in the neighbouring high-caste landowners.

To recapitulate, funeral coconut trees, which are soft and short-lived, 'embody' the recently dead. As such, they are at once loved and feared, and their survival is discouraged. Family jack-fruit trees planted in house-yards are hard and long-lived; they represent the ancestors of the families and houses (*kudumbam*) to which they are associated. Funeral coconut trees and house jack-fruit trees are both *planted*; the dead they embody are considered controllable. They are contrasted with milk trees (*paala*) and groves (*kaavu*) that grow *naturally* and materialise the uncontrollable life-force (*shakti*) of angry ghosts and spirits. Similarly to *paala* trees, which are believed to grow out of their own volition, *kaavu*s emerge *naturally*, i.e. without human intervention. These groups of trees are believed to be the depositories of dangerous and potent life-force.

Kaavus (Sacred Groves)

Kaavus are composed of various sacred and fearful trees; there are softwood ones and hardwood ones. The life-span of these trees is variable, but a *kaavu* does not disappear, for new trees are constantly emerging and replacing dying ones. *Kaavus* are prior to, and survive longer than, man-made temples with their hardwood or stone structures. This is possible because it forms a vegetal collectivity whose aggregate life endures beyond the life-span of the hardest tree, or of the most resistant stone monument. *Kaavus* exist on a different time-scale, as openings connecting this world to the nether world.

On the west side of a Hindu temple, there is usually a *kaavu*, the symbol and metonym of life-force (*shakti*) and fault or sin (*doosham*). It is a depository of dangerous fertility, a place haunted by ghosts and spirits. Groves, always situated on the outside, are clearly separated from the sacred space of temples. Yet Untouchables in Nagarajanadu represent the *kaavus* that grow on their ancestral land as their lineage temples. From the point of view of higher-caste Hindus, these groves cannot be temples. In order to explain why they are so from the Untouchables' point of view, I need to examine the people–ancestor–land relationships amongst both high castes and Untouchables. But let me first describe what *kaavus* look like.

The Nagaraja ('Snake King') Temple and Nagarajanadu *illam* (the patrilineal descent corporation of Nambudiri Brahmans) are surrounded by old and thick groves known as *sarppa kaavus* ('snake groves'). Trees in these groves are old and tall. Entangled climbers and lianas envelop the tall and mature trees. *Kaavus* are filled with bird twitters all day long, and 'snake groves' (*sarppa kaavus*) believed to host divine serpents. The divine serpents protecting the house of Nambudiris (*illam*) are greatly feared, and their snake groves are never approached at night. Despite 'modernisation', with its flow of video-recorders, personal computers, or remittances from the Gulf countries, people still believe in the life-force of sacred groves – in fact, they believe that the *shakti* of *kaavus* is far more powerful today than it was a decade ago.

During my first fieldwork in 1992–3, I could not understand why people thought that the life-force of *kaavus* had grown stronger. Upon my return in 1996, nearly three years after I left the village, I discovered in the Nagaraja Temple *kaavu* several new stone idols of Nagaraja ('Snake King') and Nagayakshi ('Snake Queen'). They had been brought there from other sacred groves that had been cut down after my departure in 1993. They were consecrated idols, and hence the containers of extremely potent *shakti*. A *kaavu* should not be cleared before moving the spirits and deities it shelters to a new abode. If an alternative abode is not provided, they will haunt the place and possess people. The risk can be reduced by calling a ritual specialist, who invokes the spirits and deities residing in the sacred grove earmarked for destruction and confines them in specific objects before taking them to a new *kaavu*, temple or 'crossing place'. Numerous sacred groves have been cleared over the last decades, and, in the process, countless spirits and deities have lost their abode. They have been moved to a few remaining groves, which, given the abnormally high concentration of spirits and deities they now host, have become exceptionally powerful. The *shakti* of the Nagarajanadu snake groves, which is much stronger now than before, has, in fact, dramatically increased *because of* the speed of modernisation.

There is another powerful, thick and old *kaavu* in Nagarajanadu; it surrounds the south, west and north sides of the village temple, called Pallippuram Mother Goddess Temple. It contains three ponds, which are located north, west, and south of Bhadrakali's shrine. Bhadrakali is the Goddess of Death, the fiercest form of the Mother Goddess. According to a goldsmith who owns a shop and sells incense and *beedi*[7] next to the village temple, humans were once (as recently as one hundred and fifty years ago) sacrificed by the northern and southern ponds. People are also known to have committed suicide in the *kaavu* of Bhadrakali temple. In addition to the two large and thick groves surrounding Nagaraja temple and Bhadrakali temple (the largest temples in Nagarajanadu), there are numerous smaller ones in the village and *punja*, to which I shall now turn.

Syrian Christians and *Kaavus*

Like the Hindus, many Syrian Christians have *kaavus* in their gardens and paddy-fields. These *kaavus*, however, belong to former Hindu inhabitants, rather than to present-day Syrian Christian landowners. The new Syrian Christian landowners may own the land legally, but they are not considered the owners of the *kaavus* located on their estates.

A Syrian Orthodox barrister I knew had an old wooden building and a *kaavu* in his garden. My Nayar neighbours (they belonged to the Kalluur *taravad*) told me that this old building was their 'ancestral house' (*aadi kudumbam*); it had life-force (*shakti*) of an ancestor who had been assassinated by a Syrian Christian rival in the eighteenth century. My neighbours added that the barrister and his family had been lighting an oil lamp in the *kaavu*; they had also been seen donating lamp oil to the village temple. Furthermore, Bhadrakali's palanquin had visited the old wooden building during the annual temple festival.[8]

I asked the barrister whether Bhadrakali had visited the old Hindu house in his garden. He evaded my question and replied that his Church prohibited such ceremonies. But he admitted that he and his family had sometimes lit an oil lamp in the *kaavu*, quickly adding, however, that beliefs in *kaavu* 'fault' (*doosham*) and 'life-force' (*shakti*) were no more than mere superstitions. If such beliefs were mere superstitions, I wondered, why then should this Syrian Christian family light a lamp in the *kaavu*? Or donate lamp oil to the goddess Bhadrakali? There were definite discrepancies between the barrister's words and deeds. Locals had two explanations for such inconsistencies. For Suusamma, a Syrian Marthomite woman, the barrister's ancestors were low-caste Hindu Izhavas, whose custom it was to light an oil lamp in the *kaavu*. In her opinion, thus, the man was propitiating his own ancestor spirits in the *kaavu*. Mariyamma, a Syrian Orthodox woman, thought differently; she said: 'When you buy land from the Hindus there may be a *kaavu* on it. If such is the case, Hindu practices must be followed, otherwise "fault" (*doosham*) will come.' Mariyamma's daughter added: 'After the death of Hindus, it is there that they are buried, isn't it? So if we don't light a lamp, *doosham* comes.' Although many Syrian Christians told me that they did not believe in the *shakti* and *doosham* of *kaavu*s, and although they called these beliefs superstitions in public, it is my feeling that they all followed Hindu customs privately; at least, they left *kaavu*s untouched.

Trees in *Kaavus*

A *kaavu* consists of trees, land and deities. Some of the trees I could identify in and around *kaavu*s included *aal* (pipal tree), *aatmaavu* (pipal and mango merged into one), *marootti* (*Hydnocarpus pentandra*), *vain* (unidentified species), *aaññili* (wild jack-fruit tree), *plaavu* (jack-fruit tree), *maavu* (mango tree), *ilaññi* (*Mimusops elangi*), *tetti* (*Ixora coccinea*), *chembakam* (unidentified species), *kaaññiram* (*Strychnos nux vomica*), *paala* (*Alstonia scholaris*), and *pana* (*Palmyra palm*). Table 8.1 lists the trees found in Nagarajanadu *kaavu*s, and summarises their ritual uses and meanings.[9]

*Kaavu*s differ in composition and character, for they belong to different deities and lineages. A grove consecrated to Muurti (a low form of Shiva) will have at its centre an *ilaññi* tree (the embodied manifestation of Muurti's potency), at which the deity is worshipped and propitiatory rites (*puja*) are performed. What I call the narrative space of *kaavu* is thus created by the interplay of the physical and material presence of

Table 8.1 Trees in or near *kaavus*, their ritual use, and types

Species	use/meanings in the ritual context	type
aal	usually surrounded by a platform, stands solitary as a sacred tree	sacred
aatmaavu	aal + maavu merged into one tree symbolises aatmaavu (soul); stands solitary as a sacred tree	sacred
marootti	nutshells are used as lamps during festivals	ceremonial
vain	latex is burnt as incense during rituals	ceremonial
aaññili	preetam is temporarily buried under this tree after death	death
plaavu	preetam is temporarily buried under this tree after death	death
maavu	used for cremation	death
ilaññi	used for cremation, related to muurtti	death
tetti	its red flowers are associated with bloodthirsty goddesses	goddess/blood
chembakam	related to red colour and hence bloodthirsty goddesses	goddess/blood
kaaññiram	preetams can be invoked at this tree, and carried to temples	evil
paala	associated with wandering evil spirits; also means burial ground	evil
pana	Yakshi sits on its top	evil

a particular tree, religious performances, and story-telling (Steedly 1993). In the *kaavu* of a Roman Catholic Pulaya of Nagarajanadu, I saw *chembakam, kaaññiram, paala*, and *tetti* trees. All these trees are associated with either bloodthirsty goddesses or 'evil' spirits. There once was in this grove a *pana* tree, on which the beautiful and bloodthirsty goddess Yakshi is believed to have sat, waiting for a male prey. It is said that the Syrian Orthodox who owned the land at the time ordered his Syrian Orthodox servant to cut the tree down. His intention in fact was to cut down and clear the *kaavu* before selling the land. The servant, so the story goes, lost his eyesight soon after having felled the *pana* tree. The Roman Catholic Pulayas I spoke with unanimously understood the servant's fate as caused by the *doosham* associated with cutting down that particular tree, itself a manifestation of the *kaavu's* superhuman *shakti*.

An Embryonic *Kaavu*

People in Nagarajanadu, both high- and low-caste, believe that a *kaavu* develops *naturally* or independently of human will. As they say, 'It is *shakti* that grows a *kaavu*.' Although most of the existing sacred groves are understood to be very old, embryonic ones, expressions of locative *shakti* in the landscape, are commonly found. In this section I describe how the 'ghost' (*preetam*) of a Nayar woman who died a good death but was neglected after cremation manifested her unhappy state by causing the 'natural growth' of a milk tree beside the earthen pot in which her bones had been temporarily buried.

Today middle-caste Hindus cremate their deceased at the south corner of the house; the bones are buried under the house jack-fruit tree, the collective representation of the house-family group. The cremation pit is filled with soil, where paddy, wheat, pulses, spices, banana and coconut are planted. Then, usually, a temporary altar made of cut-out bricks is laid down under the jack-fruit tree, where a woman of the family goes each day at dusk to propitiate the spirit by lighting an oil lamp. The wandering spirit or ghost of the dead (*preetam*) is believed to be 'twisting, turning and walking' (*ilaññu tiriññu natakkunnu*) relentlessly after cremation. If it is not 'seated' or 'released', it causes 'misfortunes' (*doosham*) to those who are responsible for its fate. After a year or so (sometimes much longer), the chief mourner digs the earthen pot out and takes the bones to a sacred 'crossing place' (*thiirtham*) on the coast, where he performs a 'sacrifice' (*bali*) and a mortuary ritual called *karmma puja*, before 'drifting' (*ozhukkuka*) the bones into the Arabian Sea. At this moment the ghost of the deceased relative (*preetam*) becomes an ancestor (*pitr*). And, like all ancestors, it 'drifts' directly from the sacred 'crossing place' towards the ancestors' abode.

There is a jack-fruit tree at the south-west corner of Bhaaskaranpilla's younger brother's house. Bhaaskaranpilla's mother's bones were buried under the jack-fruit tree nearly two years ago. But Bhaaskaranpilla's younger brother has moved out to a nearby town, so no one lights up a lamp for her ghost. A wild jack-fruit tree (*aaññili*) is growing on the west side of the house jack-fruit tree, and a young milk tree (*paala*) on its north side. The ghost's grandson, Shashi, tells me that the *paala* tree started to grow there *naturally* about a year after his grandmother's burial. The message is clear. A milk tree is associated with a wandering spirit and its passion, heat, desire and *shakti*. The ghost of Shashi's grandmother was temporarily buried under the jack-fruit tree after cremation, where it suffered neglect, for there was no one in the house to look after it. So the ghost 'twisted, turned and walked', causing a young milk tree, the physical manifestation of the ghost's unhappy condition, to grow out by the jack-fruit tree. Consequently, there are now two types of jack-fruit trees associated with death, and one milk tree associated with wandering evil spirits at the south-west corner of the uninhabited Nayar house. If no one takes the 'ghost' to a 'crossing place' on the coast and 'drifts' the bones into the Arabian Sea, the place where it currently 'twists, turns and walks' may soon develop into a small *kaavu*.

Lineage Temple

In the courtyard of the Koolatattu Nayars' lineage temple, which is located just outside Nagarajanadu, there are altogether nine shrines and platforms with seated deities. All of them are facing east. Durga, the goddess of war, is the presiding goddess. The shrine of Rakshassu (or Brahmmarakshassu), the ghost of a murdered Brahman, is located on the south-west side of Durga's shrine. On its left, one can see the shrine of Yoogiishwaran (or Yogi), a Nayar ancestor who attained extraordinary *shakti* through *tapas* or asceticism. It is worth noting that the shrine of the Nayar (Yoogiishwaran) is not only slightly smaller than that of the Brahman (Rakshassu), but also located on its left. Behind Durga's shrine and further to the west, at the *kaavu*'s edge, stand two platforms with the small shrines of Nagaraja ('Snake King') and Nagayakshi ('Snake Queen'). Yakshi's small shrine (it is much smaller than the shrines of Rakshassu and Yoogiishwaran) is located to the north-west of Durga's shrine. Arukola (or Arukaala), the spirit of a murdered Nayar ancestor, is 'seated' in the slightly smaller shrine to the left of Yakshi's. There are three small platforms behind Yakshi and Arukola, respectively that of Duutattaan (the spirit of a person who died violently), Muurtti (a low form of Shiva associated with Untouchable Parayas), and Peey (the spirit of a person who died of rabies, and also the spirit of madness associated with Untouchables). The low-status Duutattaan, Muurtti and Peey are 'seated' on shabby platforms right at the *kaavu*'s edge. Peey's platform is located at the far north-west corner; Muurtti is 'seated' to Peey's right, and Duutattaan close to Durga's shrine (see Figure 8.1).

The status of these 'evil lineage deities' is expressed by the size and location (relative to the main deity) of the platforms on which they are seated. Except for Rakshassu, 'evil deities' are all clustered on the

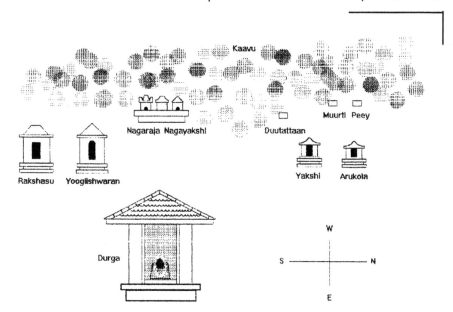

Figure 8.1 Lineage deities of Koolatattu Nayars

north-west side of the main shrine. The low status of Duutattaan, Muurtti and Peey is marked by the small size of their platforms. The location of Peey's platform further indicates that its status is the lowest of all. Muurtti comes second from the bottom in the ranking of these lineage deities. Another important distinction is between the deities that are 'seated' in the *kaavu,* and those 'seated' in the temple's courtyard. While Nagaraja and Nagayakshi, Duutattaan, Muurtti and Peey are all 'seated' in or near the *kaavu,* Durga, Rakshassu, Yakshi and Arukola are all 'seated' on the east side of the *kaavu.* The seating order of deified ghosts in the Nayar lineage temple thus replicates the principle of hierarchical inequality of castes based on ritual purity.[10]

A mature *aatmaavu* tree (a pipal and a mango merged together and symbolising the soul) surrounded by a platform stands right in front of the Durga temple. I was told that the head (*karnavan*) of a Nayar matrilineal joint-family (*taravad*) had *planted* this tree eighty years ago.[11] In other words, whereas the sacred *aatmaavu* tree at the front of the temple had been planted, the *kaavu* at its back had grown naturally (see Figure 8.2). On the basis of this information, it is possible to divide the Nayar lineage Durga temple spatially into two realms. The temple's front part forms the structured space belonging to Durga and her guardians. The size and location of the shrines and platforms express the hierarchical relationships that obtain between the goddess Durga

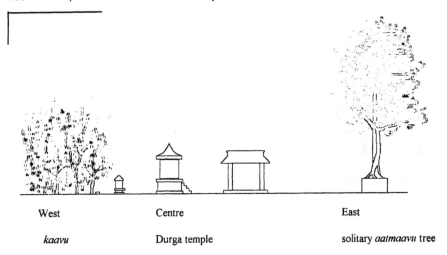

West	Centre	East
kaavu	Durga temple	solitary *aatmaavu* tree

Figure 8.2 The Koolatattu Durga temple and its two realms

and minor guardian deities. Spatially separated, and structurally different from the temple's front part, we find at the back the sacred grove
or *kaavu*, the realm of sacrifice and uncontrolled, primeval fertility,
the nether world. This is the domain of serpents, unliberated spirits
(*preetam*), wandering minor deities, and *doosham*.

A religious ceremony I witnessed in the Koolatattu Nayars' lineage
temple further illustrates this spatial division. On the morning of 28
February 1993, the day of the temple's annual festival, a Nambudiri
Brahman priest performed a *puja* at Durga's shrine, after which three
Nambudiri priests performed abbreviated *pujas* at the shrines and
platforms of the eight other guardian deities. These shorter religious
ceremonies started at Rakshassu's shrine, and moved gradually to the
shrines of Arukola, Duutattaan, and, finally, Peey, hence respecting
the hierarchical rank order from the high Goddess Durga to the
Untouchable-like divinity Peey. A different type of *puja*, aimed at
pleasing Nagaraja and Nagayakshi in the *kaavu*, was performed
afterwards at their shrines. The ceremony ended with one of the
Nambudiri priests prostrating himself before Nagaraja, thus indicating
that Nagaraja and Nagayakshi belong to a different realm, outside the
structure of divine hierarchy.

Lineage *Kaavu*

East of the Nagaraja temple, there is a colony of Pulaya former 'slaves'
(*adima*), who once were attached to the Nagarajanadu *illam*, the house

of the Nambudiri Brahman family that owns the temple. And at the centre of this Pulaya colony there is a *kaavu*, which, according to the Pulayas, does not belong to any temple, but *is* itself a temple. For high-caste Hindus, who contrast *kaavu*s and temples as two separate, and in many ways opposed, spaces, a *kaavu*, the realm of dangerous wild fertility, cannot be a temple.[12] The contradictory views of caste Hindus and Pulayas provide the key to understanding the social world as lived and experienced by Untouchables. The Pulayas live at the village's margins, that is, at the confluence of two spheres, where the village, protected by the village goddess, meets the external and uncontrolled forces of the *punja*.

The lineage *kaavu*, located on the south-west side of the Pulayas' ancestral house, has a U-shaped opening facing east. The *kaavu*'s inner part is always neatly swept with a broom. A *kaaññiram* tree, with two iron lamps thrust into its trunk, and a *paala* tree on each side, stands at the *kaavu*'s centre. Both species (*kaaññiram* and *paala*) are feared by Nagarajanadu people for their association with ghosts (*preetam*) and wandering, unliberated spirits. There are no sacred trees in or near this *kaavu*, but someone looking eastwards can remark in front of the *kaavu* a *pana* tree associated with the beautiful and bloodthirsty goddess Yakshi. As I found no visual representations of gods there, I concluded that no deity or spirit was 'fixed' to this sacred grove. This lineage *kaavu* (*kudumba kaavu*) is the 'lineage temple' (*kudumba ksheetram*) of the Pulayas. Footwear has to be removed before entering the grove, where *puja* is performed by the 'magician' (*mantravaadi*) Kochchucherukkan. *Toddy* (palm wine) and *arrack* (distilled palm wine) are offered to the 'standing' – there are no pedestals for them to 'sit' – deities and ancestors (*pitrs*) believed to dwell in the *kaavu*. Although the Pulayas call their ancestor spirits *pitr*, I suspect that *preetam*, the Nayar term for ghost, would be more appropriate from the viewpoint of caste Hindus, given that these *pitrs* are not released from this world, but haunt fields and houses, demanding food and sacrifice.

Six powerful deities and ancestor spirits of the Pulayas reside in the lineage *kaavu*. Nagaraja ('Snake King') is the owner of the soil. Three deities were brought from the Cherumturutti Bhadrakali temple (located in the hills), the Pallimood Syrian Christian church (the local St Stephen's Orthodox church), and the Pallippuram village temple (once the lineage temple of a Nayar *taravad*), where Bhadrakali is 'seated'. I do not know the provenance of the two remaining deities, Aaranmula and Ashtamuti. Nagaraja, the owner of the soil, is also the lineage deity of the Nambudiri Brahman masters. Bhadrakali of Pallippuram, the village goddess, is also an important deity of the dominant Nayars. As for Saint Stephen, he is the Saint of the powerful Syrian Christian landlords, who are more prosperous than the Nayars. The presence of high-caste master (*tamburaan*) deities in the Pulaya lineage *kaavu* seems to reflect the degree to which these former 'slaves' have been integrated into the social order dominated by their Nambudiri Brahman, Nayar and Syrian Christian 'masters'. Dumont (1959: 83) argues that 'the temple reflects the society in a simplified form'. This might be true of the Nayar lineage temples, but in the Pulaya *kaavu*, deities and spirits 'come and go' (*varuttu pookku*), moving to and fro between a number of *kaavu*s and temples. Wandering deities and spirits travel to their favourite places, where they 'sit', 'stand', or 'rest', as well as 'eat and drink'. The *kaavu*'s spatial organisation is neither hierarchical, nor relationally structured. Unstructured *kaavu*s cannot be said, therefore, to reflect neatly the dominant representation of the social order. In fact, the 'temples' of Untouchables, with their lack of temple structure, blur the dominant logic of relational hierarchy, rendering it highly ambiguous.[13] As we shall see, the Pulaya representation of *kavuus* as unstructured lineage temples has political implications.

One evening in mid-December 1992, a banana stem with a flower (the 'head' of this surrogate human), was 'beheaded' by a Nambudiri Brahman priest at the village temple. Before the blood sacrifice, Raghavan, a member of the Pallippuram Bhadrakali temple committee, explained why Bhadrakali had to be brought from Kodungalluur to Nagarajanadu as follows:

> Maybe two thousand years ago, there were many evil spirits in this place, who inflicted suffering upon local people. Kali's presence was needed to control these spirits, because only Kali can suppress bad spirits. People from Nagarajanadu, Pallimood, and other near-by villages brought Kali from Kodungalluur, and seated her at Aikkara, then at Kalluur. But Kali was not happy in these locations. At last she was brought to Pallippuram, where humans were sacrificed to please her. Many families received favours from Kali after these sacrifices and offerings.

Raaghavan is talking from the viewpoint of a Nayar, so when he says 'people of this area' he probably means 'Nayars of this area'. The Nayars brought Bhadrakali of Kodungalluur and 'seated' her on Aikkara soil (the origin of the Aikkara Bhadrakali lineage temple), and then in Kalluur land (the origin of the Kalluur Bhadrakali lineage temple). But Bhadrakali was not happy in either place. She was therefore brought to Pallippuram, the territory of the Vanmeelil Nayars (the origin of the Venmeelil Bhadrakali lineage temple). Humans had been sacrificed to please Bhadrakali, and she had reciprocated by suppressing the 'bad spirits'. Hierarchical relationships were simultaneously established between deities and between local people. Kali's relationship with the suppressed 'bad spirits', the dominant hierarchical relationship, is symbolically expressed in the village temple layout. As already discussed, caste Hindus draw analogies between the structured space of divine hierarchy and hierarchical ranking within the social field (Biardeau 1989; Dumont 1959; Wadley 1975).

In marked contrast, Bhadrakali is not necessarily present in Untouchable lineage *kaavus*, and if she exists there, the goddess is usually not 'fixed', for a *kaavu* is a 'temple' without structure, where 'bad spirits' are not suppressed or controlled by the village goddess. Within Untouchable lineage territories, Untouchable spirits and lineage deities, who are not under the control of either Bhadrakali or Saint Stephen, have the potential to afflict higher-caste people who enter their sphere of influence. Just as the Nayars brought Bhadrakali from Kodungalluur, the Kuravas brought the capricious and elusive Marutaa from Kodungalluur to their lineage *kaavu*. A Roman Catholic Pulaya who is a 'magician' (*mantravaadi*) brought the *shakti* of the heretic magician Father Kadamattam to his lineage *kaavu*. In their lineage *kaavu* the Parayas worship Muurtti, a low form of Shiva feared by the dominant Nayars. And many Pulayas worship the Bhadrakali from Malayaalapuzha in the hill area, who is believed to be far more dangerous than the Bhadrakali from the Kudungalluur plains. Untouchable lineage *kaavus* are the 'resting places' of Muurtti, Marutaa, Father Kadamattam, the Bhadrakali from the hills, and other spirits seen by high-caste people as dangerous evil spirits. Rather than reflecting the dominant ideology about the social order, their fluid presence transgresses it in some oblique and ambiguous way, and, to a certain extent, subverts it.

Untouchable *Pitrs* Are Different from Caste Hindu *Pitrs*

As I have discussed above, many high- and middle-caste Hindus now make a distinction between 'ancestor' (*pitr*) and 'ghost' (*preetam*). Whereas a *pitr* is a liberated ancestor spirit, a *preetam* is unliberated and wandering. The spirit of a dead person always starts as *preetam*, and, in the case of a good death, turns into *pitr* after the performance of mortuary rituals at 'crossing places' on the coast. If a person dies a bad death, he or she becomes a ghost that cannot easily be transformed into an ancestor. Ghosts wander and may cause misfortunes to their lineages, unless they are properly 'seated' in small ancestral shrines (*kuryaalas*) in the gardens of ancestral houses. My Pulaya, Paraya and Kurava informants do not, however, distinguish ghosts from ancestors as caste Hindus do. The spirits of dead Untouchables, who become ancestors without attaining liberation, 'stand' in *kaavus*. If an Untouchable dies violently or prematurely, his or her spirit becomes *bhuutam preetam*. These spirits are expelled from the lineage, and they wander restlessly, for it is extremely difficult to 'seat' them. Kochchucherukkan, a Pulaya 'magician', told me of such a wandering ancestor spirit, which had been 'thrown out' (*puram talliyirikkuka*) of his lineage *kaavu*.[14] Lakshmikutti, a Nayar woman, told me on the contrary that all ghosts had to be 'seated'. The difference between Nayar and Untouchable ancestor spirits is schematically summarised in Table 8.2.

Table 8.2 The nature of Nayar and Untouchable ancestor spirits

Nayar	good death	–	*preetam*	→	crossing	*pitr*
	bad death	–	*(bhuutam) preetam*	→	seated	
↓ sin						
Untouchable	good death	–	*pitr*	→	seated	
	bad death	–	*(bhuutam) preetam*	→	thrown out	

As a matter of fact, the Untouchable ancestor is equivalent to the Nayar ghost. This might be the reason why Nayars associate Untouchables with malevolent deities. The difference between Untouchable and Nayar *pitrs* is both substantial and consequential. Whereas Untouchable *pitrs* remain located in the soil, Nayar *pitrs* in the end become 'liberated', if, and as long as, mortuary rituals are performed properly. It follows that Nayar *pitrs* do not stay in the soil of their family houses, except for the bodily remains (ash and bones), which are gradually absorbed within the various vegetals planted in the cremation pit. Consequently, compared with Untouchable ancestral lands, the abode of Untouchable *pitrs*, Nayar lands are relatively 'empty'. Furthermore, in order to attain 'liberation' (*mooksham*), Nayars continuously transfer 'sin' (*paapam*) on to Untouchables through a series of 'gifts' (*daanam*). If this transfer of sin facilitates the Nayars' process of liberation, it makes it even more difficult for the Untouchables to attain liberation. And, with their lineage soil further contaminated by the 'sins' of their high-caste masters, Untouchables stand even closer to the land. If this proximity to the land is conceptualised by the Nayars as a sign of contiguity between Untouchables and 'malevolent' deities, it is for the Pulayas an expression of their being the 'rulers of soil' (*manninte adikaari*).[15]

If a *Kaavu* is a Temple, What Kind of Temple is it?

We might gain further insight by analysing the spatial and structural relation between temple and *kaavu* in terms of flows of sin and malevolence, and flows of wealth and fertility. As I have discussed in detail elsewhere (Uchiyamada 1995), the sin and malevolence contained in the 'gifts' (*daanam*) made by Nayars to Untouchables flow from the village centre, where high-caste 'masters' reside, to the village margins, where Untouchables live. On the other hand, paddy (or wealth) flows from the dangerous and fertile *punja* outside the village to the houses of high-caste 'masters' at the centre, via the labour of their Untouchable agricultural workers. Consequently, it is through the repeated practices of gift-giving and paddy production that the village is created as a symbolic space (Uchiyamada 1995).

The structural relationship existing between *kaavu* and temple is somewhat similar. A *kaavu*, with its concentration of dangerous fertility, is the depository of sin and malevolence. People say that many of the old temples in Kerala were built in former times in already existing *kaavus*. People also say that when a temple ceases to exist (whatever the reason), the site reverts to a *kaavu* (Uchiyamada 1996). *Kaavus* located behind temples are, therefore, represented as having preceded, and/or succeeded temples. Just as Untouchables labour in the dangerous and fertile *punja* and bring paddy back to the houses of their masters, *kaavus* produce lethal but profuse fertility, which is extracted and brought under control by Brahman priests within the temple spatial sphere. In this sense, the polarity *kaavu*–temple plays a part in the social world constituted by – and through – the careful regulation of the two-way flow of malevolence and fertility.

As already stated, lineage *kaavus* of Untouchables are located at the margins, where the village meets the dangerous but fertile external world. In a lineage *kaavu*, the distinctions[16] between purity and pollution, or dangerous sexuality and productive fertility, have been abolished. To recapitulate, a house jack-fruit tree lasts much longer than a funeral coconut tree; and the life-span of a temple is much longer than that of a house jack-fruit tree. How are we to conceptualise the life-span of a *kaavu* believed to have existed much before, and to last long after, man-made temples? We might suggest that *kaavus* belong to a non-unilinear, cosmogonic time, and that they constitute an opening on to a cosmogonic space.

Notes

1. I conducted eighteen months of fieldwork in 1992–3, in a village located in the Alleppey District, which I call 'Nagarajanadu' here. I returned to the village for six weeks in 1996.

2. The dyad sacred (*sudham*) and fearful (*bhayam*) is indigenous; these two terms are not mutually exclusive. The dyad is, therefore, epistemologically different from, and not reducible to, a Lévi-Straussian binary opposition of the type nature/culture or raw/cooked.

3. A sacred location where the soul crosses the (water) boundary that divides this world from the ancestors' abode.

4. Pulayas, formally 'soil slaves' (*adima*), are Untouchables who are believed to have a special connectedness with paddy-fields.

5. For the full version of this story, see Uchiyamada 1995.

6. A *karnavan* is the head of a Nayar *taravad* (or matrilineal joint corp-oration).

7. Local cigarettes.

8. As the goddess did not visit houses during my fieldwork, I could not witness her movable image visiting this old building.

9. For heuristic purposes, I have grouped *kaavu* trees into five types: sacred, ceremonial, death, goddess/blood and evil. Sacred trees are usually surrounded by platforms and found at temples. Ceremonial ones are used in festivals and rituals with lamps and incense. 'Death' trees are associated with death. 'Goddess/blood' trees are associated with capricious bloodthirsty goddesses such as Bhadrakali and Durga and her low forms. Evil ones are associated with evil, wandering deities and spirits that are greatly feared by local people.

10. Coccari (1989: 254) notes that 'Equal to the spiritual stature of the living Brahman, the Brahm [Brahmmarakshassu in Kerala] ranks high among other ghosts.'

11. When I asked the Nambudiri Brahman priest of the local Nagaraja temple about the significance of the *aatmaavu* tree, he laughed and told me that *aatmaavu* is a silly joke and a mere play on words. The Brahman priest seemed to be half-ridiculing the Sudras' attempt to Brahmanise their religion.

12. *Kaavu* is symbolically a metonym of wild fertility. The wild fertility of the grove is kept separate from, and contrasted to the temple's contained and controlled fertility (see Shulman 1980, Ch.2; see also Figure 8.2 above).

13. It is for this reason that I remain totally unconvinced by Moffat's argument about a collective 'consensus' at the bottom of the hierarchy (1979a; 1979b). Untouchables are structurally related to the higher castes. Yet Untouchables do not replicate the religion of high castes; their religious beliefs and practices do not simply 'reflect' the social structure. Moffat's argument reveals the limits of the monolithic structural approach, which is insufficient for studying process, agency, multiple subjectivity, and contested symbolic meanings.

14. Kochchucherukkan called the spirits of persons who died violently *bhuutam preetams*, or 'ghost' *preetams*. He told me on 8 April 1994 that these 'ghost' *preetams* had been 'thrown out' from the 'house/family' (*kudumbam*).

15. Similarly, sacred power was considered to be wild and capricious in ancient Tamil texts. It was inherent in persons, and was activated in certain situations. When a person died, the capricious power went out of control. It was the role of an Untouchable man to control the capricious power by taking the deceased to the forest where owls, crows, and demons live (Hart III 1975: 81–6, 133–7).

16. The meaning of such distinctions is ultimately related to the degree of strength, and controllability, of *shakti*.

References

Biardeau, M., 'Brahmans and meat-eating gods', in A. Hiltebeitel (ed.), *Criminal Gods and Demon Devotees: Essays on the Guardians of Popular Hinduism*, Albany: State University of New York Press, 1989

Coccari, D. M., 'The Bir Babas of Banaras and the deified dead', in A. Hiltebeitel (ed.), *Criminal Gods and Demon Devotees: Essays on the Guardians of Popular Hinduism*, Albany: State University of New York Press, 1989

Dumont, L., 'Structural definition of a folk deity of Tamil Nad: Aiyanar, the Lord', *Contributions to the Indian Sociology* 3, 1959, pp. 75–87

Hart III, G. L., *The Poems of Ancient Tamil: their Milieu and their Sanskrit Counterparts*, Berkeley: University of California Press, 1975

Mateer, S., *Native Life in Travancore*, London: Allen, 1883

Moffat, M., *An Untouchable Community in South India: Structure and Consensus*, Princeton: Princeton University Press, 1979a

Moffat, M., 'Harijan religion: consensus at the bottom of caste', *American Ethnologist* 6, 1979b, pp. 244–60

Shulman, D., *Tamil Temple Myths: Sacrifice and Divine Marriage in the South Indian Saiva Tradition*, Princeton, New Jersey: Princeton University Press, 1980

Steedly, M. M., *Hanging Without a Rope: Narrative Experience in Colonial and Postcolonial Karoland*, Princeton: Princeton University Press, 1993

Uchiyamada, Y., 'Passions in the landscape: ancestor spirits and land reform in Kerala, India', Paper presented at the South Asian Anthropologist Group Annual Conference held at the London School of Economics, 18–19 September 1995

Uchiyamada, Y., 'Two beautiful Untouchable women: sexuality, desire and becoming at the margins', Paper presented at the Workshop on Marginality held at the London School of Economics, 27–29 September 1996

Wadley, S. S., *Shakti: Power in the Conceptual Structure of Karimpur Religion*, Chicago: Department of Anthropology, The University of Chicago, 1975

The Second Life of Trees: Family Forestry in Upland Japan

John Knight

Introduction

Trees have long been important to human livelihoods in the mountain villages of the Kii Peninsula. In earlier centuries forest trees were the source of food, fuel, green fertiliser and shelter for villagers. More recently, the mountains have been turned into extensive timber plantations where villagers earn their living through planting, weeding, branch-cutting and a range of other silvicultural tasks, as well as felling, transporting and sawmilling. Regenerative timber forestry has come to occupy a central place in the economy of upland Japan. However, the trees in the forest have never been simply an economic resource for the people in the village. To the trees are attached a rich set of ideas, beliefs and associations. They are a site of spirits and a source of supernatural assistance, as well as a symbolic medium for human lives.

Evidence for the symbolic importance of trees in Japan is to be found, in the first instance, in a great deal of Japanese folkloric data, often applying to particular tree stands or tree species. But the modern timber plantations too, I shall argue, are an important medium through which many contemporary Japanese mountain villagers represent and understand their own lives. In the wake of the accelerated economic modernisation of upland Japan in the postwar period, a central feature of which has been the replacement of the earlier botanical diversity of the mountains by a coniferous uniformity, mountain villagers continue to associate their lives with the lives of trees. This occurs most prominently through family forestry, directed at growing timber to be used in the building industry.

In what follows, two relationships are taken up: that between trees and people, and that between trees and wood. Ideas of tree-growth among foresters, sawmillers and carpenters are associated with a number of different social relationships including marriage, the continuity of the stem family and, related to this, ties between ancestors and descendants. While the long life-span of tree stands is one feature of trees put to use in this symbolic association, an even more pivotal feature is that of the continuity between trees and wood. Timber-growers raise trees with an eye to their eventual usage as building wood. If foresters often become emotionally attached to the trees they have grown for decades, they are normally mindful that the measure of their achievement is the wood quality of the trees, and that the value of the trees is something realised after they have been felled.

There is no hard linguistic distinction between trees and wood in Japanese, as the term for tree, *ki* (木), is also used for wood. There also exists, however, a separate term for wood, *mokuzai* (written with the characters tree 木 and material 材), that distinguishes wood from trees.[1] Upland foresters stress tree–wood continuity even further when they characterise the objective of their work as giving the tree a 'second life' (*dai ni jinsei*). If upon felling the tree is rendered into building timber, this is represented as the beginning of a new life as much as ending of the old life. The tree lives on as wood in the buildings of which it forms part.

Data are drawn from the mountain villages of the Kii Peninsula in western Japan, particularly the municipality of Hongū-chō, during three spells of fieldwork – 1987–9, 1994 and 1995. In 1994 and 1995, I carried out extensive taped interviews with foresters and sawmillers in order to analyse the way in which they understand their occupations in general and the material – trees and wood – with which they work in particular.

Plantation forestry on the Kii Peninsula dates back to the seventeenth century. Up until the 1950s, fuelwood forestry co-existed with timber forestry. However, thereafter timber forests expanded, replacing the nearby fuelwood forests and extending deeper into the remote mountainous interior at the expense of the earlier (broad-leaved evergreen or Lucidophyllous) forest there. Accordingly, in the 1990s timber forests have become ubiquitous. This great expanse of timber forests should have made the villages they surround wealthy and the nation to whose postwar recovery they are productively dedicated strong. However, while timber plantations in Japan may be quantitatively impressive, many of them are qualitatively defective on account of the inadequacy of the human care they have received.

Japanese culture is commonly characterised as a 'tree culture' (*ki no bunka*). From buildings (houses, shrines and temples) to chopsticks, wood is still a ubiquitous part of everyday life for many Japanese. A further manifestation of Japan's tree culture is that people and places are often named after trees. In the mountain villages of the southern Kii Peninsula there are a great many place-names and family names containing tree characters.[2]

The Japanese *ie* or stem family is an entity that ideally transcends the lives of its individual members and is continued by means of first-son succession. The family system has been one of the key areas of debate in the sociology and anthropology of Japan. One question concerns the extent to which the *ie* has survived into the postwar period, despite its legal disestablishment in the Occupation period and in the face of the forces of urbanisation and modernisation (Kawabe and Shimizu 1994). Another has to do with the earlier ubiquity of stem families, and the claim that nuclear families have existed for much longer and on a larger scale than the representation of pre-modern Japan as an *ie*-centred society suggests (Kuroda 1994).

The concern here is with forest-owning families in upland Wakayama. Traditionally, a key focus of the *ie*'s continuity has been family property, particularly land. There is a strong correlation between the size of property and *ie* continuity. The fortunes of the *ie* as a family form were related to the concentration of landed property that existed up until the postwar land reforms. But while these land reforms redistributed farmland, in upland villages the primary form of land, forest land, was unaffected. Hence, in places like Hongū, considerable concentration in land ownership remains to this very day. Much of the data that follow is from the heirs of such large forest landholding families.

Upbringing

Foresters in Wakayama often liken tree-growing to child-rearing. The raising of the young tree saplings is characterised as parental nurturance. According to one local expression, the forester should 'treat the mountain as though you are bringing up a child' (*yama wa kodomo o sodateru tsumori de*). Foresters explain this expression by pointing out the importance of the first years of the tree's life and the necessity of giving proper care to the young tree.

As a rule, whether it is raising children or raising trees, it is the same. Like the Japanese saying 'the spirit of the three-year-old child lasts until one hundred' (*mitsogo no tamashii hyaku made*), I think that cutting undergrowth between three and five years after planting is the most important task in bringing up the tree. When you are bringing up a child, you think what sort of personality will it have, how should I bring it up? It's the same with trees ... With this sort of education – in the case of trees – you offer your love and it is honestly returned. But with human beings, even when you educate a child to grow up in a certain way, a lot of the time it doesn't go like that. But with trees, most of the time a response near to what you expected comes back.

The analogy with child-rearing extends to the way particular silvicultural tasks are imagined. Yoshimizu-san believes that while branching (i.e. branch removing), for example, is unpleasant for the tree, it is necessary because it helps the tree to grow straighter and better. Education allows people to grow straight, like a well-tended timber tree, all of whose unnecessary, lower horizontal branch-growth has been removed. The vertical, (largely) branchless tree is also pleasing to the eye: slim, beautiful and tidy. The association of growing trees with young women is, as we shall see, a recurring one.

Above all, the good timber tree is a strong tree. But telling a strong tree from a weak tree is not always straightforward. While ideally the strong tree is a beautiful one, often the reverse is the case, and the more visually impressive tree may in fact be weaker. This point was made by Shimoyama-san, a leading official of the Timber Growers' Association and himself a large forest landowner. In conversation with him and another forester, Sugiyama-san, about the difference in tree-growth on different sides of the mountains, Shimoyama-san made the following point, in arguing the merits of north-facing timber over south-facing timber: 'When you use these timbers in building, their strengths are completely different. With people and with timber [what is strongest] is that which has been bullied by nature – not like someone [referring to the rotund Sugiyama] who has been brought up in the warm.' North-facing timber might not look impressive, but it is marked by a strength related to its conditions of growth.

Shimoyama-san is in his late fifties, a war child, born in the late 1930s. Like many Japanese of his generation, he senses a big gap between those who experienced wartime and postwar privations and the younger generation of Japanese, born and raised in conditions of plenty. Younger generations of Japanese are physically larger than their counterparts in decades past. But because they have not undergone the hardships endured by their parents, they will not become stronger adults. For this older generation of foresters at least, the growth of timber trees proves to be a highly resonant analogy, one that evokes both their own experience in growing up and the generational difference between themselves and younger Japanese.

The purpose of commercial timber forestry is to grow trees quickly and lucratively. But this does not mean the bigger the better, for this would result in weak trees. A forester characterised such oversized but inferior trees in the following way:

> The tree may be big but the quality is not good. It gets fatter and fatter, but this is like a human being in the case of a fat, overfed child [*himanji*] . . . Fat, overfed children are not very healthy and they won't live very long lives. They are not the same as those people who, by doing sports like sumo or rugby, exercise and get big. There are a lot of overfed youngsters in primary school, who are much bigger than normal. It's a kind of illness in which the balance has collapsed in what they eat. No exercise. They have no powers of endurance. In the forest too, there are trees which suddenly become big, very tall and with wide growth-rings, but when the wind blows strongly these are the first trees to suffer. They are weak in the natural environment.

Japan in the 1990s is a much wealthier and better-fed society than before, but ironically this has led to a situation where many children are less rather than more healthy. Children before may have eaten meat rarely, but their bodies were somehow sturdier than those of today's children. Village children now seldom help out with farming, instead spending all their time on school homework. This man, born during the war, worries that this new pattern of upbringing augurs ill for the future. Children today would not, he thinks, be able to endure the hardships that people of his generation have. The same applies to trees: if, like the new generation of children, they are overcared for and overfed, they will certainly grow; but their large size is deceptive, because it conceals a fragility and vulnerability that will manifest itself at times of difficulty – for instance in the typhoon season.

Of course, these trees are grown for timber. It is as wooden pillars, roof-beams and planks that their qualities of strength and durability will be called on most. Dedicated foresters grow reliable timber, able to support the houses of which it forms part for hundreds of years.

The analogy between tree-growth and human upbringing recurs in the writings of the Japanese carpenter Nishioka Tsunekazu. The specific environmental placement of the tree confers on it a *kuse* or character. Trees do not simply grow, but grow in certain conditions, enduring a variety of hostile environmental forces. Accordingly, a tree develops a unique set of properties as a function of this growth location and its endurance therein. This makes for a lack of uniformity; but, far from being necessarily a handicap, these idiosyncrasies can eventually be put to the building's advantage, if used properly by the carpenter. While this makes the carpenter's job a hard one, it is also what makes it interesting and challenging. The art of traditional Japanese carpentry lay precisely in dealing with the variety of tree-growth characteristic of the Japanese mountains. The wood with which the carpenter was confronted was as variable as the mountains from which it came.

The older the tree, the more awkward or 'selfish' (*wagamama*) it tends to be. As Nishioka puts it, 'a thousand year old tree has a thousand years of character in it' (Nishioka 1993: 47). The image is of a demanding, difficult old man. The tree with character has been raised in adversity, has had a long struggle to survive, and that has accordingly acquired a hardy character. It has had to manage the elements all by itself. Nishioka sees a parallel here with human upbringing. The variability of the tree-growth in the Japanese mountains corresponds to the variability of human development in society. For example, while trees on the northern or eastern sides of the mountain must endure and grow amidst harsh winds, those on the southern and western sides and in the valley do not, and therefore develop a meek, taciturn character (*sunao de otonashiku*), making for weak wood that will not last long. They are like pampered children (*ningen de ittara onshitsu sodachi*) who grow into weak adults (Nishioka and Kohara 1978: 61). Nishioka draws a parallel between the modern Japanese wood industry and the postwar education system. Both are characterised by standardisation. But both too ultimately suffer from weakness in their 'products' – nominally mature timber and supposedly adult people.

For Nishioka, the timber from modern plantations, while it may be uniform, is weaker than that of the older growth from natural forests. It is because a tree has survived testing natural conditions for hundreds of years that it becomes suitable for use as a main house beam, which can endure those same forces for another two to three hundred years. These, however, are natural stands, not those of artificial timber plantations. Truly strong trees – those with which Japan's great temples and shrines were built and those from which durable houses are made – are those that arrive at a natural maturity of hundreds of years. In contrast, most plantation trees are not mature at all, but have been subjected to an artificially accelerated upbringing that disqualifies them for use in durable architecture. The best trees are nurtured by nature, not by Man.

Nishioka expresses exasperation with modern foresters for the way they overprotect, and therefore ultimately weaken, the trees they grow. He thus praises a two-thousand-year-old natural cypress tree, which responded to its dry conditions by penetrating a rock with its roots in order to get water. 'It was precisely because of these harsh conditions that it lived for 2,000 years. It is the same with human beings. If they are indulged [amayakashite], given anything they want, they do not turn out well. Trees are like human beings' (Nishioka 1988: 17–18). That Nishioka uses the verb amayakasu (close to the English sense of 'spoil') is significant. It is a common refrain for many older Japanese that the younger generations, brought up under conditions of postwar prosperity, have been over-indulged by their parents, so that even later on in life they expect to get what they want. Such children do not, as a result, really progress to adulthood (Doi 1973).

The point is that foresters likewise indulge their trees, creating timber stands that are dependent on them and hence do not advance to the desired state of adult strength. Such qualities of strength and durability are necessary for timber trees, no less than for human beings, because they will eventually come to form part of houses and other buildings that shelter human beings. Trees and children (especially sons) should not be pampered by those who raise them, lest they fail to attain the sturdy maturity on which the human others around them depend. Like eldest sons, trees too will one day be relied on, and this is something, Nishioka believes, that the foresters who nurture them have tended to forget.

There is another facet to the immaturity of the domestic trees used in the Japanese wood industry. It is not just that their 'upbringing' is bad, but also that they are felled too soon. The modern Japanese forestry industry fells too many immature trees. The effect of this is evident in the postwar generation of inferior dwellings and other wooden buildings erected. The vernacular term for forest thinning is mabiki. Originally referring to the removal of inferior rice-stalks from the paddyfield, mabiki was also applied to infanticide: the reduction in the number of children for the sake of the continuity of the family (La Fleur 1992: 100). Mabiki is still a resonant idiom in relation to the human world, even though infanticide is no longer practised. It gives expression to a kind of folk Malthusianism to be found in Japanese society, whereby disaster and calamities are seen to have their hidden, long-term purpose. By implication, the population of plantation trees and the population of human beings alike benefit from periodic, partial, selective eliminations. Thinning is something best done by others. This is because a forester is not a good judge of his own plantation.

> With a forest you have planted yourself, when you enter it you say, this would be a waste [if cut down], and nothing would be cut down. With thinning there is the old saying, 'make your mind up and just cut' [omoikitte kiru]. But after you have planted a tree yourself and cut the grass around it, you tend to develop a love [aichaku] for it. You feel sorry for this tree or that tree and leave it standing.

In recent decades, however, the number of unthinned timber plantations has sharply increased. Large-scale outmigratory depopulation of mountain villages, along with the deteriorating economics of forestry, has brought about a generation of what are known as 'beansprout forests' (moyashiyama) – excessive concentrations of thin, weak trees resembling so many beansprouts. This new state of plantation deterioration also evokes the use of child-rearing analogies. One former forest labourer, for example, describes his feelings of despair when, after working in the forests of larger landowners, he returns to his own family forest to find disfigured family trees, ruined by his neglect. It is as though 'you have been occupied with looking after somebody else's child, and have not given enough attention to your own child' (Ue 1984: 18).

Marriage

Felling, too, is an occasion when trees are likened to people. First of all, tree-felling is represented as death. The same Buddhist ritual idiom is invoked for the felling of a tree or the taking of a human life. Thus, just as a memorial rite of kuyō is held for ancestors (senzo kuyō), so a similar rite is held for tree spirits (mokurei kuyō) during the annual memorial for felled trees sponsored by the regional forestry industry. In this rite, like that for human ancestors, a priest recites a Buddhist sutra, incense is offered before an altar (at which is placed a tablet [ihai] inscribed with the name of the deceased), and various food offerings are made, all of which is intended to console the spirit in question. The difference between the two things is one of degree rather than kind. One difference in the two rites is the status of the death involved.

In the case of the tree spirit memorial, it is those who are responsible for taking the life of the trees who sponsor the rite aimed at securing the repose of the spirits, whereas the descendants who sponsor the ancestral memorial do so as successors whose duty to the spirit is unrelated to any direct responsibility for its death. In other words, the tree spirit memorial is a life-taker's ritual in a way that the ancestor memorial is not. There are many other such life-taking memorial rites in Japan, carried out by game hunters, fishermen, slaughterers and other members of life-taking occupations. They all share a common concern over *tatari*, or the curse of the spirit of the slain being. Cut-down trees in the forestry industry, too, may pose a danger of *tatari* to loggers.

Felling can be represented other than as killing. One sawmiller explained his occupation to me in the following terms:

Wood is a living thing. I consider the time when a tree is felled – one that has been raised from when it was very small for tens or even for hundreds of years – to be the time of its marriage [*yome'iri*]. From then on, the tree must go to work. Until then it is like a child being brought up, but then when it is felled, that is the day of its wedding . . . The sawmiller does the make-up [for the bride on her wedding day]. Then you send it [the milled timber] off to the customer. Then it becomes a house, and a fifty-year-old tree will live [as house timber] for [a further] fifty years, or a one-hundred-year-old tree will live for a hundred years. So after living its life in the earth, stretching out its roots and absorbing water, it then lives once more [as house timber] . . . The tree is brought up [eventually] to be married. It is born and raised in order to become a house, in order to become house timber.

The trees that arrive at his sawmill are like women soon to be married. What he does is to prepare them for the wedding by applying the make-up (*keshō*) that will make them into attractive brides. Like a woman, a tree is destined to become a part of a house – even, one might add, to support a house. The association between women and houses is evident in written Japanese. The word for wife, *yome*, is written with the Chinese character 嫁, which combines the character for woman 女 and the character for house 家, giving the meaning of the woman of the house. Women may even be imagined as the *daikokubashira* or primary pillar, the main physical support of the house, and one of the best and most expensive timbers of the house structure. Although the term *daikokubashira* is usually applied to the husband as household head, in contemporary rural Japan it may also be applied to the wife (Moon

1989: 106). The sawmiller's reference to the wife-like nature of timber accords with the timber-like properties of Japanese wives.

Perhaps these two interpretations of tree-felling are not quite as opposed as they may at first appear. For both dying and getting married are life-crisis transitions, and may have common elements of symbolism attached to them. Indeed, Japanese marriage has been famously characterised as a kind of symbolic death for the bride (Nakane 1967: 29). Daughters must be felled in order to make them into reliable, durable wives. The association between trees and brides is evident in the well-known 'tree spirit marriage' (*kodama yomeiri*) myth, versions of which are found throughout Japan and which has even been made into a *kabuki* play.[3] An old willow (elsewhere cypress or camphor) about to be felled to build a bridge is saved by a young man. Some time afterwards he encounters a beautiful young woman beneath this same tree, falls in love, and marries her, and they lead a happy married life. Many years later, the old willow is finally being cut down, and he discovers that his wife, now dying slowly in agony before him, is the spirit of the tree. However, in Japanese folklore tree-felling more commonly occasions marriages than ends them. This theme finds expression in the custom of planting pawlonia trees (*kiri no ki*) on the birth of a daughter.[4] When the daughter reaches twenty and a marriageable age, these fast-growing trees are already big enough to fell to use to make the chest of drawers (*tansu*) she takes with her upon marriage. Pawlonia trees are the growing dowry of growing daughters. Pawlonias are not the only planted trees that support a daughter's marriage. Although not directly used for the trousseau furniture, conifers such as cypress and cryptomeria too can be felled and sold to finance a marriage.

This association between trees and daughters tends to be more indirect today, for it is now common for forest land as such to be sold off to finance the wedding of a daughter. One Hongū man pointed out that just twenty years ago his family owned over ten hectares of forest, but that by the time he succeeded his father as family head a few years ago the landholding had fallen to two-and-a-half hectares. The reason for the depletion of the family's forest landholdings was the marriages of his four sisters in steady succession over the preceding fifteen years. Across Japan there are many local examples of what might be called matrimonial trees (conjugal pines, cryptomeria, zelkovas, and so forth) to which people make requests for finding a partner or for happy, everlasting unions.[5] Moreover, if pawlonia planting is an example of daughter trees becoming bridal wood, there are also examples of bridal trees as such. In certain areas of Japan, a bride, upon marriage and after arriving in her marital home, plants a persimmon tree. As a tree that yields much fruit each autumn, the persimmon tree symbolises the fertility expected of the bride (Umeda 1992: 62). Instead of tree-felling expediting marriage, here marriage occasions tree-planting. The association between persimmon tree and wife is reinforced by the custom of cutting down the tree upon the woman's death and using the wood to cremate her.

Marital tree-planting is not confined to individual fruit trees, but may also apply to commercial timber plantations. Examples can be found on the Kii Peninsula of commemorative wedding trees or even wedding forests. One forester, Ura-san, prepared for his wedding in the spring of 1962 by carrying out *chigoshirae*, the winter task of clearing the forest ground for planting. Spring is the season for both weddings and tree-planting. After the wedding, Ura-san, together with his new bride, planted 1,200 tree saplings. This would be their commemorative forest. The wedding mountain differs from Ura's other mountains because on it he planted expensive, high-quality saplings (from Kyushu). These species are known for their straight and sturdy growth, 'especially the *obi sugi* [a species of cryptomeria], for its growth is fast, healthy, plump and big'. He planted the saplings so that

> we would never forget that time of the wedding. Through that place [the marital forest], we could take great care of what I suppose you would call the marriage bond. As it is the case that, once married, the feelings between the spouses gradually change over the years and months, I thought that if only we could connect our marriage to nature, to cryptomeria, to the forest, we would deepen our marriage bond. That was the my thinking back then.

Maturity

A member of the regional Timber Growers' Association was explaining to me why foresters accord trees great respect, even to the point of carrying out annual thanksgiving – or gratitude-offering – ceremonies for trees. The timber tree is like a parent, he said. He then wrote down the Chinese character for parent (親 *oya*) and pointed out that it consists of three parts: 木 tree, 立 standing, and 見 to look, giving the meaning of 'one who looks at a standing tree'. A parent, in other words, is precisely one who has grown or helped to grow a mature tree from which the children can now derive the benefit. The mature tree exemplifies the parental bequest to the children. But he might equally have characterised his timber trees as ancestral, for Japanese ancestors are usually considered parental in character. Although most ancestors enshrined in the ancestral altar will tend not to be the actual parents of the living – as the altar often consists of different generations of lineal ancestor, including grandparent, great grandparent and beyond – for the extant descendants deceased parents naturally form the main focus of ancestral memorialism.

Foresters are particularly conscious of the ancestral legacy. As one landowner put it, 'I exist because there were ancestors. It is because there were ancestors that our forestry has been passed down to us. First of all, we should be grateful to the ancestors.' They are also mindful of the future. In planting and tending trees that will mature long after they themselves have died, foresters are often held up as paragons of selfless virtue, dedicated to the well-being of descendants (Himeda 1984: 49–51). The selflessness of the forester is also expressed in well-known proverbs: 'Reforesting is done for grandchildren' (*zōrin wa mago no shioki*) (Kusaka 1965: 36–7; see Figure 9.1); 'leave behind beautiful forests for the children' (*kodomo no tame ni birin o nokose*). Timber trees are often associated with the ancestor who planted them. However, raising a good forest involves more than simple planting, and includes the application of labour over a number of different generations. This is why timber forests may well be associated as much with ancestors in general as with specific ancestral planters.

In Japanese mountain villages, forests, even more than the house, can be the focus of ancestral sentiment. According to one saying, 'at *bon* [the midsummer festival] the ancestors go not to the house but first to the [family] forests' (*bon no hotoke wa ie ni ikazu, mazu yama ni iku*) (in Kusaka 1965: 149). *Bon* is the time of the annual return of the ancestors to the world of the living, and conventionally the places to which the ancestors return are the grave and the house, where the ancestral altar is located. It is against this background that the above saying asserts the overriding importance of the mountain forests in upland areas. It is the mountains, or, rather, the cultivated family forests that cover them, that are the primary locus of the stem family line.

Forests are not a commodity, something that present-day descendants are free to sell. 'If you are poor, sell off first the family belongings, then the house, and then the farmland, but do not sell the forests.' One Hongū forester explained this proverb as follows:

じいの植えた山の育つ頃に
坊やも大きくなってるで

Figure 9.1 'When the forests over there planted by grandad are grown up, you too, little boy, will be big' (Kusaka 1965: 36). From Kusaka's published volume of forest proverbs.

It refers to the old society, for nowadays forest does not have that much value. The forest is a place that produces trees, whereas the house is the place you live in and does not have any productivity . . . Before, forests could make you a lot of money and were respected. Now things have changed. In days gone by it was said, 'never sell the forests' [*yama wa zattai uru na*]. The forests are something made up of the sweat and tears of grandfather and grandmother [*jiisan bāsan no ase to namida no kesshō*], the place where you feel gratitude to the ancestors. It is something special because they have grown it for us with all their efforts. That is why it is intolerable when, in your own generation, you go and sell the land to others [. . .] For me, forest is difficult to sell. I have bought forest land but I have never sold forest land to others.

The forests take priority over everything else, even the house-dwelling, as a locus of family sentiment. Ultimately, even the house is replaceable, for it can be rebuilt with the wood from the family forests, in a way that the forests themselves are not. Not every family in the upland villages of the Kii Peninsula has extensive forest landholdings, and, while many do own some forest land, ownership is generally small-scale. For these families, the forests cannot form the basis of livelihood, which is rather the rice-fields and other fields, probably in conjunction with paid employment. But where a grandfather or other ancestor has conscientiously nurtured it, even for the modest landowning family the forest is a source of welcome, extra prosperity, allowing the family to 'fatten' itself (*futoru*). A 'fattened' family is a healthy one, one that eats well.

The Tree's Second Life

Forests contribute to family continuity not just as abstract property, but also, more intimately, as the very medium of secure, long-term family dwelling. This ideal of family forests (literally) supporting the family house is exemplified in the case of the Nishioka Tsunekazu and his family (1993: 19):

> Long ago when my grandfather built the house, he planted trees. This house lasted two hundred years. If I now plant trees, we can build a house in two hundred years' time [. . .] There was [then] an appreciation of time-spans of up to two or three hundred years, but people today do not have a sense of that sort of time-span. Instead, they think of nothing but what is in front of their eyes, the sooner the better.

What is apparent in this passage is the entwined, reciprocal relationship between houses and forests. For as the building of the house entailed the felling of forest trees, so it demanded that replacement trees be planted for the future. Just as timber-growing ensured that houses could be built, so house-building itself should trigger the planting of trees and the cultivation of new forests. From forests come houses, and these houses in turn create forests. Houses are agents of reforestation in two senses: first, because the building of the house occasions the replanting of the family mountains as above, and secondly, through the routine forestry labours of the family members brought up within, and sheltered and protected by, the house. In this

Figure 9.2 'What's that?!' 'It's Mr Wooden House, isn't it?' (Uemura 1992: 60). From a popular book on the merits of wooden houses.

way, there would always be trees and therefore houses, and houses and therefore trees, for subsequent generations of the Nishioka family.

Some landowners delight in telling of the family and forest history of their house beams. Sometimes the trees from a particular mountain associated with the family are used to erect the pillars of the family house. Manago-san is the head of a twelfth-generation family that owns 160 hectares of forest land. While he is a successful commercial forester, not all his forests are directed to market sale:

> Right in the middle of our mountains is the site of the original Manago family house. A short distance away from this, to the rear, are the ancestral graves. Close to the graves there is an area of trees which are 100 years old. There is a saying, passed down from our ancestors, which says 'as long as there is enough rice-gruel left for the next day's meal, don't cut [these trees down]'. As there are graves there, these trees should not be cut down [. . .] Only in the most dire circumstances should they be cut down.

There are about fifty or sixty of these special one-hundred-year-old trees (cypress and cryptomeria). Manago also stresses that they are 'extremely good mountain' (*hijōni ii yama*). These trees have grown into very good, thick and sturdy timber. Manago's grandfather planted them and tended to them in the early years, and this care was then continued by Manago's father. It is clear enough that if they were felled they would fetch very good prices. But the interdiction means that, barring sudden disaster, they will not be felled.

An exception was, however, recently made. Four years earlier, when Manago was rebuilding the family house, he felled three of these special trees for the entrance pillars of the house. But this felling of the trees that should not be felled did not breach the ancestral saying:

> The three trees that I asked [the ancestors] to allow me to fell were for use in our own lives. We asked to be allowed to fell these trees raised by the ancestors in order to use them as the main pillars of the house. For that, they [the ancestors] will forgive us [. . .] We used the three trees as the main pillars, put in the most visible place in the house.

These seven-metre pillars were not squared off at the sawmill but erected in their original rounded shape. Manago is clearly proud of these timbers; he points out that visitors to the house rarely fail to be impressed by them, and that they often become the subject of conversation.

Another forest landowner who built his house from ancestral forests is Yoshimizu-san. This forester states emphatically that the timbers of his house are alive as much as, if in a different way from, the trees of his forests:

> As a result of combining with people, they [trees] become logs, become desks, become pillars, and thereby re-emerge in people's places. That is where their second life [*dai ni no jinsei*] begins [. . .] Wood continues to absorb moisture, and it breathes out and breathes in. It breathes. Without fail, on a humid day a [wooden] pillar absorbs much moisture, and then when the weather is good it breathes it out. It is breathing, it is not dead. Therefore wood, right up until the end when it becomes earth [again], is not dead because it breathes . . . Take this pillar here, it is breathing right now.

He was pointing to a wooden cross-beam above the sliding doors of the rush-mat room where we were sitting. This, like the other beams and pillars of the house, he pointed out, had been grown by his grandfather. Although his grandfather died some years ago, the trees that he grew have been immortalised in the family house that they now support. The beams 'are living through the spirit of grandfather' (*ojii san no tamashii de ikite iru*). Yoshimizu never knew his grandfather directly, as he died before he himself was born, but believes that he has come to know him through the house timber. In his comments above, Yoshimizu-san was expressing the ideas of the famous carpenter Nishioka Tsunekazu (who was mentioned earlier), which are widely known among foresters, sawmillers and carpenters on the southern Kii Peninsula (many possess one or more of his books, and some have even listened to talks given by him or one of his disciples). According to Nishioka, a tree has two lives: one in the forest and the other in the building of which the tree becomes part. The carpenter's job is to ensure that the tree he works with receives a second life no shorter than the first. This is Man's duty (*gimu*) to the trees he deals with. Hence 1,300-year-old cypresses, like those used to build the famous Hōryūji temple, should be made into building timber that can last at least 1,300 years (Nishioka 1993: 26–7).

It is not, however, the case that the older the tree, the more it needs to be protected. Trees should not be left standing indefinitely. Even very old trees should be felled at the appropriate time. Not to do so, as nature protectionists argue in criticising the felling of old trees, would not be fair to the tree, because it would deny it the opportunity of living a second life as building timber (Nishioka 1993: 49). Hence, while the carpenter is partly responsible for taking the life of the tree, in fact he is granting the tree an extension of its life. But for the 'natural tree' (*shizen no ki*) to be 'reborn' as the 'building tree' (*tatemono no ki*), the tree must undergo an internal change. In earlier times it was common for a period of between three and five years to elapse between the felling of the tree and its arrival at the sawmillers. During this time the felled tree was exposed to the elements (rain, wind, snow, heat, cold), and was often left in the water, until it had completely lost *ju'eki* ('tree liquid', i.e. sap). For only sapless, hardened wood, consisting almost entirely of heartwood, is suitable for building purposes.

Conclusion

The continuity, overlap, and even identity between trees and wood forms the basis of the importance of timber forests to local families. The two phases of the life of *ki* – as tree and then as timberwood – are associated with the phases of dependency and then independent nurturance among family members in the context of the enduring house. First, tree-growing is anthropomorphically defined. Tree-growing is imagined in terms of raising children (indeed as an ideal form of child-rearing). The growth of timber trees is mediated both by the actual human labour applied to them and by (anthropomorphic) ideas about their normative growth that inform this labour process. Secondly, the growth of trees in turn forms a medium through which the human life-course is imagined, but in a way that exceeds the biological lives of family members in favour of a more enduring sense of the family. This is materially expressed, on the one hand, in advanced growth forests and, on the other, in durable wooden houses. There is, therefore, a symbiosis (anthropocentrically defined) between human lives and the lives of trees. Human beings enable trees to grow straight and to live a second life as wooden houses. The trees both enrich their growers and shelter them. Family continuity is imagined in terms of the durability of wood. Wood is thus a medium through which people can imagine transcendence.

The skewed pattern of forest landholding has meant that the conversion of ancestral forests into family houses has never been generalised among upland dwellers, and tends to be something confined to larger landowners. Nonetheless, the ideal itself would seem to have an appeal beyond those actually able to realise it. It should also be stressed that even where plantation trees do not attain a second life as family timber – the inevitable fate, of course, of most plantation timber on an estate of any appreciable size – the trees may still be seen as contributing to the family, and therefore as having a second life through the continuing family line, the descendants themselves and the worldly success they achieve.

Yet this is an age of heirlessness. Most rural families find themselves without an heir to continue the family line. Reacting to the effects of urban outmigration on villages in the 1900s, the famous Japanese folklorist Yanagita Kunio pointed to the emerging phenomenon of what he called *iegoroshi* ('domicide', or the killing of the family) in which migrants would cease to be aware of their ancestral roots (Irokawa 1985: 288–9). Families continue to die at the end of the century, just as they did at the beginning. In many mountain villages today discontinued 'dead' families greatly exceed living ones. But heirlessness means the failure not just of one sort of succession, but also of that of the trees. The normative cycle of forests–houses–forests is interrupted. Discontinued family lines are matched – indeed expressed – by decrepit family forests (if not the actual selling off of family forests). A whole generation of trees have been grown for a maturity they will never attain. Japanese sawmillers increasingly opt for foreign timber – foreign brides – and Japanese timber stands are, as a result, condemned to a wretched spinsterhood. The trees of the forest have increasingly ceased to become the wood of the village. Instead, village houses are ferroconcrete or are made from cheaper foreign timber. Dependent trees have not become nurturant houses. In this respect the forest trees recall the village parents whose children have left for the city, and who are therefore redundant as parents. They have been rejected by those they should be parenting. In the case of empty houses (*akiya*), this abandonment is literal. The nurturant second life of trees – as the supporting beams of sheltering houses – has not come about or materialised. The plantation conifers are not living the second lives they should be, they are living first lives which are too long. What might appear an impressive longevity is actually an overextended adolescence. They are suffering from an excessive tree longevity, which is ultimately false because real longevity is secured through a transformative felling, and the prospect of a kind of near-immortality. The condition of upland Japan today is a morbid one, made up as it is of mountain villages of 'dead', displaced families surrounded by conifer forests of once loved but now forgotten trees.

Acknowledgements

Ethnographic fieldwork on the Kii Peninsula (1987–9) was supported by an ESRC (Economic and Social Research Council) grant. Subsequent field trips on which this chapter draws were made possible by Wadham College (Oxford), the National Museum of Ethnology (Kokuritsu Minzokugaku Hakubutsukan) (Osaka), and the Institute for the Culture of Travel (Tabi no Bunka Kenkyūsho) (Tokyo). I would also like to thank the foresters of Hongū-chō and other parts of the Kii Peninsula for sharing with me their views on timber-growing and their knowledge on forestry more generally. Above all, I would like to express my thanks and gratitude to Mr. Kurisu Hiromasa for his assistance and friendship in the course of a number of extended visits to Hongū-chō.

Notes

1. Although this is a Chinese-style word, *kanbun*, rather than a Japanese-style word, *wabun*. The non-discriminatory term for tree/wood, *ki*, by contrast, is a Japanese-style word, and is used much more.

2. For example, arboreally named villages in the area include Ipponmatsu 一本松, Single Pine; Hiba 檜葉, False Arbor Vitae; Matsuba 松葉 Pine Leaf; Kogomori 小小森 Little Forest; Akagi 赤木 Red Tree; and Ipposugi 一方杉 One-sided Cryptomeria. Arboreally named local families include Sugiyama 杉山 Cryptomeria Mountain; Sugioka 杉岡 Cryptomeria Hill; Kuriyama 栗山 Chestnut Mountain; Kimura 木村 Tree Village; Takeda 竹田 Bamboo Field; Matsumoto 松本 Pine Origin; Matsumura 松村 Pine Village; Matsumi 松実 Pine Cone; Matsuhata 松畑 Pine Field; and Matsuba 松葉 Pine Leaf.

3. Smith (1995 [1918]: 12–18); Ashida (1995: 74); Davis (1992 [1913]: 177–80). See also Tsuda (1994: 346–7) and Taguchi (1991: 102).

4. This custom is associated principally with Fukushima Prefecture, but was also found on the Kii Peninsula. See Kimura and Tsutsui (1990: 64–5); Matsutani (1994: 164–5); Inamoto (1994: 193–9).

5. Watanabe (1994: 948); Makino (1988: 58–9); NHK (1971: 69–71).

References

Ashida, T., *Shokubutsu kotowaza jiten* (Dictionary of Plant Proverbs), Tokyo: Tōkyōdō Shuppan, 1995

Davis, F. H., *Myths and Legends of Japan*, New York: Dover Publications, 1992 [1913]

Doi, T., *The Anatomy of Dependence*, Tokyo: Kodansha, 1973

Harada, N., *Nishioka Tsunekazu to kataru: ki no ie wa sanbyaku nen* (Talking with Nishioka Tsunekazu: Wooden Houses that Last Three Hundred Years), Tokyo: Nōbunkyō, 1995

Himeda, T., *Yama to sato no fūkuroa: minzoku to fūdo e no tabi* (The Folklore of Mountain and Village: A Trip through Folklore and Local Customs), Tokyo: Haru Shobō, 1984

Inamoto, T., *Mori no katachi, mori no shigoto* (The Form of the Forest and the Job in the Forest), Tokyo: Sekaibunkasha, 1994

Irokawa, D., *The Culture of the Meiji Period* (translation edited by Marius B. Jansen), Princeton: Princeton University Press, 1985

Kawabe, H. and H. Shimizu, 'Japanese perceptions of the family and living arrangements: the trend toward nuclearization', in L. J. Cho and M. Yada (eds), *Tradition and Change in the Asian Family*, Honolulu: East–West Center, 1994

Kimura, S. and M. Tsutsui, *Mori no seikatsu dorama 100* (One Hundred Tales of Forest Life), Tokyo: Nihon Ringyō Kyōkai, 1990

Kuroda, T., 'Family structure and social change: implications of fertility changes in Japan and China', in L. J. Cho and M. Yada (eds), *Tradition and Change in the Asian Family*, Honolulu: East–West Center, 1994

Kusaka, M., *Yama no kotowaza* (Forest Proverbs), Tokyo: Zenkoku Ringyō Kairyō Fukyū Kyōkai, 1965

La Fleur, W., *Liquid Life: Abortion and Buddhism in Japan*, Princeton: Princeton University Press, 1992

Makino, K., *Kyoju no minzoku kikō* (A Travel Diary on the Folklore of Giant Trees), Tokyo: Kōbunsha, 1988

Matsutani, M., *Mokurei, heibi* (Tree Spirits and Snakes), Tokyo: Rippū Shobō, 1994

Moon, O., *From Paddyfield to Ski Slope*, Manchester: Manchester University Press, 1989

Nakane, C., *Kinship and Economic Organization in Rural Japan*, London: Athlone Press, 1967

NHK (Nihon Hōsō Kyōkai) (eds), *Nihon densetsu meishū* (A Collection of Japanese Legends), Tokyo: Nihon Hōsō Shuppan Kyōkai, 1971

Nishioka, T., *Ki ni manabe* (Learning from Trees), Tokyo: Shogakkan, 1988

—— *Ki no inochi, ki no kokoro* (The Life of the Tree, The Heart of the Tree), Tokyo: Sōshisha, 1993

Nishioka, T. and J. Kohara, *Hōryūji o sasaeta ki* (The Trees Offered Up to the Horyuji Temple), Tokyo: NHK Books, 1978

Smith, R. G., *Ancient Tales and Folklore of Japan*, London: Senate, 1995 [1918]

Taguchi, K., 'Kodama mukoiri' (Tree Spirit Husband), in Nihon Minwa no Kai (ed.), *Gaidobukku nihon no minwa* (Japanese Folktale Guidebook), Tokyo: Kōdansha, 1991

Tsuda, K., 'Kodama mukoiri' (Tree Spirit Husband), in K. Inada *et al.* (eds), *Nihon mukashibanashi jiten* (Dictionary of Japanese Old Tales), Tokyo: Kōbundō, 1994

Ue, T., *Yama no ki no hitorigoto* (The Mutterings of Mountain Trees), Tokyo: Shinjuku Shobo, 1984

Uemura, T., *Kizukuri no jōshiki hijōshiki* (Commonsense and Foolishness in Using Wood), Tokyo: Gakugei Shuppansha, 1992

Umeda, E., *Kishuki no kuni 'kikiaruki'* (Walking around the Land of Kishu Trees), Wakayama: Chuwa Insatsu, 1992

Watanabe, S., 'Meotomatsu' (The Conjugal Pine), in Inada *et al.* (eds), *Nihon mukashibanashi jiten* (Dictionary of Japanese Old Tales), Tokyo: Kōbundō, 1994

Yanagita, K., 'Japanese Folk Tales', *Folklore Studies*, XI (1), 1952, pp. 1–97 (translated by Fanny Hagin)

Yen, A., 'Thematic patterns in Japanese folktales: a search for meanings', *Asian Folklore Studies*, 33(2), 1974, pp. 1–36

Part III

Woods, Forests and Politics

Grassroots Campaigning for the World's Forests

Angie Zelter

July 1996. I am locked into a small concrete cell in a prison in England. I have been sent many cards of solidarity and support that have been stuck on to a piece of cardboard with toothpaste and propped up on the table where I am writing this. Most of the images are of wilderness areas and many are of trees and they fill me with peace and strength to continue this resistance against war, corruption, social injustice and lack of respect for all living beings on our planet.

The people supporting my act of disarmament would all see themselves as part of the ever-growing peace and environment networks, which are spreading across the planet trying to halt mankind's rush to self-destruction. Our message is '**Wake Up The Planet Is Dying**.' Our sub-text is that we can all join together, ordinary men, women, and children, across the planet, to resist and to stop the powerful destructive forces and to re-create healthy, sane and loving relationships and communities.

Our present struggle has brought us into contact with people from many cultures in every part of the world. Welsh people in the UK have joined with Inuit people in Canada to protest at low-flying military training exercises that traumatise their families and the animals they depend upon for their livelihoods. Indigenous peoples from the USA, the former USSR, China, and the Pacific have united to protest at the radioactive poisoning of their homelands from nuclear testing; and peoples from numerous countries to protest at the horrendous effects of gold or oil mining on their forests, rivers and soils. There is an acknowledgement that the worst pollution and exploitation of resources occurs on the lands and in the neighbourhoods of the poor and dispossessed, those on the 'edges' of the dominant society, those that governments and industries think they can ignore with impunity because they lack power and proper access to the 'decision-makers'. We are stretching out our hands and our hearts to peoples in rural and urban settings of the North and the South, to the poor and the wealthy, the powerful and oppressed, the victims and the victors. We are one world. We all have to change.

One of the symbols that we use in our struggles is the – spider's – web that binds and interlinks us all. But the web is always attached to the living presence of a tree. *The tree is our most potent symbol, binding and grounding us with its roots;* sheltering and protecting us within its branches; raising our spirits at the same time as stabilising our feet in the mud of the earth; giving us strength and resilience in its sturdy trunk; feeding and nurturing us with its fruits; giving us everlasting hope in the constant regeneration and rebirth of its seeds. For me, being British, the oak tree has a special resonance and significance. Let me give a few examples of how the tree has inspired the peace and environmental organisations and groups of which I have been a part.

In the early 1980s at the height of the new Cold War, I joined along with thousands of other people the peace movement, supporting CND and local peace groups. In East Anglia, where I live and where many US nuclear military bases were located, we held numerous demonstrations, vigils, blockades, and peace camps at these bases. Many of these actions were purely to point the finger, to make open and public what the state wanted to hide. These military bases were called Royal Airforce bases but were actually controlled by America's airforces. They were known as defence bases but were actually offensive and threatening to our fellow global citizens in other parts of the world. They were said to be 'conventional', until we exposed them as nuclear. We often took seeds from wild flowers and from our favourite trees and scattered them around the fences and threw them over the gates in a continuing ritual that has been repeated at many destructive and deceitful sites across the country. We hardly ever discussed – or planned – these actions; they seemed a very natural thing to do; they were intuitive responses to evil and death. Sometimes, we went into the bases and planted as many trees as possible before being arrested and charged with 'criminal damage'. But what we were doing was sowing the seeds of life to counterbalance the death and destruction emanating from military bases located in isolated rural areas of great beauty that were once common lands that were taken away from the people.

Looking at our banners you can see the tremendous overarching significance of trees for us. One of our most beautiful and best-loved, entitled 'Women For Life On Earth', is of a huge tree within the branches of which you find peace symbols: white doves, peace cranes, CND signs, candles, rainbows, webs, flutes, and people of all colours dancing and hugging flowers. In 1986, during the unwarranted and abhorrent US attack on Libya's capital, Tripoli, when residential areas were bombed from planes that flew from my local air bases, my family felt the need to plant a grove of trees in our large garden to express our remorse at our government's connivance in such a crime, and to express our faith and hope in the future. Planting trees is a common response to insecurity and trauma; but it is also a form of celebration. Then we developed a community woodland with money raised locally, and tree planting organised by local people themselves. As many people asked to plant trees to commemorate private births, deaths, marriages and other significant occasions, we decided to put aside several acres of our local community woodland for this purpose. Community members now go in their own time; no permission is needed to plant a tree; any member is free to make his or her own ceremony. We all feel a deep need to plant and care for trees. But this deep yearning is hard to fulfil in Britain, where land access is so restricted. Our land distribution is just as skewed as in places like Brazil, with a very small percentage of landowners owning the vast bulk of the land and allowing very little public access.

Trees can live for thousands of years; a continuity with the past, present and future; a soothing, calming and stable presence. Maybe this is why they are such a pervasive symbol for this age of speed, transience, short-term gain and individual ownership. There is a comforting wonder when we contemplate ancient trees, for they will outlast all the petty problems of humanity. But will they? Some of our deepest spiritual instincts are being challenged by the rate and scope of the present destruction of forests occurring across the planet; tropical, temperate and boreal forests are *all* threatened.[1]

It is no step at all from the peace movement to the environment movement – back and forth. From the threat of instant obliteration from a nuclear warhead, to the slow poisoning by radiation, to the knowledge of the military's being one of the most serious and wide-spread polluters on the planet, to concern and anger over the felling of our forests. Sometimes the link is hurtfully direct, like the defoliants used to kill the mangrove and tropical forests in Vietnam. Throughout the 1980s, the Greenham Common Women's peace camp brought together thousands of women from many different walks of life. It was there that we first discussed the links between our fears and the problems faced by our society. The nuclear holocaust nightmares of our children; the threats to innocent civilians in other countries misnamed by our government as 'the enemy'; the horror and waste of the arms trade our country was encouraging for short-term financial gain; the unfair global trading system and Third World debt; slavery and the continuation of colonialism by the misuse of the economic power of the industrialised nations and the large transnational companies; the lust for money and the mean, short-sighted grab for the material resources of other countries with little regard for the effect on local peoples. Property and profit seemed to rule. We had no respect for our political 'leaders'.

So much so that we recognised the danger of leadership and its corrupting power. We rotated our own, and had a much-loved slogan we were fond of sharing: 'We have no leaders – the stars are in the sky.' Our own ethical values and those we taught our children were sorely at variance with those of our institutions and industries. Ordinary people felt helpless and disempowered – dispirited. We were being told we lived in a democracy and could vote for whoever and whatever we wanted, but it wasn't working. Citizen's charters were issued and occasional public inquiries allowed, but the odds seemed stacked against any real popular participation in the running of our lives. Britain was divided, our communities were breaking down. Britain was torn, dirty, ungenerous and dying from within. The light in people's eyes was going out and hate was growing. But, at Greenham, we discovered through active involvement in the peace movement what all repressed people have discovered: that we *do* have power if we work together, and if we have hope. At sites across the country, in our thousands, we defied the military machine.[2] We cut through the fences every night, danced on the nuclear bunkers, planted trees in the scorched earth, smiled, gave flowers to the soldiers within, and above all else, we sang. We sang from our hearts and souls our songs of resistance and power. Every movement has its songs; they just spring out when you leave behind the dead, grey, lonely, and television-dominated world of careless consumption to find again your humanity and strength. We cried together our pain, our fear, and our growing power. One remarkable day, 40,000 women encircled the US base at Greenham and the ten-mile perimeter fence was breached in numerous places. We all carried the lessons of Greenham home with us. We won that battle; after our continuous ten-year presence at the peace camps around the Greenham base, cruise missiles were eventually dismantled and the base is now closing. Many of the women who went to Greenham naturally expanded their activities into the environmental movement.

Locally, the resistance and fight against nuclear weapons has naturally encompassed the 'civil' nuclear plants, which actually provide fissile material to the military, and which operate under the same kind of secrecy as the military do. 'Accidents' and their effects (i.e. leukaemia) only come to light many years later. The Chernobyl accident alerted even the most ignorant, as the health and environment effects are still felt – or even growing – ten years later. The radioactive legacy has not gone away as we were told it would. One unexpected environmental consequence was the take-up of radiation by the forests of Belarus. If there was ever to be a large forest fire we would have another Chernobyl! Man has created something that can outlast the lifetime of even the most ancient tree; the half-life of plutonium is 24,000 years. What an awesome abuse of our 'rationality'.

My concern and love for trees became more focused when I was asked if I would join a group of Earth First! activists taking part in an international support action for the hunter-gatherer Penan of Sarawak in Malaysia. I agreed, and spent four months in Sarawak in 1991. We met with several Dayak peoples and talked about the destruction of their forests, homes and communities – their life – in order to provide timber to sustain extravagant and wasteful lifestyles in the industrialised countries. Our international group blockaded some timber barges, stopping work on parts of the Baram River. We protested at the logging of the Penan's forests, and asked that native customary land rights be respected. We spent two months in prison in Miri, the same prison where hundreds of Penan had been sent some years before, at the height of their logging road protests. This was a good example of cross-cultural grassroots activism, and it has inspired many.

This kind of transglobal solidarity is essential at both community and spiritual level. One can feel just as isolated when fighting a large company in the middle of a forest in Sarawak, as when confronting a large company in a small English town. Sometimes, the companies are even the same! Certainly the same forces are at work everywhere. The global trading system connects those companies robbing the Penan of their forests with British companies marketing the products made from Penan trees in my local superstore. The bananas that are sold in my grocer's store are grown in plantations smothered with polluting chemicals that are destroying the health and water supplies of my global brothers and sisters working in near-slavery conditions on land that has often been cut from beautiful old-growth forests against the wishes of the local people. Since returning from Sarawak, I have been working almost continuously on forest issues. Other campaigners work on different issues, but we all feel linked, because the major catastrophes facing our planet are interconnected; none can be solved without solving the others. We meet often on demonstrations, blockades and lobbies, and, increasingly, at the AGMs and gatherings of transnational companies and world institutions like the World Bank and the G7 country meetings. But these are becoming less effective methods of resistance. We are moving on to more direct forms of protest and trying to build up alternative structures, communities and ways of life.

One of the most vital protests in Britain today is the anti-roads campaign. This is a broad-based movement urging fair and equitable public access to transport through a cheap, public mass-transit system for everyone rather than individual cars only for the better-off. This movement is resisting the destruction and conversion of our country-side into ugly tarmac and concrete, and the deaths of thousands of people in road accidents. The protest especially centres on the pollution that causes major respiratory diseases in young and old, as well as catastrophic climate change through the production of greenhouse gases and ozone layer depletion. The anti-roads campaign is taking on some of the largest and most powerful transnational companies, the oil industry and the car industry. And, once again, the tree is domin-ating the campaign as a symbol of resistance, endurance, strength, hope and beauty. In the M11 campaign, it was the attempted protection of an ancient sweet chestnut tree on the site of the proposed motorway (which was to destroy 350 houses) that focused the attention and protest of local people. Some activists decided to live in their tree-house in the chestnut tree, where they had their mail delivered. School-children wrote letters to the tree-house, and their parents and grandparents joined hands with them to surround the ancient tree, trying to protect it with their bodies. The road builders destroyed the tree in the end, but not before legal history was made. This was the first time an eviction order was served on a tree-house dweller. The tree was felled, but another local community was radicalised, politicised and woken up to the struggle for a just and beautiful world. The people who tried to protect the old chestnut tree began to articulate, and have faith in, their own common sense. They resented the new roads, as these would only encourage more cars. There is not enough room or fresh air in Britain for everyone to have a car. We have to share, the majority of cars have to be taken away, and there has to be public transport. Other campaigners have even ritually 'killed' their cars by burning them and burying them nose in the ground, tail in the air. All this to chanting, singing and dancing. Yes, this is all coming back as we rediscover our strength and hope and reclaim our land! Even tribes are being formed in an attempt to rebuild the community life that modern, industrial life has broken. The Lizard Tribe, for example, has formed to protect an area of high conservation value to the west of Norwich near Wymondham; and the Donga Tribe, to resist the desecration of Twyford Down.

The present conflict going on over the M66 at Newbury in Berkshire epitomises the struggle. Here you can see the different values clashing. The alternative lifestyles and new vibrant cultures are confronting the old, tired, authoritarian and monocultural status-quo. Here, young and old, and straight and alternative, have left their 'normal' homes and set up camps in treetops. They have built walk-ways to connect the trees. The tree spirits may have left the site temporarily at the onslaught of the bulldozers, tarmac, and sometimes violent struggles taking place there. But the campaigners have entered into the branching tops, trying to stop the massacre of yet more trees. They tie themselves to the branches, and risk their lives as the 'security' forces drag them down by force. This is the British equivalent of the famous and inspiring Indian Chipko movement, where women hugged the trees to prevent the logging of ancestral village forests. By April 1996, there had been around 800 arrests, 10,000 trees killed, and 34 protest camps evicted along the route of the proposed Newbury Bypass, and this at a cost of approximately ten million pounds. The Department of Transport is considering a six million pound fence to surround the proposed route, in preparation for the next battle aimed at stopping the building work. All this to 'protect' the road from the very people the authorities say they are building the road for! Many of my friends were intimately involved in the Third Battle of Newbury, as it has become known. And a battle it was, with underground defensive camps, with disaffection and desertions from the conscripted security forces into the rebel/guerrilla camps, with treetop occupations, and with specialist climbers and massed ranks of protesters. Some 6,000 turned out for the 11 February 1996 rally, which received wide media coverage.

The tree defenders loved 'their' trees, which they regarded as magical, and in which they invested so much emotional energy. After three months of treetop living, the energy charge is such that one feels transformed. One woman who had lived in her tree-house for over three months said she felt she was communicating with the spirits of the trees. A man remembers feeling elated every time he was climbing to the top of the tree he was defending at Seaview Camp. His muscles felt particularly alive from weeks of climbing up and down on ropes and branches. He was eventually forced out of 'his' tree by security men in 'cherry pickers'. When the tree was felled, he felt utterly heart-broken. A poem pinned on a tree at one of the camps said:

Let it not be said
And said unto your shame,
That there was beauty here
Before you came.

People were desperately angry at the destruction of beauty and life that was going on all around them. Chain-saws lopped branches off indiscriminately, trees crashed down – with little regard for security. Protesters wandered around in a despairing daze, some bleeding from the rough handling by the security guards. One such guard taunted them, saying they should be using their time more productively by planting trees! He made no reply to their questions of how they could recreate the old trees, the heathland, the water meadows, the ancient bogs, the sites of Special Scientific Interest, and the two battle sites from the English Civil War . . . One friend said it was difficult to grasp the age of some of the trees along the Newbury Route. Some had been alive with the Roundheads and Cavaliers, and would have lived for many more years. At Newbury, there were the mystical tree-dwellers, who saw trees as the symbols of the Countryside, that is, of the most visible, the most impressive, and the oldest ecological landscape in the nation. The countryside is the sole focus of their struggle to save the environment. But Newbury was also the land of the ground-dwellers, those who spoke in terms of the car problem, anti-roads, and concrete lives.

In Britain, we destroyed nature many centuries ago, and since, we have been left with a bland, domesticated, man-made environment. This is why we feel so passionate about the few fragments of nature that are left; and this is why we want to protect them. Many of us mourn our lost wilderness, our departed wolves. As we look at much of the urban squalor and agro-industrial sabotage that surrounds us, beautiful views scarred by electricity pylons, battery chicken farms, factories, roads, rubbish tips, sewage outfalls, monocultural farms, and tree plantations, we feel emptiness, alienation and desolation. Those few areas of marshes or native woodlands, and even of parks and public spaces, are all we have left; so we treasure them greatly. The branches of our movements interweave, connected as they are by the longing for a wholesome, loving world. Local anti-roads campaigners pickaxe the newly-laid tarmac of yet another by-pass and plant trees in the middle to 'close' the road and return it to a public space filled again with living beings. Urban resisters reclaim the streets by setting up bollards at either end, and inviting all the neighbours on to the hastily rolled-out carpets. Games are put out for the children, and all have a picnic. Each group tries to re-establish the community links severed by the car's dangerous and unconscious thundering by. Protesters are trying to stop the industrial mega-machine that is by-passing *their* local needs.

The story is repeated across the planet. Ordinary local people are not consulted, their rights are trampled upon, their lands taken away from them, their local markets destroyed, and their strength, dignity and confidence stripped away. Everywhere, in Britain and in Ogoni land, in the USA and in Colombia, in Australia and in Thailand, people have lost or are losing their self-sufficient, autonomous and proud cultures. They are turning to despair, disintegration, drugs and a slow cultural death. And now the trees are dying too! Look around you! And it's not just the trees. The mass extinction of millions of our fellow living species is currently taking place. Biological and cultural extinction are intimately connected. We have allowed the transnational companies and national governments to get out of balance and become narrow-minded, cancerous and dangerous. The aims and objectives of many of our institutions and companies have resulted in the impoverishment of huge sections of our global community. It is therefore time for us all to appeal to every human being to behave with full awareness of the consequences of our actions on all life forms, on the soil, the water and the air. We must make the links obvious to everyone. We must continue to encourage the spiritual awareness of wholeness, so we can all feel once again our interconnectedness. This knowledge and aware-ness are not hidden too deep. Everyone with a little prompting can find this awareness within.

A recent project of *Reforest the Earth* asks people to make a cloth square for a quilt on forest issues. We have received hundreds of beautifully embroidered, painted or woven squares, which are then sewn together to make a 'forest cover'. The beauty, diversity, pain and hope expressed show that many of the links *have* been made. There are many animals and plants; cars crossed out, big dams and oil wells extinguished and replaced with bicycles and wind farms; there are tree-stumps and a bewildered logger looking confused at a desert with no trees left for him to fell; there are islands drowning in a rising sea, plants and people shrivelling under a widening ozone hole. But there is also peace and hope shown in brown, red, yellow and cream hands clasped in peace; as well as replanting in the deserts. So much knowledge and passion shown in just a few yards of cloth . . . People are aware of what is happening, and they are beginning to do something about it. The pendulum continues to swing!

Over the last few years, indigenous groups in the Amazon have been asking citizens' groups in Britain to help them protect their forests. Britain is the major market for the top-quality cuts of Brazilian mahogany. Much of this quality mahogany is stolen from indigenous lands. I therefore started, with others, an organisation called CRISP-O (Citizens Recovery of Indigenous Peoples' Stolen Property – Organisation). We walked into stores and sawmills in Britain, and simply took out the Brazilian mahogany to hand it in to the nearest police station as stolen property – stolen by the big Brazilian logging companies and then shipped into Britain from Belem. We charged the store owners with handling stolen property. We called our actions 'ethical shoplifting'. These and other direct actions, like blockades of the shipping ports and office occupations of the major importing agents and importing companies, have led us into direct confrontation with the directors of many of the timber companies, as well as with the Timber Trade Federation. However, at the same time, we organised a Women's Negotiating Team to set up a dialogue and find a way out for these companies, while protecting the forests and their peoples. We agreed to stop our direct actions if they would agree to talks and changes in their trading activities. These talks are still continuing and some companies are beginning to change their buying policies. The judicious use of peaceful direct action continues also!

Scandinavian environmental groups and the Saami people have also contacted us for joint action to help save the few boreal old-growth forests left. We have tried to link producer and consumer countries, and to link grassroots campaigns across the globe. Ordinary people everywhere are rising, and *are* supporting each other by making the connections. The Newbury Bypass tree-dwellers received support letters from the Ogoni people of Nigeria. The activists campaigning to Save Oxleas Wood received funds from the Brazilian Rubber Tappers, who had raised money to help the Londoners save their trees in the same way as they were attempting to save theirs in Amazonia. The time has come for more creative direct action by those global citizens with a global conscience. We must build the alternatives as we go along. We are either all winners or all losers; we must transform our societies from within, and we have to do it ourselves, peacefully, lovingly and with patient – yet strong – determination. And we are!

That is one of the reasons why I am still sitting here in Risley prison in Cheshire. Four of us formed a D.I.Y. disarmament group called *Seeds of Hope – East Timor Ploughshares – Women Disarming for Life and Justice*. We peacefully disarmed a Hawk fighter aircraft that was ready to be exported to Indonesia. Indonesia is ruled by a ruthless military dictator, Suharto, who has killed one million of his own people since he came to power. He has also caused the death of around one-third of the population of East Timor in the twenty years of its illegal occupation: he murdered one in every three people! We decided to disarm this plane so it couldn't be used to kill more innocent villagers. We felt that our responsibility as global citizens was to try to prevent this genocide by stopping British Aerospace and the British government's aid to the Suharto regime. Equipped with ordinary household hammers, our group carefully hammered on the sensitive parts of the plane, causing around two million pounds' worth of damage. The Indonesians have said they don't want the plane repaired ('it is jinxed now'), so they have ordered a completely new one. But the anti-arms trade campaign continues.

My hammer was decorated with a sword being transformed into a ploughshare and with acorns germinating into little oak trees. Before the action, we wrote down our feelings of despair, pain and anger at the destruction of our beautiful planet and burnt the writings. We mixed the ashes from this 'despair' with our seeds of 'hope' (acorns and sunflowers). We each took a handful of ashes and seeds on our action, which we spread around the plane, and gave to the police. Meanwhile, here in my cell, I draw strength from the growth of people's movements everywhere. We have everything we need to create a better world – it is within us. Let us join hands, let us celebrate our different cultures and experiences, and let us unite in our love for trees and understanding that the planet we all share is fragile. Together, we can reforest our planet and our souls.

Notes

1. UK Forests Network, *Forests Memorandum and Forest Charter*, Norwich: UKFN, 1994. 'Forests Memorandum' was produced by British NGOs to explain

the causes of, and suggest solutions to, the rapid extinction of the world's forests.

2. Zelter, A. and A. B. Bharadwaj, *Snowball, Gandhi in Action,* Norwich: UKFN, 1992. *Snowball* consists of the personal statements made by anti-nuclear protesters to give to the police and courts when arrested in the mass civil-disobedience campaign against nuclear weapons called 'Snowball'.

Northwest Coast Trees: From Metaphors in Culture to Symbols for Culture

Marie Mauzé

The analysis of symbolism, a complex notion covering many different meanings and definitions, is riddled with difficulties. The first problem is to identify the level of reality that anthropology seeks to analyse. Are fieldworkers restituting the practices and ways of thinking of specific local people, or are they merely fleshing out a plausible account?[1] Such questioning may be put even more forcefully to an analyst relying on her intuition and common sense. This is what an anthropologist must do when attempting to interpret texts or data recorded in various situations, and collected in a mixture of languages: the informant's, the ethnographer's, and, even, a third (national) language native to neither of the two. The data anthropologists work with are already the product of native exegesis, or of the ethnographer's interpretation, or both. There are at least three aspects to the problem of analysing symbols: the concepts defined by the local culture; the concepts of the anthropologist's own culture; and the meta-language referring to anthropological categories or concepts. The anthropological discourse may be grounded within some kind of alleged reality, but it gains its autonomy by offering arbitrary interpretations. This arbitrariness constitutes the very substance of the anthropological discourse produced within the framework of specific technical terms and academic conventions. I have myself never conducted thorough research on Northwest Coast tree symbolism. To find relevant data I had to 'dig' in various monographs, some written about a century ago by a whole generation of ethnographers, among them Franz Boas. Their concern was to salvage what they could of societies and cultures they perceived as dying. Their aim was to gather as many data on as many topics connected with a supposedly 'traditional' society as possible. Interestingly, the information on trees contained in these early writings falls under the most diverse headings: 'religion', 'metaphorical language', 'technology', 'prayers', 'healing', 'medicine', 'mythology', 'basketry', etc. This very list of 'labels' shows that I am dealing with heterogeneous data. I am fully aware of the somewhat arbitrary nature of my attempt to tie bits and pieces together in order to create a synthetic account of the symbolic meaning of trees in Northwest Coast social life.

The significance of tree symbolism on the Northwest Coast – especially cedar symbolism – has been widely acknowledged, but has never been seriously studied. A thorough anthropological analysis of the cognitive models trees provide to the many native groups who inhabit this area has yet to be provided. It is only fair to mention Hilary Stewart's *Cedar, Tree of Life to the Northwest Coast Indians* (1984), a comprehensive study of cedar technology. However, despite its encyclopaedic character, Stewart's study does not provide a complete treatment of tree and wood symbolism. I should also add at this point that animals in this region of North America play a much greater and more explicit role in native conceptualisations of the world than trees do. By contrast, today, trees or, rather, forests have become a central focus in native political life. For the last twenty years or so, Native peoples supported by environmental groups have struggled for the preservation of old-growth forests and have taken legal actions to stop logging on lands they are claiming as their ancient territories (M'Gonigle 1988). Native peoples have been mobilising for years to preserve their culture and history. While their efforts were for some time concentrated on potlatch, their cardinal institution and a key cultural symbol, they are, in the current highly politicised context of land claims, focusing on the preservation of old-growth cedar forests. These forests symbolise cultural renewal, as well as the strength of Indian identity. Trees and forests, as synecdoche or metonymy[2] for the whole Northwest Coast Indian culture, are today endowed with a mystical aura. Doubtless these representations are influenced by ideas borrowed from the North American pan-Indian movement and from the many environmentalist groups now existing throughout North America.

In this chapter, I analyse two types of discourse on Northwest Coast trees: (1) the 'traditional' discourse, which is internal, and rooted in practice and experience; and (2) the contemporary discourse, which is explicitly targeted on a large – White and non-White – public. Both discourses are multivocal. The traditional discourse is mainly concerned with relationships between trees and human beings, the transformation of trees into wood, and the biological features underpinning the use of trees as metaphors of strength and longevity. The contemporary discourse is part of an overall strategy for the advancement of native positions towards self-government. It also expresses environmental concerns, and, as such, is both similar to the ecological discourse (especially on the issue of non-economic values), and opposed to native 'pro-development' aspirations. There are native communities where the defence of logging jobs takes priority over forest conservation (M'Gonigle 1988). The traditional and contemporary discourses differ in their way of conceptualising the mode of relation established between trees and human beings. If in the traditional context these relations were experientially rooted, they are today seen to be part of a conscious return to spirituality. For a growing number of Native people, ecologists and New Age adepts alike, native spirituality takes the form of a mystical quest in which trees and forests have an important role to play as mediators. It is, moreover, being converted into a mode of adaptation to the world.

The Importance of Trees on the Northwest Coast

The cedar (red and yellow) is the most common species to grow along the forested coastline of the Pacific North-west, which is characterised, from the Yakutat Bay in the Gulf of Alaska to the Columbia River in the south, by a marine, moist and temperate climate. Hemlock, spruce,[3] alder and fir trees also grow profusely. Native peoples have used such remarkable natural resources to create a rich material and symbolical world. Distinctions between species and varieties within species were elaborate, and recognised differences in wood and bark quality were exploited in a vast range of domestic and ritual contexts. The wood of the cedar was economically and culturally so central that it was known as the 'tree of life' in many Northwest Coast languages; this led ethnographers to refer to Northwest Coast Indians as 'Peoples of the Cedar' (Stewart 1984). A recent article published in a Kwakiutl local museum newsletter (*U'Mista News* 1995) and entitled 'Survival of the Cedar People' illustrates that Native people have today adopted this expression as a term of self-reference.

Cedar trees were used in the production of a variety of products designed to meet both daily and seasonal needs. The great insulating properties of cedar wood, a particularly light and soft wood, are due to its cellular structure. The inner bark, which is both resistant and flexible, is easy to work. Throughout his or her life, an individual used not only the wood, bark and roots, but also the withes and leaves of cedar. Women specialised in preparing and weaving cedar bark and roots, and men in wood processing techniques, from tree-felling to plank-splitting and carving (Stewart 1984; Turner 1979). Massive beams and planks for longhouses, chests for food storage, dug-out canoes, boxes, and ceremonial objects were all made of cedar. Heraldic, mortuary and house poles were carved out of cedar; and the wood used in the making of various utensils and implements, such as harpoon shafts, hooks, fishing floats, combs, drums, and so forth, was also cedar. Whereas household basketry was made of cedar bark and roots, the fibrous part of the bark was used for matting, cordage, garments, diapers and shrouds for the dead. Tree products were also valued as efficient medicines to cure a great variety of illnesses (Boas 1921, 1966; Gunther 1973; Stewart 1984; and Turner 1979).

Keeping in mind that trees are experienced very differently in mundane and ritual contexts, let us now examine the role of the cedar tree in the socio-religious sphere. The existence of cedar crests evidences the tree's significance, even if the term is somewhat improper,[4] the notion of 'crest' here functioning less as a classificatory marker than as a means of recognising the tree's enormous contribution to human welfare. The Haida Indians adopted the cedar tree as their crest. Swanton (1905: 143, 268) reports that some members of the Haida Raven clan tattooed it on their forearms. The Kwakiutl Indians exhibited button blankets ornamented with the 'tree of life' during ceremonies. Amongst the Skokomish Indians, the cedar is a cultural hero who brings fire to the people. One of the Skokomish myths tells about the cedar's ability to transform, through the power of a song, a family of half-human, half-salmon beings into true humans (Pavel *et al.* 1993: 59–60). One of the Kwakiutl tribes still considers Red Cedar Man (*Hawelkwelatl*) as their ancestor. Red Cedar Man saved his family by sheltering them inside a red cedar tree during the great flood. He then learnt how to perform the red cedar bark ceremony, the main winter ritual of the Kwakiutl Indians.[5]

The Tree, the Group and the Individual in Northwest Coast Indian Languages

Compared to zoological idioms, which are very common in Northwest Coast languages, botanical idioms are relatively few.[6] For example, the descent group or *numaym* is more commonly portrayed as an animal. In some cases, however, contrastive metaphors of trunk and roots are found, as in Kwakwa'la, the language of the Kwakiutl, where they express the contrasting positions of chief and group members. The chief, the 'post of our world' (*?upik*), is also known as 'the only one standing in the world', 'the cedar that cannot be spanned', and 'root of the tribe'. These metaphors[7] express the chief's status and greatness with reference to tree parts (trunk and roots) and their characteristics. The chief's ancestors are said to be 'the root of the tree'. The hierarchical structure of the *numaym* is also expressed through a tree idiom. The chief, who in animal metaphors is represented as the 'head', has now become the body of a great cedar tree; the group as a whole forms the tree's branches, and the commoners the 'men of the trunk'. Some Kwakiutl groups used the word for 'the post of heaven that holds up the sky' (*o!pek*) to characterise the chief (Berman 1991: 83–4; Boas 1921: 836; 1929: 234–5). The *o!pek* is visualised as a bridge to the sky, who links distinct worlds together. Applied to the chief's person, the metaphor defines the chief's ability to establish relationships with the underworld, the earth and heaven. When a chief and his heir die together, it is said that 'both tree and root were killed' (Curtis 1915: 113). Tree symbolism expresses both rootedness in the past, and continuity in the future.

Trees, Life and Death

Given their biological characteristics, trees make ideal metaphors to convey the notions of growth, strength[8] and longevity. Trees (especially cedars) that tower above seventy metres and are a thousand years old[9] provide suitable cognitive models for native theories of human and social experience. Throughout his or her life a Northwest Coast Indian performed many private and collective rituals, which all included, in one form or another, the use of cedar. To ensure a child's good health, the Kwakiutl either wrapped the placenta in cedar bark or buried it at the foot of a live cedar tree (Boas 1921: 606–7). Before receiving a name, a child's bond to life was considered extremely brittle; so the absorption of the placenta – a living substance – by a tree known to live such a long life was seen as helping the child to establish a stronger link to life, and live a long life as well (Walens 1981: 110). The Lummi, who also placed the afterbirth in the stump of a large and robust tree, would fasten the placenta to the topmost limbs of a cedar tree if they wanted the child to grow brave and courageous. Many Tlingit rituals aimed at extending the life-span focused on a tree growing at the edge of the forest. Soiled baby diapers and the dishes and clothes of secluded pubescent girls were burnt and pounded on to old trees stumps to ensure that infants and young girls would live a long life (de Laguna 1972: 764, 522, 528). The same tree was used to tie the clothes of a survivor during rituals aimed at preventing the recurrence of drowning (de Laguna 1972: 538). A bewitched person had to go into the forest to pray to the trees, or confess his or her wrongdoing (Boas 1966: 157–8; Curtis 1915: 77; de Laguna 1972: 735). The spiritual force of trees was thought to ward off the dangers associated with witchcraft and illnesses. It was also seen as a means to attain the degree of cleanliness required for participating in rituals, following the belief that cleanliness attracted the good will of supernatural beings. Cedar wood and bark were considered to have special cleansing properties, particularly effective against the pollution associated with death. Among the Kwakiutl, one could protect one's body from decaying like the corpse one had been in contact with, by rubbing the contaminated skin with cedar bark floss (Curtis 1915: 54). Trees, therefore, were clearly central cultural vehicles for the communication of significant ideas and values.

Trees, moreover, were associated with human mortality, in marked contrast with stones, symbols of immortality. A Tsimshian myth dealing with human origin tells the story of Elderberry Bush and Stone laying in labour at the same time. Elderberry Bush gave birth first, and this is why, says the myth, humans are mortal and their skin soft. Had Stone been the first to give birth, people would be immortal beings with a skin as hard as stone (Boas 1930[1895]: 278; 1916: 620; Cove 1987: 51–2). The Tlingit's creator and cultural hero Raven is immortal, for he is made of stone (de Laguna 1972: 856). The Tlingit also say that Raven, the trickster, created men out of rotten wood or leaves. This is why people are mortal. After the flood, Raven tried to make people by using both a rock and a leaf, but the rock was too slow, and the leaf too quick, so humans came from the leaf, and were, therefore, doomed to die (Swanton 1909: 462). The opposition between trees and stones is not as clear-cut in rituals as it is in myths. Stones were sometimes associated with long life. The Tlingit, for example, who surrounded secluded young girls with stones symbolising their future children, hoped that the latter would live a long life (Kan 1989: 388).[10]

Attitudes towards Trees

Philippe Descola (1992: 114–15) has observed that '[A]nimic systems do not treat plants and animals as mere signs or as privileged operators of taxonomic thought: they treat them as proper persons, as irreducible categories.' Indeed, on the Northwest Coast, trees are endowed with many human characteristics. Trees have a sentient life, they have a 'soul', and are capable of feelings and thoughts just like people (Boas 1921: 1220; 1927: 616; 1966: 155; de Laguna 1972: 822). They respond to the sentiments humans hold towards them, and if they cry upon dying, it is to express the pain people feel at the sight of a dead tree (Pavel *et al.* 1993: 76). The Kwakiutl consider a cut down tree to be 'killed' (Curtis 1915: 11). Trees are also endowed with the faculty of speech. The Bella Coola, for instance, considered that trees and people could speak to each other, and, although human beings had forgotten the language of trees, trees could still understand human speech (McIlwraith 1992 [1948]: 91–2). One could talk to a tree, and address it in prayers. Being proper people, trees were treated like people.

In many Northwest Coast languages, a term-for-term correspondence is established between constituent parts of human physiology and vegetal elements. Trees are made of flesh (wood) and skin (bark) (Walens 1981: 51). They are conceived as having physical characteristics similar to those of humans, such as faces (Boas 1966: 157), arms and legs. Like humans, cedar trees wear clothes. Amongst the Tlingit, the stages of tree growth and maturation are talked about in terms of fluids and tissues. A mature tree – from one foot to two feet in diameter – is called *sha'gee* (from *sha*, 'blood'), owing to its bark's reddish colour. In reference to the immature character of its wood, a young tree is named *tuckle*, literally 'cartilage' (Emmons 1903: 233–4). However, these equivalences of attributes or, rather, these mutual connections of attributes do not apply at all levels. If a real identification – as, for example, in Kwakiutl thought – exists between animals and humans, such is not the case between trees and humans, or, at least, a similar identification has never been clearly documented.

Let us take the equivalence between trees, animals and human beings with regard to sexual life and reproduction.[11] Whereas sexual intercourse between humans and animals forms the central theme of numerous myths, very few myths deal with sexual intercourse between humans and trees. One of these rare exceptions is the Tlingit myth 'The image that came to life' (Swanton 1909: 181–2), which tells the story of a young Haida chief whose wife died soon after the wedding. Crushed with grief over such insuperable loss, the chief asked a carver to make a statue in his wife's image out of cedar wood. He dressed the sculpture with his wife's clothes, and, considering it a living being, began to copulate with it. Some time later the carving, which had so far never talked, started to produce a sound like that of cracking wood.

The chief soon found a young tree growing underneath the wooden carving. As Lévi-Strauss remarked (1993: 174), 'Plants (trees) can only beget plants (trees); a wooden woman can only give birth to a tree' (Lévi-Strauss 1993: 176, my translation). The matter is entirely different when it comes to sexual intercourse between humans and animals. Humans and animals beget humans *and/or* animals, for animals are considered to be made of an inner substance which, being essentially human, has been transformed into an animal form through the animal skin. Consequently, sexual relationships between animals and humans, unlike those between humans and trees, are not subject to moral disapproval. A Tsimshian version of the above myth actually specifies that to take a wooden statue for wife and to copulate with it is utterly immoral (Lévi-Strauss 1993: 175).

Trees, especially cedar trees, were considered to be animate beings imbued with both material and spiritual value. They were believed to possess a spirit or a living force that humans should respect when interacting with trees. Conversely, this living force or vital energy could be communicated to humans, and help them throughout their lives.[12] This living force explains why wooden objects were regarded as living substances. The reddish colour of cedar wood, equated with blood, gave it the supernatural force that the Kwakiutl called *nawalak*, the spirit flowing through the tree's vital parts. For the Kwakiutl, all objects made of cedar wood or bark (poles, planks, ceremonial paraphernalia, and so forth) were alive, for they were the products of the transformation of 'something' alive. In Goldman's (1975: 19) words, wooden objects 'are forms of life that undergo transformations, becoming all other forms. From this point of view one does not speak of images carved in wood, but of wood transformed [...].'

Like many animistic systems, the cosmic world (the total sum of what existed) of the Northwest Coast peoples was essentially fixed in terms of quantity. The universe, to and from which nothing could be either added or subtracted, formed a complete and closed-in circuit within which a constant amount of soul-substance was flowing, and, despite its continuous transformations, preserved (Goldman 1975; Mauzé 1993). In this system, based on the understanding that 'natural beings possess their own spiritual principles and that it is possible for humans to establish with these entities personal relations of a certain kind – relations of protection, seduction, hostility, alliance, or exchanges of services' (Descola 1992: 114), humans and non-humans had developed a relationship based on mutual reciprocity, mutual need and mutual care for each other's existential and reproductive needs.

The need to exploit and utilise natural elements was fully recognised by Northwest Coast peoples. But so was the obligation to treat them with reverence and respect. Thus house-builders or canoe-makers did not fell trees at random. The soundness of the wood of a tree destined to be cut down was first tested by chiselling a hole in the trunk. When planks were needed, they were sometimes split from a standing tree. This practice was not only advantageous in terms of time and energy-saving; it also protected the tree's life. It is with the same respect for a tree's life and continued growth that women harvested bark with extreme care, always leaving enough bark on the tree for sap circulation to continue, and choosing trunks that would not be harmed by the partial removal of their bark. A canoe-maker would always fast and pray in order to find the right tree. Before cutting a tree, the Kwakiutl would pray and offer gifts to its spirits; the Tlingit would lit a fire and pour oil or some other aliment to feed the tree spirits (de Laguna 1972: 735). Before taking a board from a living tree, a house-builder would address the tree by saying: 'We have come to beg a piece from you today' (Curtis 1915: 11). A standing tree was called *ketsoq* in Kwakwa'la, literally 'begged for'. A man about to fell a tree would ask the trunk to fall in the right direction, begging it not to hit other trees on its way down, and not to land too heavily on the ground (Boas 1921: 616–17). The Tlingit used to scatter eagle down on the felling site to prevent falling trees from injuring fellow-trees (de Laguna 1972: 735). Such procedures, based on gratitude and on the acknowledgement that trees were giving up their lives for the benefit of humans, were directed at ensuring a good supply of natural resources for future years. It is because they explicitly and emphatically acknowledged the central role played by the life-giving cedar in their lives, that Northwest Coast native peoples addressed them with supplicatory expressions such as 'Long Life Maker', 'Life Giver', 'Healing Woman', or 'Friend and Supernatural One'.[13] The reproduction of trees, like that of all other living beings, was considered to depend on ritual performance. This is why tree-fellers, canoe-makers and bark-collectors performed appropriate rituals to release the souls of trees, a necessary condition for their rebirth. With proper ritual treatment, the organic part (flesh, skin, or their equivalent) could be consumed or used, while the soul remained intact. However, Goldman (1975: 3) notes that '[T]he specific relationships between men and plants, and between men and animals are significantly distinctive. Plants may require generalized respect, but because of their closeness to the human species, animals make demands comparable to those of humans.' Did the preservation of the generalised social sphere equilibrium depend on a relationship of reciprocal substitution between humans and trees to the same extent as it depended on the reciprocal substitution between humans and animals? The question remains open.

Trees, Culture and Politics

Northwest Coast rhetoric on sacred trees makes heavy use of metaphors, which can be understood, misunderstood, debated and interpreted; it is, therefore, inherently 'open-ended'. It is also, to borrow Armin Geertz' insightful analysis of Hopi prophecy, both 'authoritative', for it 'consists in a series of dogmatic statements', and inflective, in the sense that 'meaning can be changeable, malleable, and absorbing new details and interpretations [...]' (Geertz 1992: 9–12). I approach the issue of tree symbolism in contemporary Northwest Coast Native discourse as an empirical problem, and do not claim that my analysis exhausts all possible interpretations. The core data under analysis in this section come from two publications funded by the 'National Native Alcohol and Drug Abuse Program' of Health and Welfare Canada, which focus on the 'sacred tree' and the 'tree of life' as main symbols of native welfare and identity, and from an article published three years ago. This article, entitled 'Too Long, Too Silent: The Threat to Cedars and the Sacred Ways of the Skokomish' was written by three authors, a 'traditional spiritual leader', an 'assistant professor of education' and 'an attorney'. It illustrates very well the context in which Native environmentalist and political discourses are emerging today. Emphatically presented as expressing Native views, with phrases such as 'our tribe', 'in a traditional voice', or 'survival of our traditional culture', this article has a clear political message to deliver: the protection of old-growth forests symbolised by cedar trees is the necessary condition for the survival of Native culture. Its objective is to convince the Federal Government that old-growth forests are sacred sites, which, therefore, should fall under the protection of the 1978 American Indian Religious Freedom Act.[14]

'Traditional' worldviews and perceptions of nature undoubtedly inspire the new Native discourse on the environment, which is also influenced by deep ecology ideals. Given that Native people are widely seen to behave respectfully towards – and live in harmony with – nature, and given that they are often considered to be genuine ecologists, or, even, North America's first conservationists,[15] the complementarity of contemporary Native and environmentalist discourses is not surprising.

Moreover, Native people do not hesitate, in their efforts to build political alliances with environmentalist groups, to invoke the myth of pre-contact harmony.

Deep ecologists argue that the natural environment has intrinsic value. In Altman's (1994: 17) words, '[D]eep ecology holds that life is interconnected at the most fundamental levels, and that we must strive to listen to and understand the other voices of nature in order to better perceive the needs of our planetary home.' The views of deep ecologists centre on a 'natural contract' – in opposition to a 'social contract' – which would grant rights and protection to natural elements. As pointed out by Luc Ferry (1992: 28, my translation), '[M]an is no longer considered to be at the centre of the world; it is therefore no longer essential that he receives protection from himself; rather, it is now the cosmos as such that should be protected from human beings.' This kind of discourse ontologises natural beings in a way slightly different from the way in which 'traditional' Native discourse does. Here, the matter is not that trees can potentially become human beings, but, rather, that they are *moral beings*. Some of the expressions chosen by the authors of the article mentioned earlier are revealing: 'The threat to Cedar', 'the wanton genocide of other beings', 'the fate of Cedar is so precarious', or 'the slaughter of Cedar' (Pavel *et al.* 1993: 53, 55, 56, 75). Trees are seen to contain the knowledge humans need to deal adequately with other living species. The destruction of trees is equated to a loss of culture, and a lack of respect for both humans and non-humans. The idea that the Golden Age era (when the relationship between humans and natural entities was entirely based on reciprocity) has ended, and that the demise of any one species threatens the world's equilibrium, on which this romanticised vision is founded, find a parallel in the precept that people must now protect endangered species, for, by doing so, they protect themselves as well. For the Skokomish spiritual leader, one of the essay's authors:

[T]he traditional educational system [...] provides human beings an opportunity to hypothetize that if another life form is in danger, then human beings are also in danger. If danger to another species is disregarded, this behavior could be manifested within the tribe and could lead to warring [sic] of the other people against one another. Protecting other life forms from extinction, particularly Cedar, then becomes the principal means to protect humanity.

In positing 'natural' beings as fundamental objects this statement explicitly centres on the idea that the survival of nature and especially of trees will depend on the will of human beings. Somehow this point of view is true to the traditional native idea that species need each other to live and reproduce. Trees are sacred. One is struck by the extensive use Native people make of the word 'sacred' in North America and, indeed, elsewhere in the world. The word 'sacred' has been so over-used in political contexts, that its original meaning is now almost undetectable under the layers of new meanings. These meanings, derived in part from the Western New Age notion that religion and nature are one and the same thing, refer to specific relations between societies and their natural environments. Consequently, Native peoples are adopting as theirs the slightly misleading conception that everything in 'Indian' life is 'sacred', because Indian cultures do not distinguish a separate religious domain (Feest 1995). The expression 'sacred trees', therefore, could be interpreted as a motto that reifies both culture and religion. I am tempted to see in such Northwest Coast representations of nature and conceptualisations of relationships between humans and natural beings the creative work of Native leaders involved in land claims and repatriation of native artefacts issues within specific judicial contexts (Feest 1995: 33–42).

Symbols, concepts and notions may be borrowed from other North American Native groups, or from Western philosophy. They may combine distinct local belief systems to produce a generic system of thought, in which each constitutive element has equal value, and can serve any cause. The notion of sacred trees, for example, has been characterised in the following way:

> A tree becomes sacred through recognition of the power that it expresses. This power may be manifested as the food, shelter, fuel, materials used to build boats, or medicine that the tree provides [...]. Sacred trees have also provided beauty, hope, confort, and inspiration, nurturing and healing the mental, emotional, and spiritual levels of our being. They are symbols of abundance, creativity, generosity, permanence, energy and strength (Altman 1994: 9).

This characterisation and philosophy are found in almost identical terms in the booklet on sacred trees produced by the 'National Native Alcohol and Drug Abuse Program' of Health and Welfare Canada:

For all the people of the earth, the Creator has planted a Sacred Tree under which they may gather, and there find healing, power and wisdom, and security. The roots of this tree spread deep into the body of Mother Earth.[16] Its branches reach upward like hands praying to Father Sky. The fruit of this tree are the good things the Creator has given to the people: teaching to show the path of love, compassion, generosity, patience, wisdom, justice, courage, respect, humility and many other wonderful gifts (Anonymous 1984: 7).

Trees do not merely symbolise moral values; they also epitomise the loss of nature and purity. Indeed, given their great longevity, they are thought to be the living witnesses of the idealised pre-contact period that preceded the era of destruction brought by the white man:

Because many of the old-growth Cedar predate the coming of the white man, they are our link to more pure times before the land was desecrated and razed [...] We need a place where old-growth trees, especially the Red Cedar, live along with young trees; where we know our shrines will be unmolested; where we can obtain Cedar for ceremonial purposes; where we can go for retreat and meditation with our Grandmother, the Cedar; and where we can take our spiritual baths unmolested (Pavel *et al.* 1993: 64).

This statement, aimed at presenting convincing arguments on the historical link between Northwest Coast people (in this case, the Skokomish), the cedar tree and old-growth forests, should thus be read as a political statement in defence of ancestral lands on the ground that they are sacred and essential for religious practices. Spiritual leaders often try to give more weight to what they say by using Christian analogies. For example, they may define a sacred site, a significant element of aboriginal religion, through Christian idioms. A sacred site thus becomes a place 'where Cedar grows in a natural state' (Pavel *et al.* 1993: 73) and where '[Northwest Coast Indians] take the new initiates of [their] ancient secret society for purpose of isolation, meditation, spiritual cleansing, ritual bathing and schooling. [These sites are their] church, [their] school, [their] drugstore, and [their] monastery. The things that dwell in these sites are the teachers of [their] people' (Pavel *et al.* 1993: 77-8). The author (ibid.) adds in a similar vein that: '[T]he old-growth Cedars are our holy shrines, just as the church of the Dome of the Rock is held to be the birthplace of the Christ. The old-growth Cedar is equally holy to us.'

In promoting cedars to the status of sacred trees, Native peoples are fighting against massive clear-cutting.[17] Cedar preservation is more often a matter of cultural and political survival than one of ecological survival. Many groups in British Columbia are promoting research on aboriginal forest management practices, for example, culturally modified trees (CMTs).[18] CMTs, moreover, are proofs of the long history of occupation of Indian ancestral territories. As such, they are also citable for land claim litigation purposes (Stryd and Eldridge 1993). Native discourse rarely focuses on the conservation of biodiversity or the balance of the ecosystem from a Western point of view; it rarely deals with local forestry politics on reservation lands. It should not, therefore, be confused with Western environmentalist discourses. The two may actually conflict, as in the recent case of two chiefs from the sensitive area of Clayoquot Sound on the West Coast of Vancouver Island, who recently approved new logging permits, allowing the clear-cutting of ancient forests in that region, despite the fact that Native peoples now have veto power over such decisions.[19] In former times, tree representations, relations between men and trees, and ritual activities involving trees were all constituted on the basis of techno-economic relationships. My contention is that the modification of these techno-economic relations has allowed the development of an asserted discourse rooted in political and social strategy.

Conclusion

This chapter has first offered a survey of the various symbolic uses of trees found in the Northwest Coast ethnographic literature. The data examined here are necessarily heterogeneous; and, as the ways in which trees are talked about, used in ritual contexts, or socially included are so varied, no unique meaning has been attached to tree symbolism. The second part of the chapter has explored the making of tree symbolism by native leaders, who piece together fragments from aboriginal conceptualisations of trees with bits from contemporary ecological Western discourse. It would be illegitimate to lump together in a single category the various symbolic practices found and suppose them to form a single vehicle for mental representations. Were one to find symbolic unity, it would be at the cost of ethnographic truth, for it could only be achieved by creating a new and separate level of discourse. Meaning defined through use can never be unitary.

Acknowledgements

I am grateful to Maurice Bloch, George Lenclud and Laura Rival for their helpful suggestions. I also wish to thank Margaret Seguin for providing me with invaluable information.

Notes

1. See in particular Bloch (1992) on this debate. Bloch (1992, 1993) proposes a new direction of investigation that I am following here.

2. Lakoff and Johnson (1980: 36) remark that '[M]etaphor and metonymy are different kinds of processes. Metaphor is principally a way of conceiving of one thing in terms of another. Metonymy, on the other hand, has primarily a referential function, that is, it allows us to use one entity to stand for another.' The authors also point out that 'in the case of metonymy THE PART FOR THE WHOLE there are many parts that can stand for the whole'.

3. Economically the most important wood in the Northern area.

4. Plants and trees are actually not widespread as crests. As noted by M. Halpin (1984: 27) 'Plants form a very small category of crests of limited distribution' among the Tsimshian-Gitksan. According to a Kwakiutl woman, the design of a tree on a button blanket is called *Gwa'ka'lee'la'la'*, which means 'tree of life'. 'Our use of cedar', she adds, 'is symbolized here' (in Jensen and Sargent 1986: 43). The cedar or 'tree of life' as a crest is not a clan or a *numaym* crest; it should be considered a visual symbol reflecting a people's practice.

5. After the flood, *Halwelkwalath* changed his name for *Tseqame*. He was taught to weave cedar head bands, wrist wrings and ankle rings. *Tseqame* then taught the red cedar bark ceremony to the neighbouring tribes.

6. According to Margaret Seguin, the Tsimshian language has seven counting systems based on the classification of what is counted. One of them is for long things and the classifier morpheme is based on the word for tree (M. Seguin, personal communication).

7. See Sandor (1986: 103), who notes that 'metaphors always express equivalences, the point being that some equivalences, i.e. identifications, are considered as metaphoric because they cannot be accepted as literally true, as direct predication'.

8. Commonplace expressions such as 'as strong as a cedar' were currently used (Curtis 1915: 94).

9. Even a fallen tree remains sound for about a hundred years, thanks to protective oils and their fungicidal properties.

10. De Laguna (1972: 538) refers to stones as a means of protection against premature death in the case of a woman who has lost her first husband.

11. To my knowledge, this domain has never been investigated. Lévi-Strauss (1993) touches upon this question when referring to the status of the North-west Coast artist and his work.

12. The power of the cedar was said to be so strong that the tree's inner force could be absorbed through contiguity, just by leaning one's back against the trunk.

13. The same honorific names were also used for animals. Sometimes, kinship terms, for example, Grandmother (Pavel *et al.* 1993: 64) or Elder Sister (Boelscher 1988: 22), were used as marks of respect.

14. In Canada neither the *Constitution Act* nor the *Charter of Rights and Freedoms* provides any specific guarantee of First Nations' religious freedom.

15. See for example the last chapter ('Indian Wisdom for Today') in *North American Indian Ecology* (Hughes 1996). The author asserts that Euro-American society has a lot to learn from the Native American way of thinking and practice, if it wants to find the right answers to the ecological crisis.

16. On the North-west Coast, the notion of sacred is now connected to the idea of harmony with Mother Earth (Pavel *et al.* 1993). It has been demonstrated that the notion of Mother Earth in North America is part of the mythology invented by Western scholars. It is not a historical and ethnographic reality for all Native American Indians. However, the fictive notion of Mother Earth is accepted with almost no discussion by contemporary Native environ-mentalists, for whom Mother Earth has become *the* symbol of their struggles (Gill 1990: 129–43).

17. Their battles over land use are supported by local artists. Yuxweluptun (Lawrence Paul), a Salish artist who 'risks [...] the clichéd affinity between native and nature [...]' (Townsend-Gault 1995: 17), for he 'is not painting landscape but land claims' (Townsend-Gault 1995: 7), considers himself a political activist. He denounces the coloniser's disastrous impact on the colonised environment in works such as *Clear-Cut Logging on Native Sovereign Lands, Shaman Coming to Fix* (1991); *Reservation Native Surrounded by Supernatural Clear-Cuts* (1993); *MacMillan Bloedel Eco-System Destroyers and their Preferred Weapons* (1994).

18. A CMT is 'a tree which has been intentionally altered by Native people participating in the traditional use of the forest' (Stryd and Eldridge 1993: 184).

19. Another example is that of the Makah band of Washington State, which announced in May 1995 its plans to harpoon five grey whales a year (the species has recently been removed from the list of endangered species), an action symbolising the survival of the band's traditional culture. Such actions are likely to threaten the support of environmentalists for aboriginal rights.

References

Altman, N., *Sacred Trees*, San Francisco: Sierra Club Books, 1994

Anonymous, *The Sacred Tree*, Lethbridge, Alberta: Four Worlds Development Press (Funding provided by National Native Alcohol and Drug Abuse Program of Health and Welfare Canada), 1984

Berman, J., 'The Seal's Sleeping Cave: The Interpretation of Boas' Kwakwa'ala Texts', unpublished doctoral dissertation, University of Pennsylvania, 1991

Bloch, M., 'What goes without saying: the conceptualization of Zafimaniry society', in A. Kuper (ed.), *Conceptualizing Society*, London: Routledge, 1992

—— 'Domain-specificity, living kinds and symbolism', in P. Boyer (ed.), *Cognitive Aspects of Religious Symbolism*, Cambridge: Cambridge University Press, 1993

Boas, F., *Tsimshian Mythology*, Annual Report of the Bureau of American Ethnology, 1909–1910, Washington, DC: Government Printing Office, 1916

—— *Ethnology of the Kwakiutl*, Bureau of American Ethnology, Thirty-Fifth Annual Report, Parts 1 and 2, Washington, DC: Government Printing Office, 1921

—— 'Religious terminology of the Kwakiutl', *Festschrift Meinhof*, Hamburg, pp. 386–92, 1927. Reprinted in *Race, Language and Culture*, 1940, New York: The Free Press

—— 'Metaphorical expressions in the language of the Kwakiutl', 1929. Reprinted in *Race, Language and Culture*, 1940, New York: The Free Press

—— *The Religion of the Kwakiutl Indians* (Columbia University Contributions to Anthropology, Part 2, translations), New York: Columbia University Press, 1930

—— *Kwakiutl Ethnography*, edited by H. Codere, Chicago: The University of Chicago Press, 1966

Boelscher, M., *The Curtain Within. Haida Social and Mythical Discourse*, Vancouver: University of British Columbia Press, 1988

Cove, J., *Shattered Images. Dialogues and Meditations on Tsimshian Narratives*, Ottawa: Carleton University Press, 1987

Curtis, E., *The North American Indian*. Vol. 10, *The Kwakiutl*. New York: Johnson Reprint Company Ltd, 1915

De Laguna, F., *Under Mount Saint Elias. The History and Culture of Yakutat Tlingit*, 3 vols, Washington: Smithsonian Institution Press, 1972

Descola, P., 'Societies of nature and the nature of societies', in A. Kuper (ed.), *Conceptualizing Society*, London: Routledge, 1992

Emmons, G. T., *The Basketry of the Tlingit*, 1903. Reprint Edition with Appendices, 1993 by the Friends of the Sheldon Jackson Museum for the Sheldon Jackson Museum, Alaska State Museums, Division Libraries, Archives and Museums Sate of Alaska

Feest, C. F., '"Repatriation": a European view on the question of restitution of Native American artifacts', *European Review of Native American Studies*, 9(2), 1995, pp. 33–52

Ferry, L., *Le nouvel ordre écologique. L'arbre, l'animal et l'homme*, Paris: Grasset & Fasquelle, 1992

Geertz, A., *The Invention of Prophecy. Continuity and Meaning in Hopi Indian Religion*, Los Angeles: University of California Press, 1992

Gill, S., 'Mother Earth: An American Myth', in J. Clifton (ed.), *The Invented Indian. Cultural Fictions & Government Policies*, New Brunswick (USA): Transaction Publishers, 1990

Goldman, I., *The Mouth of Heaven. An Introduction to Kwakiutl Religious Thought*, New York: John Wiley & Sons, 1975

Gunther, E., *Ethnobotany of Western Washington. The Knowledge and Use of Indigenous Plants by Native Americans*, Seattle: The University of Washington Press, 1973

Halpin, M., 'The structure of Tsimshian totemism', in J. Miller and C. M. Eastman (eds), *The Tsimshian and their Neighbors of the North Pacific Coast*, Seattle: University of Washington Press, 1984

Hughes, J. D., *North American Indian Ecology*, 2nd edn, El Paso, Texas: Texas Western Press, 1996

Jensen, D. and P. Sargent, *Robes of Power. Totem Poles on Cloth*, Museum Note No. 17, Vancouver: University of British Columbia Press in association with the UBC Museum of Anthropology, 1986

Kan, S., *Symbolic Immortality*, Washington: Smithsonian Institution Press, 1989

Lakoff, G. and M. Johnson, *Metaphors We Live By*, Chicago: Chicago University Press, 1980

Lévi-Strauss, C., *Regarder écouter lire*, Paris: Plon, 1993

McIlwraith, T. F., *The Bella Coola Indians*, 2 vols (1st edn 1948), Toronto: University of Toronto Press, 1992

M'Gonigle, M., 'Native rights and environmental sustainability: lessons from the British Columbia wilderness', *The Canadian Journal of Native Studies*, 8(1), 1988, pp. 107–30

Mauzé, M., 'Preservation, Transformation and Power in the Kwak-waka'wakw Worldview', Paper given at the Conference on *The*

Symbolics of Spirit and Power in North American Native Traditions, Ottawa, 1993

Pavel, M., G. B. Miller and M. J. Pavel, 'Too long, too silent: the threat to cedar and the sacred ways of the Skokomish', *American Indian Culture and Research Journal*, 17(3), 1993, pp. 53–80

Rival L., 'The growth of family trees: understanding Huaorani perceptions of the forest', *Man* 28(4), 1993, pp. 635–42.

Sandor, A., 'Metaphor and belief', *Journal of Anthropological Research*, 42(2), 1986, pp. 101–22

Stewart, H., *Cedar. Tree of Life to the Northwest Coast Indians*, Vancouver: Douglas & McIntyre, 1984

Stryd, A. H. and M. Eldridge, 'CMT Archeology in British Columbia: The Meares Island Studies', *BC Studies*, 99, Autumn 1993, pp. 184–227

Swanton, J. R., *Haida Texts and Myths: Skidegate Dialect*, Washington: Bureau of American Ethnology, Bulletin 29, 1905

—— *Tlingit Myths and Texts*, Washington: Bureau of American Ethnology, Bulletin 39, 1909

Thomas, K., *Man and the Natural World. Changing Attitudes in England 1500–1800*, Harmonsworth: Penguin Books, 1984

Townsend-Gault, C., 'The Salvation Art of Yuxweluptun' in *Lawrence Paul Yuxweluptun. Born to Live and Die on your Colonialist Reservations*, Vancouver: Morris and Helen Belkin Art Gallery, University of British Columbia, 1995

Turner, N., *Plants in British Columbia Indian Technology*, Victoria: British Columbia Provincial Museum, 1979

Turner N., R. Bouchard and D. Kennedy, *Ethnobotany of the Okanagan-Colville Indians of British Columbia and Washington*, Victoria: British Columbia Provincial Museum, 1980

U'Mista News, August 1995.

Walens, S., *Feasting with Cannibals*, Princeton: Princeton University Press, 1981

Representatives of the Past: Trees in Historical Dispute and Socialised Ecology in the Forest Zone of the Republic of Guinea, West Africa

James Fairhead and Melissa Leach

Introduction[1]

Since foresters and botanists first saw the forest patches that surround the villages in Kissidougou prefecture of the Republic of Guinea, they have considered them quite literally as 'nature': the last vestiges of the Upper Guinean forest block's northern extension. Supposing that the soils and climate of the region should support forest, they assume that it once did, and that the forest patches present today are relics of this past forest cover: a heritage that has survived the savannisation wrought elsewhere by local inhabitants (Adam 1948; Aubréville 1949; Chevalier 1933; République de Guinée 1988; Schnell 1952). For the region's Kissia and Kuranko[2] inhabitants, by contrast, these forest patches are quite literally cultured: encouraged to form through habitation and management, and the focus of cultural practice and social memories (Fairhead and Leach 1996).

In this chapter, we focus on issues concerning the origin and representation of these forest patches, their constituent trees, and other trees in Kissidougou's landscape. We begin by sketching some principal aspects of forest–savannah dynamics in the broad terms in which Kissia and Kuranko understand them, and as inseparable from everyday practice, long-term settlement and land-use history. Yet, as landscape features with histories, forest patches and their constituent trees do not have a single historical or symbolic significance shared by those who live with and use them. The diverse ways in which trees are represented partially reflect types of use, value, access and control. Furthermore, inasmuch as trees can mark events in social and political history, assertions concerning their origins and status can become strong statements in social and political disputes, as well as in those over material resources. Just as when foresters consider these forests as 'natural relics' they construct them as international and national heritage over which their institutions claim custodianship, so local land, tree rights, and claims over trees can be contested through struggles over cultural meanings (cf. Berry 1989; Moore 1993). Thus, although trees and forest patches are 'culture' in every sense of the word, we do not seek to identify a particular, 'authentic' cultural vision and knowledge of them; rather, we want to expose the field of interests and discourses within which they are represented. This perspective has the further advantage of avoiding casting these forests as relics of an indigenous culture in the modern world, in which forest conservation depends on the conservation of a particular culture (cf. Clad 1985; Wilson 1993).

Central to our perspective is an emphasis on the practical and everyday; on the ways that understandings of landscape components and ecological processes are linked to everyday interaction in landscape use. In this respect, several authors have emphasised the need to apprehend things experienced but not voiced; terming this the 'unmediated', 'non-representational' or 'practical knowledge' that is 'responsible for the phenomenal givens that people ordinarily apprehend' (Atran 1990; Rival 1993). But while it is important not to overlook this aspect of knowledge for lack of overt representation, it does place the analyst in a theoretical and political quagmire. As Fardon (1986) argues forcibly, when dealing with unrepresented experience, the interpreters and the theories of unrepresented knowledge they wield gain a privileged and unaccountable position in representational discourse – discourse that, as Ferguson (1990) and ultimately Foucault remind us, may have powerful instrumental effects. The danger of imputing excess symbolic association to issues concerning trees is all the more acute given the present Euro-American preoccupation with trees and forests. Recognition of this intractable problem underlies our interpretative emphasis on what villagers say. The fact that interpretation of landscape history and dynamics in local discourse relates not only to issues of ecology but also to the material results of access to and control over resources provides a further reason for concentrating on villagers' own diverse discourses. Historical ecology – like cultural ecology – cannot be restricted to a positivist exercise of understanding the status and evolution of landscape in relation to its use. It must also comprehend the political context in which different assertions about these are made.

Settled Islands in Savannah

Most of Kissidougou's 800 or more villages lie in open clearings in the middle of dense, semi-deciduous forest patches. These patches are small relative to the area of the surrounding savannah, within which they lie as distinctive islands. That the distribution of forest islands follows the distribution of settlement provides a strong spatial image of a basic local principle: that settled social life promotes forest establishment. It is the needs and activities associated with habitation that create reasons and enabling conditions for eliminating fire and concentrating fertility and woody resources around settlements, thus promoting the establishment of forest in previously savannah conditions.

Forest patches are also associated with once-inhabited village and farm hamlet sites (in Kuranko *tombondu*; in Kissie, *ce pomdo*). Villagers suggest that these forests exist today as the legacy of the everyday lives of past inhabitants. In Toly, one of the villages we studied, at least twelve such sites were identified. Five are associated with descent groups now living in the village. Their small forest islands have been carefully preserved. The other old sites are now farmed and fallowed, like the rest of the landscape. In the Kuranko study village, there were more than ten such old sites, each associated with particular founding families. Local observation that human settlement enables forest to establish contrasts sharply with the dominant perceptions of foresters and ecologists, here as elsewhere in the forest–savannah transition zone, that human activity has only a destructive or at best benign effect on forest cover (cf. Furley *et al.* 1992). Within local perspectives, the fact that forests are a corollary of settlement – a social creation – contrasts them with other parts of the landscape that owe their form to less overt management, or even to the unmediated agency of God. For such forest patches the questions of who created and shaped the island, and when and how, carry salience in issues of access and control over its resources.

Forest patch distribution also follows the distribution of water in the landscape. Sometimes, settlements are themselves established by a rocky outcrop that concentrates water, the better to enable forest growth, or beside a stream, using and extending its strip of gallery (riparian) forest to form an encircling island. In other cases, water-related forest patches exist separately from village sites: in the network of gallery and inland valley swamp forests that dissect the landscape, and in the small forest patches on rocky hills that have good water reserves.

Villagers also recognise how certain forms of cultivation improve soil–water relations by promoting water infiltration and its storage. They thus encourage the establishment of dense vegetation by tipping the successional balance against savannah grasses. Such changes result especially from the long-term application of gardening-like cultivation techniques in savannahs (Leach and Fairhead 1994). The repeated mounding and organic matter incorporation during 'gardening' of peanuts and root crops 'opens' and 'ripens' the soil, making it 'oily', and creating conditions in which trees can more easily establish once gardening ceases. Such patches of long-occupied and worked 'anthropogenic' soils with improved water relations are a characteristic of old habitation sites (*tombondu*) where there used to be gardens. And where farmers purposefully ripen soils elsewhere, they metaphorically liken the resulting land to the land of such old sites (*i ba sene san siama, du di mo, a di ke tombondu di* – if you cultivate for many years, the soil will ripen, it will become *tombondu*).

The concentration of woody vegetation in lived in, socialised spaces is likened by villagers to its concentration on termite mounds. The spatial association between termite 'settlements' (mounds) and forest patches in many ways parallels the association in the human world, providing Kissia and Kuranko with a powerful metaphor for their own impact on vegetation. Villagers have a profound understanding of termite social organisation, and recognise in it a social world parallel to their own: one of male and female chiefs, and of different categories of workers (cf. Fairhead and Leach 1994). Recognising the concentration of fertility and water availability in and around termite-worked soils, farmers take advantage of certain types of termite mound as 'gardens' for vegetable planting. But if not cultivated by people, soils improved by termites tend to develop dense woody growth. In this sense they parallel gardens, which develop a distinctive woody vegetation when fallowed. Similar pioneer tree species are typical of both cases (e.g. *Allophylus spicatus; Bridelia ferruginea; Nauclea latifolia; Newbouldia laevis*).[3]

The landscape also accommodates another parallel 'social' world, of djinn spirits (*nyina*). Villagers describe *nyina* as of many types and characters – as many as there are human beings – and too many to know, although many sorts are named. They consider them to have a 'social' existence, with many parallels to that lived by people, but also with some inversions of human social norms. For example, *nyina* live in towns and houses and make farms, but they eat their rice cold. People with special gifts of vision can strike up alliances with particular *nyina*. Exceptional abilities in farming, hunting or wealth-acquisition seemingly at odds with a person's social status are often explained in terms of *nyina* 'help'. However, because they can also make unexpected physical attacks or outrageous demands, villagers generally consider the proper and safe relationship between human and *nyina* society as one of separation and respectful distance. Such a relationship is sometimes secured through ritual offerings (cf. Jackson 1977: 37). While diverse landscape forms such as large rocks and pools are favourite resting places for *nyina,* there are also *nyina* villages (*nyina so* in Kuranko). Habitual *nyina* settlements, like human settlements and termite settlements, are generally associated with forest patches. Kuranko often refer to forest patches on rocky outcrops or groundwater-fed gallery forests as such *nyina's* places. Equally, some individual trees (often *Ceiba pentandra, Afzelia africana* or *Bombax buonopozense*) are also considered as the homes of particular *nyina*. Felling any such patches or trees without *nyina* consent and appropriate sacrifices can prompt harmful revenge. Certain chiefly lineages ascribe their power partly to an alliance they established with a particularly powerful *nyina* when the village was founded (cf. Jackson 1977: 36–7). In addition to securing the upholding of chiefly authority and that of ruling families, offerings to this *nyina* assure generalised prosperity. In Sandaya such offerings are made at a particular *Afzelia Africana* tree on the edge of a *Carapa procera* forest, widely regarded as the principal *nyina* village.

Representations of Forest Island Creation and Enrichment

For both Kissia and Kuranko, forest islands around villages play important roles in protecting the settlement from dry season bush fires, high winds and excessive heat. They also provide convenient sources of forest products and shelter for tree crops and social activities. In past periods of warfare, they were central to settlement fortification.

Today, villagers encourage forest island development more or less deliberately in the course of everyday life, occasionally by tree planting, but principally by creating the fire and soil conditions that favour forest regeneration in savannah. Villagers create fire-breaks to prevent annual savannah fires destroying their thatched houses and garden fences, largely through everyday activities that reduce the quantity of inflammable grasses on the village margins. Men collect thatch and fencing grass there, and families frequently tether their cattle in the forest patches during the farming season, as grazing and trampling diminish grass quantities. Early in the dry season, young men and elders alike set and monitor a controlled burn that eliminates the fuel for more threatening late-season fires. Thus protected, village-edge areas develop dense semi-deciduous moist forest vegetation over the years, and, as the island of forest expands, grass collection and grazing are gradually moved further out. The fertilisation of village-edge soils by the deposition of human and animal faeces, ash and household waste further encourages forest development. Villagers sometimes garden for a limited period around an inhabited settlement specifically to encourage forest establishment by removing grasses and ripening the soils. But the link between gardening and forest patch formation is more commonly manifested when once-gardened village and farm hamlet sites are abandoned, or when a new settlement is established on an old garden site.

While forest-promoting activities can be deliberately targeted, the individual activities that contribute to forest establishment are frequently undertaken without this outcome in mind. Forest island development in this sense depends on the diverse activities of village members, and not on deliberate management by community institutions. In certain villages, some elderly men and women – usually of landholding lineages – represent the formation of forest patches as occurring in a punctuated, but intentional way. Leaders of descent groups that claim founder status in a territory, and the political authority associated with this, often emphasise how their ancestors arrived in empty, relatively inhospitable savannah and initiated the beginnings of a forest island and a settlement there by planting 'starter' trees. As one Kissi elder said of his village, Yiffo: 'The firstcomers planted cotton trees. There is still one which carries the name of the planter' (cassette Ki39).[4] Some of these trees are attributed origins that emphasise the extraordinary capabilities of village founders (e.g. at Fondambadou an initial *Erythrophleum guineensis* tree grew from the founder's powerful staff placed in the ground). But founding trees are normally remembered more prosaically as individuals of fast-growing species that were transplanted from wildlings to suppress fire and accelerate rapid forest succession within their protection (using, for example *Triplochiton scleroxylon* and *Ceiba pentandra*).

Frequently, one – or more – of these founding trees becomes a marker of the establishment of an alliance or 'contract' with the land spirits: the contract that ensures a place for human settlement and reproduction, and for productive farming, hunting and fishing to sustain it. In Kuranko, it is usually the founding family that manages this contract and makes the sacrifices necessary to maintain it, often with the assistance of trained chief hunters or specialist 'medicine holders' (*basi ti*). In Kissi villages the land contract enshrined in foundational trees is usually managed by a family reputed to have been the first to bury a member in the new settlement: a role that is distinguished from political chieftaincy, which is assumed by other possible village founders. As an elder in Ningbeda succinctly put it: 'You have founded a village, you go, you build, he whose child dies first, it is he who is the land chief; even if you are the first in the village, you are not the land chief' (cassette Ki2). The representation of forest island origins in terms of the planting of initial trees is significant in upholding relations between lineages. For ruling families, the trees remain markers invoking historical planting events that legitimise their current social and political status.

Other 'punctuated' views of forest island origin draw on the planting of trees and establishment of forest islands as fortresses. From this perspective, the rings of large silk-cotton trees (*Ceiba pentandra*) and *Bombax buonopozense* encircling the village, which form a conspicuous feature of forest islands, are represented as having grown from the stakes of the stockades that were used in combination with ditches and closely-interplanted thorn bushes and lianas in pre-twentieth century fortification strategies. As the rings of closely staked cotton trees grew, trees were often trained for particular purposes. Some would have their apical meristem cut to promote a dense branch-spreading and interlocking crowns for maximum concealment, shade, and grass suppression and hence fire control. A few such trees would be fertilised and trimmed of their lateral branches to encourage rapid upward growth into lookout trees and gate posts. The training of trees to take on different forms – whether the spreading form known by Kuranko as *bolonani* (four arms/ branches) or tall straight forms suitable for timber – is a common practice in the region.[5]

For most village men and women, however, forest island development, if considered at all, is represented in a more gradual way. The origins of forest islands are simply the logical extension into the past of processes experienced in the present. It is unremarkable that the gradual, cumulative effect of diverse activities on savannah village margins should be the establishment and expansion of a belt of woodland. It is by no means all residents who relate a specific history of origin of the forest island they inhabit, especially if they have come from other localities as male immigrants or as wives moving to their husband's home at marriage. Among them, many suppose that the forest around their village has 'always' existed, while noting in other contexts that everyday activities cause the gradual extension of forest island area. Within this perspective, the rings of cotton trees tend to be interpreted as the overgrown relics of the living fence poles of past garden sites. People point out how effectively fence poles 'take' in fertile garden soils, and these tree species are among those used to make garden enclosures today. Such attribution of the origins of tree species or forests to everyday activities and gardening appeared to us to be particularly common among those with relatively little influence over lineage affairs, whether women or men. In effect, it locates forest island origins away from the domain of lineage politics, within which they are relatively powerless, and places it instead in a domain over which they have relatively more control (cf. Cashman 1991).

In addition to fortification, villagers have enriched and altered the species composition of forest islands for a wide range of purposes. As people of different gender, age and social position use and value island resources in different ways, the species composition in forest islands comes to reflect the patterning of socially varied priorities, albeit mediated by people's differential ability to realise them. Use priorities also change over time, so forest islands acquire a layering of changing enrichment legacies. From the first, forest islands were enriched with kola trees (*Cola nitida*), earning the Kissidougou region its ascription as part of *Worodu* (Kola-land) within Mande-speaking West Africa. The nuts produced in this area carry high value not only in local health and cultural practice, but also as an important trading commodity in long-established forest–savannah commerce. Women are culturally prohibited from planting and harvesting (though not trading) kola, but men frequently transplant wildlings and thus acquire individual control over the resulting tree, wherever it may be in the forest island. Both Kissia and Kuranko also plant kola with the buried umbilical cord of a newborn baby, to 'grow up with the child'. From the 1930s, men began to plant coffee in forest islands. Labour and tenure arrangements have excluded almost all women from this. When necessary, forest islands were extended to house more coffee, and were adapted by removing undergrowth and selectively thinning the canopy, leaving some trees for shade and valued timber, fruit and oilseed resources (e.g. *Afzelia africana, Khaya grandifoliola, Parinari excelsa, Elaeis guineensis*). More recently, coffee profitability has declined and bananas have come to be favoured as forest island tree crops, along with fruit trees, which are planted by women and children as well by men. All these tree crops are individually owned by their planters as heritable property. While some village forest islands are divided into individualised plots, complicated inheritance patterns and more spontaneous transplanting mean that people often have individual tenure over trees scattered throughout the island.

Other valued tree species also become concentrated in forest islands through their selective preservation, and occasionally transplanting. Tenure over such trees and their products is, however, frequently ambiguous. Those who nurture particular timber or medicinal trees in their coffee or kola plantations, for example, assert in conversation that these trees belong to them. Yet others can assert that the trees are under more generalised village control, on the grounds that they are there fortuitously, 'planted by God', and thus feel no obligation to respect the plantation owner's claims when seeking the produce. Oil palms are particularly ambiguous in this respect, whether in the forest island or on agricultural land elsewhere. Land under repeated cultivation tends to become enriched with oil palms, both because of the fire-protection that cultivation affords, and because of the self-seeding that palm-oil processing in fields encourages. Here, there is ambiguity between the claims of present cultivators, who may feel that through their using the land for several years, the palms are theirs; of those who cultivated the land in the past, claiming originally to have enriched the land with the palms; and of those who claim that the palms were 'planted by God' and are thus freely accessible to anyone.

'Sacred' Institutions in Forest Islands

Social memories evoked by the forest island are made explicit in the shrines devoted to past inhabitants and cult figures. The silk-cotton and *Triplochiton scleroxylon* trees planted by founders often become sites where present lineage members seek ancestral beneficence, often through sacrifices. In many forest islands, village hunters maintain an altar to the locality's most renowned hunters, who trace the ancestry of their skills and success ultimately to Mandenbori, the legendary father-figure of all hunters. In Kissi forest islands, a place is reserved for the burial of the first-dead children of each family, who unlike other people are buried 'with the land' rather than among the living in the inhabited village, and whose death is neither recognised nor mourned. Those buried in this way are locally termed *cuei pieeo*, literally 'child (buried in) the leaves' (Paulme 1950: 514): the leaves of *Newbouldia laevis*, a pioneer forest species that reproduces vegetatively and comes to dominate the burial site. Within most Kissi forest islands, there is an additional shrine to the chief land spirit (*Luande*), managed by the land chief lineage and with access strictly limited to initiated members of the men's society.

The men's society (*tooma vanpiandua* in southern Kissi areas) is an institution or 'secret society' that trains young men, during at least two initiation stages, in skills and knowledge central to male social roles. Initiates also learn to manage important aspects of community and inter-village life, as well as political relations. Schooling and society business take place in a delimited part of the forest island, which provides the necessary concealment of activities from women and non-initiates. The boundaries are made clear to potential trespassers by the planting of distinctive *Dracaena arborea* trees. The installation of this specialised arena for men's society business, and of the 'medicines' (*koan*), special plants and expertise needed to run the institution, is an important sign of a well-established, politically influential settlement, as distinct from a subordinate hamlet or farm camp. Women have a parallel initiation society (*tooma vanlandua*), which similarly educates young initiates, transacts women's business, and holds gender-specific knowledge, especially concerning fertility and reproduction. Women's society affairs are conducted at streamside locations, where shrines to female ancestors are maintained. The place is usually concealed from men and non-initiates by a forest patch, often a part of the village forest island.

In Kuranko regions, men and women also maintain particular forest spaces for initiation activities, often in the village forest island. Equally certain areas of the forest carry ancestral significance, and others are reserved for activities of men's societies such as *komo*. Several more northerly Kissi areas have these institutions rather than the *tooma* type found further south. Indeed, across all localities, there is great variation in secret society institutions. Throughout history, these have been acquired and discarded in different areas as they have gained and lost popularity. MacCormack (1980), for example, describes how Sherbro people nearer the coast 'bought' the joint male–female form of *tooma* from specialists invited from Kissi regions. Exclusively male societies that teach particular warfare skills, such as talking drums, have spread during the last two centuries from an origin that many Kissia trace to Loma country. In this respect, and as D'Azevedo (1962) has emphasised, secret society organisations – and their particular forms of vegetation manipulation – should be understood as a regional, rather than as an ethnic phenomenon.

Most forest islands thus contain male and female 'sacred' places. Yet their quality derives from the installation of the institutions in them, rather than inhering in any sacredness of 'forest' as a category in Kissi thought. This institutional quality equally applies to parts of the forest only, not its whole. These points have often been overlooked by foresters, who have attributed the preservation of forest relics around villages to their sacred character: in effect seeing them as islands of pristine nature in an otherwise profane and degraded landscape. The French term for the institutions, *forêt sacrée*, only serves to emphasise this vision. This perception, held by botanists in Guinea since the 1930s (e.g. Chevalier 1933) and persisting today among conservationists in Guinea and Africa more widely, erroneously attributes forest preservation to cultural beliefs about the forest and nature. Such a misperception is made possible only by considering local thought within Western notions of nature and culture.

Forest Representation in Ethnic Identity and Political Discourse

Foresters' and botanists' perception of the ethnic basis of *forêt sacrée* institutions have contributed to the stereotyping of the Kissia as a 'forest people', like other groups further south (Loma, Guerze), with cultural proclivities towards forest conservation. Since the early colonial period, the Kissia have been contrasted ethnically with the more northerly 'savannah people' of Mandinka origin – including Kissidougou's Kuranko populations. In the context of historical and ongoing southwards Mandinka migration, their fire-setting in savannah farming, honey collecting and hunting was considered responsible for southwards savannisation (Adam 1948). Where Kuranko lived within forest islands, this was perceived as a habit acquired from the Kissia, as it is by modern foresters and environmental policy-makers. This ethnic stereotyping of forest-related behaviour overlooks Kuranko practical knowledge and experience of forest island formation, as well as the fluid character of ethnic affiliation in a region of long-standing migration and political turbulence. Where Kuranko immigrants have moved into Kissi villages, they have often been incorporated into Kissia society and land management. Indeed, many supposedly 'forest' Kissi families can trace descent from a Mandinka family of savannah origin.

Nevertheless, as local politics have articulated with wider political structures, certain Kissia have come to draw on such stereotypes in their own assertions of identity. Islamic Mandinka groups have long played key roles in forest–savannah commerce, and, as powerful traders, have at times represented a threat to Kissia community cohesion and politico-economic interests. This was the emphasis of a man's description of his southern Kissi village in modern times: 'We do not have strangers here; the Mandinka came, but the youth chased them away because they were enriching themselves on the one hand and distracting the young girls on the other' (cassette Ki47). In such circumstances, attributions of forest-related behaviour can provide a powerful way of emphasising difference: 'When the Mandinka lived here, this was an open clearing. Wherever Mandinka sit down, you will not see forest' (cassette Ki 47).

During Guinea's First Republic, the regime of the President Sekou Touré pursued a 'demystification' policy, encouraging villages to move out of the mystified obscurity of their forest islands and into 'the open': the enlightened clarity and modernity upheld by the regime's cultural values, and the roadside world more accessible to the state's demands (Rivière 1969). This policy drew on and reinforced both ethnic stereotypes and their forest reference. It upheld the ideals of social clarity and of openness and simplicity in language and expression: of clear 'savannah language' (*kan gbe*) and lifestyles. These were already part of Mandinka (and Kuranko) self-representations, in contrast with the secrecy and obscurity of the forest culture and languages that they find difficult to learn; but they now became significant in maintaining a favourable relationship with the State. Many Kissia perceived Sekou Touré's regime as Mandinka-biased, and the attempts it made to evict Kissia from their forest islands and suppress *forêt sacrée* schools were interpreted as attempts to disempower the Kissi institution that had hitherto defended Kissia from Mandinka domination, whether cultural or military. The political conditions from 1958 to 1984 therefore reinforced the significance of forest symbolism in Kissidougou's local and ethnically-charged political discourse.

In this context, the privileging of the forest in national and international environmental discussions, and the images of forest loss and of threatened relics projected by the forestry service, have come to coincide with the broader politico-ethnic interests of the Kissia. Such interests were heightened in the run-up to Guinea's multi-party elections in December 1993. Sharing one forest – where the forest islands of neighbouring villages have come to touch each other – is one of the strongest metaphors of Kissi political solidarity, linked as it used to be to alliance in warfare and secret society initiation. The idea that the Kissi region could (even recently) have been united within one forest provides a politically appealing vision of unity, as does the analysis of forest loss as due to Mandinka immigration. The memory of forest islands as literal fortresses strengthens the association between forest and political defence in a modern world in which Kissi men's societies are still training youth in fortification and warfare techniques. Although the interpretation of forest islands as threatened relics is most often voiced within the politically influential urban Kissi community, it can also be heard in villages when rural Kissia use environmental images to make politico-ethnic points.

Felling Trees and Forests

Kissidougou's inhabitants consider neither forest islands nor the trees within them as objects for eternal preservation. Nor do they share foresters' reverence for the most voluminous trees. While large individuals are valued for fortification, shade, and certain food and ritual purposes, for many food, medicine and woodworking uses (poles, carving etc.) smaller trees are preferred, either from younger forest island growth or surrounding fallows and savannahs. Large forest hardwoods are difficult to work with local technology, and, as they get old, may become dangerous, threatening injury and house damage from unexpected tree or branch falls during seasonal high winds. In the past, specialist tree-fellers from more southerly Guekedou-Kissi, Loma or Mende localities where men's bush schools give training in high-forest felling skills and medicines (Leach 1994) would be invited in to remove troublesome overgrown trees. When this was impossible, the whole village would have to relocate.

These days, the same service can be performed by inviting in one of the numerous private chainsaw operators now active in the Kissidougou area. Since the early 1980s, commercial timber felling has become big business. But although in some circumstances villagers profit from it, it is generally a source of major tension. Given that the state forestry service claims a monopoly right to grant permits for timber felling, villagers' capacity to control it is extremely limited. State control over a list of forest species, part of national forestry policy since the early colonial period, is based on the idea of these trees as endangered 'natural patrimony'. This vision and its legal institutionalisation competes with customary tenurial claims over trees that villagers make on the grounds that the trees developed because of settlement, cultivation or active preservation. Despite the high value of their timber resources, villagers have generally been unable to negotiate higher returns than a standard one plank in ten. Loggers cannot begin work in a village without the chiefs' and elders' permission, but permission is hard to refuse given the weight of urban authority that the loggers have or claim. Urban-based younger men with authoritative village relatives sometimes profit as intermediaries in these arrangements. Once loggers are in the village, it is difficult to control which trees they fell.

Young men and women are often angry about tree felling on econ-omic grounds, as they receive so little of the value. A mature *Afzelia africana* tree would pay a young man's brideprice if he could realise its full cash returns. But those who fell and saw trees usually operate with pseudo-state consent and under the local authority of the village chief, who can claim that the trees are under village, not individual authority, especially if the plantations are no longer worked. The plot-holders might thus receive minimal compensation for damage to tree crops, but no direct timber revenues, and thus be angered by their loss of tenurial control as well as their personal financial loss. And felling the trees special to particular lineages is normally lineage members' prerogative, feasible only after careful ritual preparation, sacrifices to ancestors and negotiations with spirits to move elsewhere. Lineage members fear adverse consequences for their families, as well as for the loggers, if they are felled. Women resent the felling of conveniently located fruit and nut trees when these are cut for timber, although they gladly make use of the firewood available from plank remnants. It is such diverse concerns that are at stake when loggers fell trees, not the loss of the large trees *per se*. Nor does the felling of large forest trees compromise the future integrity of the forest island, which continues to be valued and maintained for the diverse reasons for which it originally formed.

In some cases, villagers themselves have felled whole forest islands. But this has been only following their abandonment as residential places, when inhabitants have moved to a new settlement site. Forest island uses diminish once they are no longer inhabited, and as villagers shift their attention to the new forest island developing around the new site, they consider it only sensible to convert large parts of the old one to agricultural land to take advantage of the highly fertile soils beneath it. Such instances have been used by environmentalists as evidence of the destructive tendencies of local land use practices towards forest 'nature'. But for Kissia and Kuranko, the same practices are simply part of the dynamic character of forest patches, which now, as always, come, go and shift as social settlements do.

Conclusions

The significances of Kissidougou's forest islands and the trees within them are as many as the discourses that relate to them, and the positions of different people within these discourses. Forest islands thus acquire very different meanings depending on who one is, and whether the attention is on everyday provisioning and village protection, village origins and lineage political relationships, the power and military structures of men's societies, the control over fertility in women's societies, the economic value of tree crops and timber, or assertions of ethnic identity and relationships with the State. This is equally true for the significances of particular tree species and, indeed, of particular trees. As representatives of the past, forest islands are not only represented differently according to people's interpretations of resource value, but are also, in effect, a living archive – a repository of layered social memories – albeit one open to socially differentiated interpretations.

Given that representations of trees and forests are contextual and socially differentiated, the temptation to identify a shared set of 'cultural' meanings – a single indigenous knowledge – is misplaced. Doing so would obscure social difference and suppress less prominent intellectual and social positions. It would give the false impression that such knowledge can be examined in isolation from broader economic and global processes. Such a view is clearly untenable in Kissidougou, given that attitudes towards forest islands have been shaped by war, national and international environmentalist ideas and institutions, and shifts in regional and international trade.

Diverse as they are, local views concerning vegetation nevertheless contain little that resembles Western views of 'nature' in general, and Western representations of these so-called relic forest patches in particular. Indeed, many Kissi and Kuranko representations transcend the basic Western division between things natural and things cultural. Ecology can be socialised, so that forest islands or particular trees are thought of in terms of the social processes of which they are a part (cf. Croll and Parkin 1992). And inasmuch as ideas of society (and reproduction) are embodied in settlements, so the changes in soil and vegetation associated with settlement are thought of as an integral part of the settlement process, not as society acting on a conceptually distinct environment. This social–forest patch association has its counterpart in the termite and *nyina* worlds, which Western thought would relegate to the natural and supernatural, but which Kissidougou villagers take more as reflections of their own sociality. Stressing the social character of forest patches in the landscape is not to imply that the spaces between them are in some sense a-social. But they are socialised in different ways, in the domains of farming, hunting, gathering and fishing, in sharp distinction from the islands of settlement and settled reproduction (Fairhead and Leach 1996).

The visions of nature that inform conservation policies should also be seen as socialised, located in particular social and historical circumstances. These visions have constituted Kissidougou's forests as 'natural' relics, and as of regional climatic and global significance; part of global inheritance. For conservationists, Kissidougou's environment is degraded and degrading, and subject to current crisis as these last relics themselves lie endangered. The ability to construct forest patches as nature is thus integral to environmental crisis narratives that, as Roe notes more generally, are 'the primary means whereby development experts and the institutions for which they work claim rights to stewardship over land and resources which they do not own' (Roe 1995: 1065).

Notes

1. This chapter is a slightly revised version of a paper entitled 'Culturing trees: socialised knowledge in the political ecology of Kissia and Kuranko forest islands of Guinea', which will appear in K. Seeland (ed.), *Nature is Culture* (1997, IT Publications). It has been equally co-authored by Melissa Leach and James Fairhead, and draws on fieldwork and analysis carried out also by Dominique Millimouno and Marie Kamano. The research was funded by ESCOR of the then Overseas Development Administration, whom we gratefully thank; opinions represented here are, however, the authors' own, not those of DFID. Many thanks are also due to the villagers in Kissidougou prefecture with whom we worked and to our Guinean collaborators: Projet Développement Rural Intégré de Kissidougou (DERIK), Direction Nationale des Forêts et Faune (DNFF) and Direction Nationale de Recherche Scientifique (DNRS).

2. Kissia is the preferred and correct plural term for the people who speak Kissie, a language categorised within the Mel group of West Atlantic languages. Kuranko is a dialect of Maninka, part of the Mande language group.

3. Villagers' understanding of termites' vegetational effects as metaphorically associated with people's effects on soil and vegetation is missed by ecologists of the region. While they now appreciate the ability of termites to promote forest establishment in savannah (Hopkins 1992), they consider this only as a 'natural' phenomenon, rather than a 'settlement-social' one analogous to human activity.

4. Cassette citations refer to the list of over 100 recordings of discussions concerning local agro-ecology and history that we collected, transcribed and translated during the research.

5. Foresters, by contrast, tend to attribute tree form only to natural conditions, assuming heavily branched individuals to have grown up in savannah or forest clearings, and tall straight ones – the 'forest form' – in forest. They thus wrongly infer that all forest-form trees on more open land are relics of deforestation.

References

Adam, J. G., 'Les reliques boisées et les essences des savanes dans la zone préforestière en Guinée française', *Bulletin de la Société Botanique Française* 98, 1948, pp. 22–6

Atran, S., *Cognitive foundations of natural history: towards an anthropology of science,* Cambridge: Cambridge University Press, 1990

Aubréville, A., *Climats, forêts et désertification de l'Afrique tropicale,* Paris: Société d'Editions Géographiques, Maritimes et Coloniales, 1949

Berry, S., 'Social institutions and access to resources', *Africa* 59 (1), 1989, pp. 41–5

Cashman, K., 'Systems of knowledge as systems of domination: the limitations of established meaning', *Agriculture and Human Values* 8 (1&2), 1991

Chevalier, A., 'Les bois sacrés des Noirs de l'Afrique tropicale comme sanctuaires de la nature', *Comptes Rendus de la Société de Biogéographie,* p. 37, 1933

Clad, J. C., 'Conservation and indigenous peoples: a study of convergent interests', in J. McNeely and D. Pitt (eds), *Culture and Conservation,* London and Sydney: Croom Helm, 1985

Croll, E. and D. Parkin, 'Cultural understandings of the environment', in E. Croll and D. Parkin (eds), *Bush Base: Forest Farm: Culture, environment and development,* London: Routledge, 1992

D'Azevedo, W. L., 'Some historical problems in the delineation of a Central West Atlantic Region', *Annals, New York Academy of Sciences*, 96, 1962, pp. 513–38

Fairhead, J. and M. Leach, 'Termites, society and ecology: perspectives from Mande and Central West Atlantic regions', Paper presented at the African Studies Association (UK), Lancaster, September 1994

Fairhead, J. and M. Leach, *Misreading the African Landscape: society and ecology in a forest–savannah mosaic*, African Studies Series, Cambridge and New York: Cambridge University Press, 1996

Fardon, R., 'Protestations of ignorance, or things left unsaid?' Paper presented at the EIDOS conference, SOAS, June 1986

Furley, P., J. Proctor and J. Ratter (eds), *The Nature and Dynamics of Forest–Savanna Boundaries*, London: Chapman & Hall, 1992

Hopkins, B., 'Ecological processes at the forest–savanna boundary', in P. A. Furley, J. Proctor and J. A. Ratter (eds), *Nature and Dynamics of Forest–Savanna Boundaries*, London, Chapman & Hall, 1992

Jackson, M., *The Kuranko: dimensions of social reality in a West African Society*, New York: St Martin's Press, 1977

Leach, M., *Rainforest Relations: gender and resource use among the Mende of Gola, Sierra Leone*. Edinburgh: Edinburgh University Press and Washington: Smithsonian Institution, 1994

Leach, M. and J. Fairhead, 'Ruined settlements and new gardens: gender and soil-ripening among Kuranko farmers in the forest–savanna transition zone', in I. Yngstrom, P. Jeffery, K. King and C. Toulmin (eds), *Gender and Environment in Africa: Perspectives on the Politics of Environmental Sustainability*, Edinburgh: Centre of African Studies, 1994

MacCormack, C. P., 'Proto-social to adult: a Sherbro transformation', in C. MacCormack and M. Strathern (eds), *Nature, Culture and Gender*, Cambridge: Cambridge University Press, 1980

Moore, D., 'Contesting terrain in Zimbabwe's Eastern Highlands: Political ecology and peasant resource struggles', *Economic Geography* 69 (3/4), 1993, pp. 380–401

Paulme, D., 'Fautes sexuelles et "premiers morts" dans une société africaine', *Journal de Psychologie Normale et Pathologique*, 1950, pp. 507–24

République de Guinée, *Politique forestière et plan d'action*, Conakry, 1988

Rival, L., 'The growth of family trees: understanding Huaorani perceptions of the forest', *Man* 28 (4), 1993, pp. 635–52

Rivière, C., 'Fétichisme et démystification: l'exemple guinéen', *Afrique Documents*, 102/3, 1969, pp. 131–68

Roe, E., '"Except Africa": postcript to a special section on development narratives', *World Development* 23(6), 1995, pp. 1065–70

Schnell, R., 'Contribution à une étude phyto-sociologique et phyto-géographique de l'Afrique Occidentale: les groupements et les unités géobotaniques de la région guinéenne', Dakar, *Mémoires de l'I.F.A.N,* 18, 1952, pp. 41–236

Wilson, A., 'Sacred Forests and the Elders', in E. Kemf (ed.), *The law of the mother: protecting indigenous peoples in protected areas*, Sierra Club: San Francisco, 1993

Modern Forestry: Trees and Development Spaces in South-west Bengal, India

Krishna Sivaramakrishnan

During the last decade groups of villagers in south-west Bengal have mobilised to protect certain second-growth forests in the region. This process of local cooperation within villages and between villagers and the State is called Joint Forest Management (JFM), and has become a forestry development scheme in many parts of India. My larger project explores the ways in which, as a development regime pertaining to forest management, JFM is a historical product of colonial state-making.[1] In this chapter I will confine myself to how JFM creates a contested development space by briefly presenting and analysing competing narratives that have been generated about the origins of JFM.

Viewed from the analytical perspective of state formation, JFM appears to engender several versions of what we might call its origin myth. All of them contain commentaries on the possibilities for development, the locus of necessary expertise and the notion of village community so readily employed in development projects. As the State in India has always assumed responsibility for both maintaining order and initiating change,[2] each narrative also evaluates the State's agency in shaping and implementing development projects that would transfer power from State to society. Through these narratives we can also identify the wide variety of actors – human agents, their institutions and ideas – whose conflicts and coalitions are defining JFM. For simplicity we may classify the players as villagers, NGOs and government officials; but while doing so we have to remain aware of the internal fractures within these groupings. Competing accounts of JFM origins are generated as much through friction within these groups as they are a product of struggles between them.[3]

These narratives are important because they construct 'a tricky space where lives are told and stories lived' (Steedly 1993: 15). As images of the past and visions for the future, and conflicting representations that are mobilised in struggles to shape specific political results, development narratives describe shared spaces in which social and State agents act. Operating in these development spaces, agents articulate diverse social locations and subject positions to constitute their history and identity. These development spaces need to be studied as material landscapes that are at the same time imagined, and must be imagined in order to be experienced.

Representations play an important part in social action. Therefore, 'how knowledge, power and agency are represented and responsibility attributed in different situations . . . are issues of interest' (Hobart 1993: 13). Development narratives become institutionally embedded policy paradigms that are difficult to dislodge (Hoben 1995). They are also transformed historically through changes in institutions and constellations of interests. Through their varying accounts of the same events, narratives become discursive strategies, working to organise and win property claims, limit social freedom and legitimate State intervention (Carr 1986; Cronon 1992; Fortmann 1994; Hoben 1995; Peters 1992; Roe 1991). Narratives, as the most spontaneous form of historical representation, are a means to appreciate all social formations and identities; including the processes of state-making. A number of scholars have amply demonstrated the immense possibilities of such an approach (see for example Amin 1995; Chakravarty 1992; Duara 1995; Norman 1991; Stoler 1992; Stone 1979; White 1984).

Forest as a landscape, a repository of environmental services, an economic resource, a cultural heritage, a food source for landless tribes: these are some of the important representations, symbolic constructions, through which the politics of rhetoric and managerial practices intersect in sites like the dry deciduous sal (*Shorea robusta*) forests of south-west Bengal.[4] How exactly was a particular place caught up in these translocal discourses, and how did it reconfigure them? To comprehend that we need to situate ourselves in the field and then proceed to the construction of development spaces there.

People, Landscapes and Trees in South-west Bengal

Bandhgora, where I did fieldwork for this study, is part of the Jhargram administrative subdivision, the Jhargram Development Block and the Bandharbhola Forest Beat, in the Jhargram Range of West Midnapore Division (see Figure 13.1). The little market town of Jhargram is a few miles away, and all the villagers of Bandhgora go there on the weekly market day, and sometimes on other days in the week to seek work,

MAP

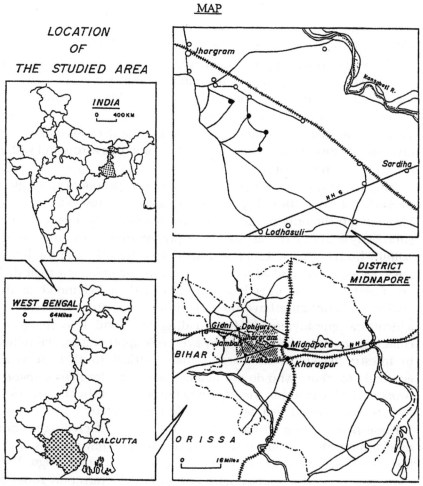

* Shaded circles indicate villages of intensive fieldwork

Figure 13.1 Map of Midnapore district, West Bengal, India

buy food and clothes, and sell vegetables from their home gardens and fuelwood from the forests. Jhargram is also the seat of the Raja, erstwhile *zamindar* (landlord), who lives in the dilapidated *rajbari* (palace) on the outskirts of town facing the equally broken-down but much revered Savitri temple, believed to be at least three hundred years old.

The temple has the usual *pukur* (pond) adjacent – a muddy body of water in which the present Raja's grandfather is reputed to have bathed regularly – and is partially concealed by an impressive grove of sal and mahua (*Bassia latifolia*) trees that are probably a hundred years old or more. That these trees remained uncut for so long is evidence of this being in some way a protected copse – a sacred grove. We are wont to imagine that such a *jaherthan* (place of worship) will contain real virgin old growth; but that is mostly not the case.[5] The forests, nested in the patchwork landscape of paddy-fields, grassy uplands and scrub regeneration, take on specific cultural meanings both as wooded estates and individual trees. In Bandhgora I lived amongst Mahato, Santhal and Lodhas, who share some of these meanings and differ in others. Variations in their understanding of trees in their lives were shaped by divergent historical experiences of forest use and loss across and within these broad ethnic groups.

Being the poorest and most forest-dependent people of the region, the Lodhas are now the only people who regard the forest as a sanctuary. They remain the only people who know it intimately, can traverse it effortlessly without the assistance of pre-existing trails, and extract skilfully from it the scant supply of small game (mostly hare and jungle fowl), roots, tubers and edible wild plants that supplement their diet. The forest also most directly contributes to their livelihood, as the Lodhas of Bandhgora have no agricultural land and only seasonal agricultural employment.[6] Head-loading fuelwood into Jhargram, collecting roots and herbs valued by ayurvedic apothecaries, and toiling in forestry development works remain critical to their survival, especially for those who do not migrate seasonally for *narmal khat-thé* (work in the lowlands) in the adjoining blocks east of the Subarnarekha river, where irrigated *boro* (winter) paddy is cultivated.[7]

These people seem to have eluded the touch of civilisation and development that became a State project within a few decades of the first incursions of British rule into the region over 220 years ago. They thus remain, in the scrubby sal forest–savannah transition zones of south-west Bengal, as the most glaring evidence of a persisting political frontier in the heart of India. Not surprisingly, as foresters – and NGOs alike – involved in promoting JFM said several times during my fieldwork, the Lodhas pose the biggest challenge to the project of rural development forestry.

For Mahatos the forests, principally the sal tree, have come to signify the vestiges of wealth that the landscape once contained, its ravages marking their dwindling natural capital in the struggle for development. Sal, an excellent hardwood, is valued by them for its qualities as building timber, for houseposts, plough handles, and cart construction. Its leaves serve both as excellent fodder and raw material for fashioning a variety of domestic utensils. The sal resin is used as both insecticide and incense. *Mahua*, among sal's most numerous associates, provides vital nutritional supplements. Its inflated corolla is used to prepare liquor, and the oil expressed from the seed is used as a substitute for butter. The fleshy, succulent flower is dried and used as a complementary staple to rice, mainly by the Santhals, often extending a family's supply of rice for a couple of months.

Most villages have discrete populations of single ethnicity, and they fall on a continuum that combines class, community and ecology in the following manner: (1) *Mahatos* are the most prosperous, engaged mostly in wet rice cultivation on good low-lying inundated fields (*aman/jola*). Their relationship to forests is almost completely commerc- ialised and managerial. Even in the *zamindari* era, headmen and village watchmen were most often drawn from the Mahato community, who thus frequently exercised control over forests and enjoyed special rights to timber. (2) *Santhals* occupy, both hierarchically and physically, the middle of the three-tier scenario. They also cultivate wet rice, but do not own so much good paddy land. Rice, maize and a cassava-like vegetable locally called *alti* are their main food. These crops are grown on unembanked *dahi* (upland) plots, where water does not stand. (3) *Lodhas* are clearly on the bottom of the economic scale, and the most recently sedentarised group. They own very little land, live in the most intimate relation with the forest, and are perceived as the key to forest protection, an idea that their organic intellectuals are already turning into political capital. The Lodhas are most dependent on gathering and hunting, especially forest fowl. Forest products contribute most to their subsistence.

So in the patchwork of *aman*, *dahi* and jungle lands that characterises the landscape, we can think of the Mahatos as the main exploiters of the *aman* niche, the Santhals of the *dahi* niche and the Lodhas of the jungle. Predictably, the Santhals are the ones most interested in animal husbandry. They keep the widest range of domestic animals, apart from hunting a number of forest fauna, since *dahi* land is the area most used for grazing. This is not to suggest that they do not use the other parts of the landscape. In fact all these groups possess, in varying quantities, access to all the types of land, and draw sustenance from all manner of land-based occupations supplemented by coolie work, service, trade and such non-agricultural modes of employment. My schema is, therefore, merely a starting-point, and not to be understood as identifying watertight sociological compartments. I propose this many-sided socio-ecological continuum, not so much to distinguish the relationship of various groups within the peasantry to the State, nor even to trace the emergence of ethnic and community identity in their midst, but to focus on the plurality of representations that such a continuum reveals about the forests, without reifying in rigid association particular visions with distinct groups. Friction within the continuum is crucial to shaping the over-arching 'peasant position or view' that is in turn necessitated by an imposed structure like the JFM programme.[8]

Creating Development Spaces

Much recent writing has examined the ways in which forests enter the imagination of Western peoples, though such research has often focused on literary or artistic national cultures (Cartmill 1994; Harrison 1992; Schama 1995; Thomas 1983). Similar writing in South Asia is less in evidence, though the extant literature draws on similar sources, such as classical texts, folklore, and the anthropology of tribal religions.[9] Such work informs us of the widely shared and enduring aspects of the cultural meaning of forests in national, regional or ethnic groupings, and provides us with concepts to examine the local politics of forest use and management. In these specific contexts we can also find these concepts being deployed, negotiated, transformed, adopted and rejected; while others can also be identified that are not generally associated with the usual cultural repertoire of symbolic representations of nature among any particular community.

The case of JFM, a scheme of forest regeneration based on unprecedented cooperation between 'traditional enemies' – foresters and peasantries – has conjured up a rich variety of such representations of forests and their uses.[10] These narratives both describe the scheme and influence its implementation. Their study can tell us much about forests and the human imagination, where the interaction of ideas no longer the preserve of any one culture are, nonetheless, generating a unique field of arguments and actions. Taking such an approach this chapter will examine narratives surrounding JFM in Bengal. In particular by examining the discussions about the origins of JFM, and their characterisation of forests as a development space, I would like to describe how the narratives construct diverse meanings around forests and their management, through interpretations of governance and scientific forestry.

Since participatory development is the overall formula, the struggles naturally centre on who should get more voice. This leads to both the State and NGOs defining their supervisory or training role; and some villagers asking for more autonomy. In the process categories, redolent with historical inference, are constituted and utilised. Of particular note in this regard are notions of community, control or jurisdiction, and expertise. I later on return to definitions of these categories as they are formed in debates about JFM. At this point all that is needed is a better appreciation of JFM stories and their ramification for the construction of national development spaces.

Having said that, the need for brevity will allow me to sketch out only two narratives. They have been constructed to sustain my focus on issues of participation in joint forest management. One is the distilled product of official discourses on JFM's origins, and the other a standardised account from villagers belonging to a long surviving forest protection committee in western Midnapore. Such authorised narratives are salient because they become central to policy debates and local politics. I begin with the account of JFM origins rendered by one group of villagers.

Local Initiatives

A few months after I had been in the field, I began to collect material on how village leaders perceived the origins of JFM in their area. The story of the Haldanga forest protection committee mirrors, in many respects, the issues they raised and is, therefore, discussed in detail below. I expected to get the standardised narrative or the polished, carefully crafted public version of why and how the villagers mobilised to protect their forests. I was also aware that such a prepared telling 'hardly exhausts what we might wish to know about power' (Scott 1990: 14). But just as the production of standardised narratives reveals struggles over boundaries that are drawn between what is made public and what is kept hidden, its proffered outcome – of orthodoxy and consensus – can denote the shape of the community, whose boundary is so managed through struggle.

We were seated in concentric circles on the school-room floor, with a few children perched in the open barless windows. The distribution of wealth and standing in the village was mirrored in the way people sat around that day. Members of Singha households, clearly the élites, sat close. Mahatos and Santhals, petty cultivators mostly, brought up the rear. Lodhas, labourers all, were standing in a scatter outside, though many had chosen not to come. The task of narration was assumed by three prime organisers of the committee. The discussion, lasting several hours, was recorded in Bengali; the translations and editing are mine. What follows is a highly abbreviated version of their consolidated story.

About sixteen years ago, there were concerted efforts all around this region to extend cultivation at the expense of the forests. A few young men decided to ask people to clear fields elsewhere, as forests were valuable. There was considerable tension and conflict, but with the support of elders these men were able to prevail. In 1985 the village joined the Zila Parishad rural development research project to prepare village development plans. This proved to be a very educative process, and was a different experience from earlier forest protection which, my informants said, was not based on real awareness.

In 1988 the forest beat officer, pleased that villages were protecting the forest, promised that he would secure government assistance if the committee survived. This was a difficult task, because the committee would have to last longer than the other usual village committees, like those organised for specific events or festivals. But work in rural development planning since 1985 had created an organisation that came in handy. At the time forest destruction continued apace. There were scuffles with villagers of neighbouring Sirsi that could not be resolved through the *panchayat* (local elected self-government body). But the department helped solve the problem. Yet again, there was a violent dispute with the Belpahar forest committee. Many people were hospitalised and the forest department helped defray some of the costs of treatment. From the beginning the foresters were sympathetic.

Then the Haldanga committee heard about micro-planning and how the forest department would undertake schemes to benefit the villagers. Comparing the JFM scheme with land reforms, where sharecroppers had been guaranteed 75 per cent of the crop, they asked why JFM would give only 25 per cent of the produce to the village committee. The forester explained that in addition to direct profit sharing, another 25 per cent of the net proceeds would be spent on village development. This would be in the nature of indirect compensation. Considering the inadequacy of development work undertaken by the *panchayati raj* institutions after 1978, the Haldanga forest protection committee was motivated to continue in the expectation of additional investment in village development. Since then the forest department has prepared two roads to the village. But villagers found that the works have not been satisfactory, and money has not been spent well. They pointed out the defects in the public works. After two meetings with the Divisional Forest Officer and the District Magistrate, they were taken on a tour of other Forest Protection Committees (FPC). In Chatnasol Range they saw Hatimara FPC. From 1989, when the Government Order on JFM was passed, progress made under the scheme has remained slow and unsatisfactory.

This account (which I have liberally edited and paraphrased) is fascinating for its engagement with development discourse. It traces a path marked by many shared milestones, the social forestry project, rural development research, working through *panchayats*. While careful to intimate the role of villager initiative, this narrative quickly locates itself within the learning, progress and cumulative gain metaphors of development discourse.

But what is particularly salient, and is only alluded to in this standardised narrative, is the way in which the cooperative conservation community is formed and maintained through several exclusions. The violent exchanges with neighbours, the Lodhas who remain spoken for but silent, the poorer villagers who were prevented from encroaching on forests for farmland, are all episodes and absences that are passed over in the story as told. We are reminded by cryptic allusions and strategic omissions in this story that when environmental protection is to be accomplished through the exclusion of certain people from the use of a resource, it will follow existing patterns of power and stratification in society. While my example illustrates social stratification along ethnic and class lines, this argument would hold equally for other forms of exclusion, and hence vitiated community participation, notably gender (see Jackson 1993, and Agarwal 1997).

Clearly development discourse is being appropriated and modified by village élites in ways that bear the stamp of local political imperatives. To that extent, these agents of community forestry, like the people Stacy Pigg (1992: 495) wrote about in Nepal, 'do not perceive the ideology of development as culturally foreign'. They are also delineating a critique of government policy, even as their local initiative is diffused through prolonged cooperation with foresters into the world of government schemes. This critique is crucial to maintaining the fragile community forged in the face of internal fracture and external hostility, for it declares the need for government support, and chides the government for being tardy in providing the support that would legitimate and make feasible the continuance of the community. Most importantly, this critique is not derived from the anti-modern or pre-modern realm of social identity. Through this critique a new community is being created, by reminding the government of certain populist aspects of development discourse that created the space for forest protection committees in the first place.

State Reformism

I will now turn to the distilled official version of how the forest department in Bengal came to be institutionally disposed towards facilitating the emergence of JFM. In interviews and more casual discussions, foresters of all ranks repeatedly alluded to the recurrent violence and atmosphere of suspicion that prevailed in the first decades following the transfer of forests from landlords to the State government in south-west Bengal. A senior Conservator of Forests in West Bengal recounted the numerous raids on village markets he led in the early 1970s as a Divisional Forest Officer, particularly one in June 1973 that resulted in several deaths as the police opened fire on defiant villagers. In his words, 'confrontations and conflicts were so intense that hundreds of forest staff [. . .] lost their lives fighting to defend forests from illegal extraction and over-exploitation' (Palit 1993: 4). Another forester recollected his days raiding and destroying head-loads seized from villagers *en route* to local markets. His memory of sustained violent conflict with villagers through the 1960s and 1970s coincided with the introduction of scientific management in south-west Bengal forests, acquired from abolished landlord estates around 1955.

In all these accounts, poor performance under a production forestry regime and the introduction of social forestry and accelerated land reforms under successive Left Front governments after 1977 converge to impel a transition in forest management. As a result, in the official narratives of JFM's origins, the period from about 1960 to 1980 has become a time to forget. But some 'progressive' foresters do recall this period, for such recollection serves to underscore that an opportunity was lost to break the mould of colonial, custodial, forestry and collaborate with people in forest conservation and development. In their story of the forest department's evolutionary progression into the benign enlightened present, the mid-century decades mark the passage through darkness, the early learning years. Such learning of course advances through the misty morning light of social forestry. The West Bengal social forestry project of the 1980s has thus gained an important place in marking the transition to JFM, though it failed to achieve most of its welfare targets. How did this happen?

Social forestry dictated a shift in departmental working styles, along with a wider political devolution that occurred concurrently in Bengal. It proved to be a major effort on the part of foresters to plant trees on lands outside State forests. In addition the project resulted in farmer nurseries that were created to generate the large supply of seedlings required for the massive afforestation programme. Strips were usually planted on government lands along roadsides, canal banks, railway lines and embankments. They were supposed to be protected by villagers, who had to be persuaded, as a modicum of plantation survival was necessary to secure additional funding for the project activities in different districts. Village wood-lots utilised *panchayat* wastes and other community lands. Farm forestry was basically subsidised private tree-planting. All these components required in varying degrees the cooperation of villagers and local bodies, thereby placing foresters in a position where they had to sell their schemes. Since all this was done in the name of affording improved supplies of fuelwood, non-timber forest products and wage labour, foresters could now participate in existing rural development discourse as agents and vendors.

As many foresters pointed out to me, they learned and took part in 'technology extension', something earlier confined to the agricultural sector. To the degree that extension involved transfer of technical knowledge, foresters mostly seemed pleased to be cast in this wisdom-dispensing role. But another face of extension is transparency of government purpose. This requirement was at times a point of contention between senior officials and field staff. The Subordinate Forest Service Association had encouraged its members in the field to draw senior officials on tour into public discussion with villagers about departmental schemes and their objectives. This strategy could often cause considerable embarrassment to the senior official on the spot, given the generalised hostility of villagers to the forest department in the phase prior to social forestry.

While social forestry transformed the forest department into a development agency, it also interacted with the wider political and administrative devolution under way in West Bengal under the Panchayati Raj Act. Since 1978 the Left Front Government had organised elections to a three-tier local government structure called *panchayats*. Local responsibility for land reforms, education, and a host of social services had been transferred to these bodies. By 1986 they were integrated through a series of government orders into social forestry. As official publicity frames the account, 'the experience of West Bengal Social Forestry Project, select JFM experiments in Midnapore since 1970s, and motivation by departmental staff and Panchayat officials spread "people's" participation like wildfire in south-west Bengal' (Roy 1992: 12).

To sum up, both villagers and foresters seem to agree that the changing institutional environment of forest management and its relationship to the rhetoric of development were important for the emergence of JFM. Where they diverge is in their account of agency, or the motive force behind the rearranged social relations that made forest protection committees possible. These disagreements become central to the politics of contesting forest management, because through JFM forests are being defined as sites of development, opening to reconsideration rules and policies framed a hundred years ago. If the government's *ex post facto* rationalisation of its role is transparent, equally the original community of conservation-minded villagers eludes definition. In fact, the limited examples taken so far leave us with a contradictory set of glimpses into this community: of youth inspired equally by modern education and the wisdom of elders; of 'traditional élites' repositioned as subalterns and organic intellectuals in a poor and remote village; of woods being protected as much for the planted, much maligned, eucalyptus as for naturally occurring sal, the indigenous species that bears special cultural significance locally. We shall, therefore, conclude by considering some of the wider implications of these contradictions and ironies.

Forest Politics, Development and State-making

Development discourse, through the language of technical expertise, is easily bent to the cause of those foresters who wish to contain and direct the process that in the language of enthusiasts is 'community resurgence' and for official purposes is 'rural awakening'. This tendency is expressed by a series of separations – between the scope of local initiative and the regime of central direction, between the role of indigenous knowledge and the necessary inputs of science – that foresters as the experts in regeneration are instituting in JFM. I shall discuss the resultant conflicts and the issues raised by them through the ideas of community, control or jurisdiction, and expertise that I alluded to in my introduction. Arguably the symbolic and material contestations over JFM are negotiations of these categories of social meaning and action.

First comes the issue of identifying the bounded entity nominated as the village community that is actually engaged in forest protection. The symbolic importance of JFM, for the social activists and non-governmental development specialists involved, is its periodic recharging of energies through self-renewal.[11] Thus one pattern in the reporting on JFM is fresh detections of spontaneously organised committees. Much of this derives from a perception that sees the formation of forest protection committees as anarchic and hence simultaneously an example of radical politics and grassroots democracy at work.[12] There can be several objections to this.

The few instances discussed so far more plausibly reveal the working of local leadership through connections outside the village, and the leaders' explicit experience and knowledge of government agencies and development discourse. Such shaping of community does not derive from any intrinsic community ethic, and may in fact batten on existing asymmetries of power in the village.[13] In this situation, the primordial community is more often produced by the study of cosmologies and timeless high culture that stresses system maintenance and function-alism, a social science preference, rather than the ebb and flow of social practice. But this flawed notion has informed massive investments in community development schemes in South Asia in the 1950s and 1960s, and continues to offer powerful support to most environ-mentalists.[14]

To the contrary, my fieldwork suggests that the local mobilisation witnessed in connection with JFM participates in the logic of new agrarian movements, which cannot be understood as struggles for grassroots democracy simply because a broad spectrum of rural people have been moved to make demands on the State. But we do find specific cultural-material processes influencing an emerging pattern of assoc-iational politics. Which brings me to the second theme, the long-standing tension between State centralisation and local control.

Current debates on these issues frequently recapture the flavour and substance of historical conflicts.[15] Despite a fairly draconian law that itself came out of heated debate within the colonial State, forest management as practice remained imbricated within the very basis of productive relations; hence rules, policy resolutions and working plans frequently created a gap between grand design and particular context that made room for negotiation.[16] Through this pragmatic and contingent mechanism developmentalist States have passed or been made to concede greater power and flexibility to rural élites and forest users in agricultural modernisation, forest management regimes. The colonial State in India had an abiding desire for legitimacy, so the central contradiction often became a balancing act between practising expropriation and seeking consent. This created 'a sphere of struggle around State laws and policies' (Bhattacharya 1992: 147; see also Thompson 1975 and Mitchell 1991).

Without consolidating the colonial State in any particular way, we can say there emerged a development regime that carried within it the tension between central authority and local control over natural resources, and carried over many epochal divides to remain with us in the current debates about JFM. This tension was central to the most recent round of controversy, reminiscent of the agitation against the Forest Bill during 1982–4, which was sparked by The Conservation of Forests and Natural Ecosystems Bill of 1994. This draft legislation provoked a commentator in *Down to Earth*, the leading environmental news journal of India, to remark that 'JFM is likely to limit community action within the framework of official planning. The proposed draft bill narrows the scope of participation by making community institutions subservient to the will of the forest department' (Roychoudhury 1995: 27).

Being taken over by the central government and pushed as a state-sponsored modular democratisation of forest management has both standardised JFM and engendered a new level of modification. In Midnapore district alone wide variation can be observed in the practices of different village committees. While in some villages lopping of the sal tree supplemented collecting leaves, grass, flowers, mushrooms and biomass from associates like *kendu* (*Diospyros melanoxylon*) or *asan* (*Terminalia tomentosa*), in others the regenerating forest was completely untouched. The attempts by foresters to carry out multiple shoot-cutting to enhance stem growth in sal coppices were viewed with suspicion in some villages, and occasioned the exasperated comment, 'the villagers have to be trained, they resist shoot cutting and this retards the growth of sal saplings'.[17] In many parts of Bengal and western India, the rules framed by the FPCs are in violation of forest law; but they are allowed to persist.

On the contrary, the quest for de-centred democracy, which has made allies of liberalisers and anti-modern or post-modern traditionalists, cannot escape the danger of falling into the hands of conservative élitism. Communities that are forged across fault lines of gender, ethnicity and class bear the impress of state-making (Bright and Harding

1984). Some of the common disputes arising from the new communities forged through JFM are based in the disruption of old ones, which become visible in the moment of their denial. Thus forest areas have been demarcated as the JFM preserve of one village, ignoring the access granted to another in a colonial revenue settlement. In other instances JFM has become the latest vehicle of pastoralist expropriation. If the localisation of control partitions the protected forest spaces in terms of proximity and primary access, another divide is instituted by the localisation of management and its concern with requisite knowledge.[18]

The third issue, then, is the matter of expertise. In JFM this question has been approached so far by defining Non-Timber Forest Products (NTFP) as being of special significance to the 'local community' and correspondingly placing timber and poles in a wider economy.[19] On this base has been built a superstructure of segmented expertise, seeking to reserve for official science the domain of silviculture. Is JFM a concession to local autonomy that is substantially different from the leeway given to local foresters in scientific forestry? In both cases, the forest department is concerned with the viable technical strategies that would compose the forest management regime. While they do not have annual control forms, through the FPC information sheet, the silvicultural prescriptions and the control of budgets that are used for annual forestry operations, the forest department does standardise and control centrally the activities and decision-making in an important area of JFM.

By maintaining a planting component in JFM the forest department incorporates into local issues the wider concern with types of regeneration. Natural regeneration is something that is 'low technology', especially in coppice management. The standard prescriptions are for multiple shoot-cutting and rotational coppicing, which requires labour in short spells at roughly three-year intervals. A curious reversal of environmentalist discourse, on the question of indigenous species versus exotics, is offered by some FPCs. Contrary to the usual claim that the resurgent community is resentful of exotics, farmer preference for exotics has seeped into JFM. Elites hope to maximise their benefits from JFM through the percentage rule. Foresters are left pushing native fruit trees and other NTFP producers in the name of development. This narrowing of local knowledge and meaningful participation to the sphere of NTFP brings together strategies of market-led development currently in favour, and the older concern of the forest department to secure village labour in different ways for their projects.

These are the ways in which the opening of forest areas to JFM schemes has transformed erstwhile commercial and conservation spaces into a contested development space. FPCs have begun to leave their imprint on this space. Foresters are intent on preserving their control (in the final instance) through silviculture, a knowledge that through manuals and working plans is claimed as their exclusive preserve. Given the participatory framework, this leaves the awkward question of what should be conceded to the domain of local knowledge, where under the rules of JFM villagers are skilled practitioners. The answer, jointly provided by environmentalists and development specialists, is the knowledge of NTFP collection and processing (like making sal leaf plates, or pressing *mahua* seed for oil). In contrast, FPC leaders, like those of Haldanga we heard from, frequently compare JFM to Operation Barga. They are referring to the historic land reform of the 1980s, where share-croppers were entered in the record of rights and recognised as tenants on agricultural lands. The rhetoric of *bargadari* returns focus resolutely to sharing the merchantable produce of JFM areas.[20] It shows that some groups in the peasantry are asserting a right to these forests in a manner that attacks the private versus public distinction instituted through forest management by the colonial State and maintained into the present working of JFM.

Such integration of landscape and managerial knowledge, resisting separations the foresters wish to maintain, is well illustrated by the annual disagreements between villagers and foresters on firing the forest floor. Fire facilitates washing nutrients down into the fields of cultivators. The mulch formed on the forest floor may help forest growth, but the burnt slash benefits agriculture downhill. The foresters have even dug trenches and drains in the forest to collect and distribute nutrients derived from decomposing litter within the forest. By burning, the villagers collect these nutrients as ash mingled in surface run-off following pre-monsoon showers. Other *in situ* benefits of firing, notably the greater facility afforded to hunting and grazing, are again things the foresters would rather eliminate, as they recreate older conflicts over forest access. Even micro-planning, envisaged as the mechanism for FPC involvement in 'technical aspects' of forest management, has become subordinate to the working plan, with its scope confined to the enumeration of 'people's' needs.

These tussles between FPCs and foresters reveal alternative conceptions of development and empowerment through a scheme like JFM. Numerous senior officials apprehended and commented upon the friction that JFM has caused between *panchayats* and FPCs. *Panchayats* loom large on the local scene in Bengal. They exemplify the infrastructural reach of the regional State, but also become institutional sites most vulnerable to social appropriation, in the dialectical manner discussed earlier. With the emergence of FPCs as a new, more local level of associational politics, *panchayats* are also sites of central reassertion. We are then required to theorise this process of state-making.

JFM is created through its implementation, but is also a product of specific historical processes that separate, for analytical purposes, into two streams. One could be called patterns of representations. The other could be called a cumulation of institutional arrangements. For example, in directing JFM towards particular areas, seeing some sites as more suited to the programme, government agencies have called up their versions of regional development history, in which have combined their perceptions of specific landscapes and the people living there. Hence the business of seeing small tribal villages in the forest–savannah transition zone as the desirable focus of JFM.

These representations are related to institutions in political society or the public sphere through the themes of community, control and expertise. I will conclude by briefly touching on their utility for the study of state-making. The idea of community was most often translated in forest policy as the locus of governance, that is the level at which the State does not create institutions but battens on what it perceives as existing and sturdy community institutions. This externalisation of managerial transactions is also an externalisation of costs and a recognition of areas of darkness in State knowledge. Hence the definition of community also serves to define the limits of direct control. Control remains a tricky business. If, on the one hand, it stands on the shoulders of community, on the other, control also attempts to bend community to its needs. There is, then, at work in JFM, as in forest management earlier, a tension between using the community and destroying it.

Expertise relates most directly to representations of the forests, or the idea of woods as social symbols. Clearly a certain type of forest symbolised what was economically desirable to managers. Several arrangements could produce that forest. The one ultimately preferred was usually chosen because it allowed State expertise to dominate and thereby facilitated control. In this chapter I have pointed to the ways in which JFM remains captive to that predilection and thus fails to realise its promise of radical devolution in forest management in Bengal. The lasting irony, of course, is that the unavoidable imperfections of the system make desired policy goals elusive, helping to cast suspicion on expertise itself. JFM then becomes the latest phase in a longer history of redefining community, control and expertise in the forests of south-west Bengal. In this most recent phase the sal tree and its principal associates, such as *mahua* and *kendu*, have become icons of development spaces in the forests of south-west Bengal.

Acknowledgements

The research on which this chapter is based was carried out as part of a larger project entitled 'Revising Laws of the Jungle: Changing Peasant–State Relations in the Forests of Bengal'. This research was assisted by a grant from the Joint Committee on South Asia of the Social Science Research Council and the American Council of Learned Societies with funds provided by the Andrew W. Mellon Foundation and the Ford Foundation. Financial support for this project was also provided by the Wenner-Gren Foundation for Anthropological Research; the Center for International and Area Studies, Yale University; and the Program in Agrarian Studies, Yale University. A version of one section of this chapter was presented at the Annual Meeting of the American Anthropological Association, Washington DC, November 1995. Another version was presented to the University of Canterbury Conference on Trees and Woods as Social Symbols, Wye, January 1996. An expanded version was also presented to the Workshop on Participation and the Micropolitics of Development Encounters, Harvard Institute for International Development, Harvard University, May 1996. I thank participants at all these meetings, and also Linda Angst, Maurice Bloch, John Cinnamon, Renald Clerisme, Fred Cooper, Margeret Everett, Akhil Gupta, Angelique Haugerud, Peta Katz, William Kelly, Patricia Mathews, Nancy Peluso, Pauline Peters, Laura Rival, Jim Scott, and Christina Wasson for reading and commenting on various earlier versions.

Notes

1. 'Development regime' is used as defined by Ludden (1992). Such a historical and processual understanding of development contradicts the analyses of Ferguson (1994) and Escobar (1995). For a detailed discussion of state-making as the processes of establishing, strengthening and limiting the

structures and institutions of official power in society, see Sivaramakrishnan (1996: Chapter 2).

2. The contradictions and tensions arising from this complex charge are well discussed by Kohli (1990).

3. Representative accounts by NGO-based experts, development agencies, and government officials can be found in Poffenburger and McGean (1996), Poffenburger (1995) and Palit (1993). Most of these accounts elaborate their description of pre-colonial harmony with nature in tribal society following the influential work of Gadgil and Guha (1992).

4. According to recent estimates, notified sal forest lands in West Bengal occupy 4,700.59 square miles, in two zones. In the north, in the Himalayan foothills, *bhabhar* and *terai* tracts; and in the south-west, mostly in the lateritic belt along the border with Bihar (Joshi *et al.* 1980). Sal is a large, gregarious tree, and tends to dominate the canopy of the late successional forest. The lower Himalayan alluvial terrain is the zone of moist sal, and the south-west Bengal lateritic plateau fringe is the zone of dry deciduous sal. My fieldwork was in this undulating lower Bengal region (see Figure 13.1).

5. As Bishnu Soren of Antapati was to inform me in one of our various discussions about the changes in the Bandhgora landscape, *jaherthans* were changed periodically as settlements shifted, or new areas were cleared for cultivation and others lapsed into jungle. Sometimes administrative action, like the demarcation of village boundaries, occasioned a move for the *jaherthan*. In the hierarchy of sacred groves found among the Santhals in particular, the larger regional sites of worship were more permanent and the smaller ones dedicated to individual hamlets could move more frequently.

6. The sole authority on Lodhas, P. K. Bhowmick, also studied Lodha villages in Jhargram. His information on their socio-economic conditions, when compared with mine, shows no improvement in their status in the last forty years – that is no tangible benefits of development in independent India (see Bhowmick 1963: Chapters 2–4).

7. Only one-third of the Lodha families in Tiyakati went *narmal khat-thé* in the winter of 1993–4.

8. This capacity of collectivities to engage the State is formed by the 'conformation of regional cultures in response to the reorganization of power relations in space' (Lomnitz 1994: 262). For a more detailed description and analysis of regional culture in south-west Bengal see Sivaramakrishnan (1996: Chapter 10).

9. Gadgil and Guha (1992) is the best recent introduction to the subject. In contrast to these highly literary and élite culture-based approaches, I am more interested in the study of attitudes to trees and forests rooted in material culture and the intimate interplay between imagination, memory and experience in the daily routines of life (see Rival 1993 and Bloch 1995).

10. We now have many studies of the conflicts between the forester and the tribes, peasantries, cottagers and other rural communities in both European and colonial contexts. A small list of excellent studies in this genre would include Thompson (1975), Guha (1989), Peluso (1992), Schmink and Wood (1992) and Sahlins (1994).

11. The idea that small, homogeneous tribal villages possess an innate conservation community that was re-awakened by JFM is pervasive in the development rhetoric surrounding the programme, and was faithfully spouted at me by foresters at all levels during fieldwork, both in my fieldsite and the adjoining forest ranges that I visited periodically.

12. The term 'anarchism' is used in this chapter to describe spontaneous collective action, characterised by loosely organised non-hierarchical co-ordination of the sort that obtains when 'organization [. . .] established freely, socially, and above all from below [. . .] comes from all sides to create nodes of coordination, natural centers to serve all these points' (Voline as quoted in Guerin 1970: 43). These analyses use a notion of community that emphasises its face-to-face character, wide participation in decision-making, commonly held values and ties of reciprocity. Its archetype is small-scale tribal societies based on low-technology subsistence economies. For further discussion of these categories and their problems see Taylor (1982) and Douglas (1986: 26–46).

13. For a fine illustration of this point, see Tsing (1993: 73–103). As Giddens (1994: 126) puts it, 'traditional communities can be, and normally have been oppressive. Community in the form of mechanical solidarity crushes individual autonomy and exerts a compelling pressure towards conformism.'

14. For community development see Tennekoon (1988) and Woost (1993). For environmentalism see Sivaramakrishnan (1995).

15. In many ways, what happens today re-enacts the struggle that went on within the colonial State before the Indian Forest Act of 1878 was enacted and extinguished a range of customary rights of villagers. The making of the 1878 Act has been well discussed in Guha (1990) and Rangarajan (1994). But the matter did not end there. The 1878 Indian Forest Act remained ambiguous on systems of management to be introduced and provided tremendous latitude for regional administrations to fashion interpretations of its provisions that emerged from their particular contexts.

16. Compare the distinction between statute law and forest law made in Thompson (1975), who shows how the latter was more attuned to the daily realities of dealing with the multitude of demands and pressures in the English forests of the eighteenth century.

17. B. S. Pratihar, Additional Divisional Forest Officer, West Midnapore, interviewed 29 July 1992.

18. As a scholar of official discourse puts it, 'the power that is modern mastery

both derives from knowledge and requires knowledge of a particular kind [. . .]
experts are the bearers of such knowledge' (Ashforth 1990: 5).

19. There is now a whole corpus of field studies conducted under the
umbrella of the JFM National Support Group research network that compute
and describe the local benefits flowing from NTFPs. Notable examples for Bengal
are Malhotra *et al.* (1992), Malhotra *et al.* (1993) and Lal *et al.* (1993).

20. My findings in this regard, based on informal discussion with FPC leaders
in my fieldwork site and neighbouring forest ranges, were confirmed by some
field foresters (range and beat officers) with whom I also spent considerable
time in informal settings.

References

Agarwal, B., 'Environmental action, gender equity and women's part-
    icipation', *Development and Change* 28, 1997, pp. 1–44

Amin, S., *Event, Metaphor, Memory: Chauri Chaura, 1922–1992*, Berkeley:
    University of California Press, 1995

Ashforth, A., *The Politics of Official Discourse in Twentieth Century South
    Africa*, Oxford: Clarendon, 1990

Bhattacharya, N., 'Colonial State and agrarian society', in B. Stein (ed.),
    The Making of Agrarian Policy in British India, 1770–1900, Delhi:
    Oxford University Press, 1992

Bhowmick, P. K. *The Lodhas of West Bengal*, Calcutta: Punthi Pushtak,
    1963

Bloch, M., 'People into places. Zafimaniry concepts of clarity', in
    E. Hirsch and M. O'Hanlon (eds), *The Anthropology of Landscape:
    Perspectives on Place and Space*, Oxford: Clarendon, 1995

Bright, C. and S. Harding (eds), *State-making and Social Movements: Essays
    in History and Theory*, Ann Arbor: University of Michigan Press, 1984

Carr, D., *Time, Narrative and History*, Bloomington: Indiana University
    Press, 1986

Cartmill, M., *From a View to a Death in the Morning*, Cambridge: Harvard
    University Press, 1994

Chakravarty, D., 'Postcoloniality and the artifice of history: who speaks
    for 'Indian' pasts?', *Representations* 37, 1992, pp. 1–26

Cronon, W., 'A place for stories: nature, history and narrative', *Journal
    of American History* 78, 1992, pp. 1372–6

Douglas, M., *How Institutions Think*, Syracuse: Syracuse University Press,
    1986

Duara, P., *Rescuing History from the Nation: Questioning Narratives of
    Modern China*, Chicago: University of Chicago Press, 1995

Escobar, A., *Encountering Development: The Making and Unmaking of the Third World*, Princeton: Princeton University Press, 1995

Ferguson, J., *The Anti-Politics Machine: 'Development' Depoliticisation and Bureaucratic Power in Lesotho*, Minneapolis: University of Minnesota Press, 1994

Fortmann, L., 'Talking Claims: Discursive Strategies in Contesting Property', paper presented to the Weekly Colloquium, Program in Agrarian Studies, Yale University, 1994

Gadgil, M. and R. Guha, *This Fissured Land: An Ecological History of India*, Delhi: Oxford University Press, 1992

Giddens, A., *Beyond Left and Right: The Future of Radical Politics*, Cambridge: Polity Press, 1994

Guerin, D., *Anarchism*, New York: The Monthly Review Press, 1970

Guha, R., *The Unquiet Woods: The Ecological Basis of Peasant Resistance in the Himalaya*, Delhi: Oxford University Press, 1989

—— 'An early environmental debate: the making of the 1878 Forest Act', *Indian Economic and Social History Review* 27(1), 1990, pp. 65–84

Harrison, R. P., *Forests: The Shadow of Civilization*, Chicago: University of Chicago Press, 1992

Hobart, M., 'Introduction: the growth of ignorance?', in M. Hobart (ed.), *An Anthropological Critique of Development: The Growth of Ignorance*, London: Routledge, 1993

Hoben, A., 'Paradigms and politics: the cultural construction of environmental policy in Ethiopia', *World Development* 23(6), 1995, pp. 1007–21

Jackson, C., 'Environmentalisms and gender interests in the Third World', *Development and Change* 24(4), 1993, pp. 649–77

Joshi, H. B. *et al.* (eds), *Troup's Silviculture of Indian Trees*, Dehradun: Forest Research Institute, 1980

Kohli, A., *Democracy and Discontent: India's Growing Crisis of Governability*, Cambridge: Cambridge University Press, 1990

Lal, S. K., A. K. Das, A. K. Raj and M. S. Kundu, *Status of Nontimber Forest Product Collection and Marketing at the Primary Collectors and Wholesalers Level: A Case Study of Raigarh Forest Protection Committee in Ranibandh Range of South Bankura Forest Divsion of West Bengal*, Calcutta: Ramakrishna Mission Loka Shiksha Parisad, West Bengal, 1993

Lomnitz, C., 'Decadence in times of globalization', *Cultural Anthropology* 9(2), 1994, pp. 257–67

Ludden, D., 'India's development regime', in N. Dirks (ed.), *Colonialism and Culture*, Ann Arbor: University of Michigan Press, 1992

Malhotra K. C., M. Poffenburger, A. Bhattacharya and D. Deb, 'Rapid appraisal methodology trials in southwest Bengal: assessing natural forest regeneration patterns and non-wood forest product harvesting practices', *Forests, Trees and People* 15/16, 1992, pp. 18–25

Malhotra, K. C., D. Deb, M. Dutta, T.S. Vasulu, G. Yadav and M. Adhikari, *Role of Nontimber Forest Produce in Village Economy*, London: ODI Rural Development Forestry Network Paper 15d, 1993

Mitchell, T., 'America's Egypt: the discourse of the development industry', *Middle East Report*, March–April 1991, pp. 18–34

Norman, A. P., 'Telling it like it was: historical narratives on their own terms', *History and Theory* 30(2), 1991, pp. 119–35

Palit, S., 'The future of Indian forest management: into the twenty-first century', *Joint Forest Management Working Paper* 15, National Support Group for Joint Forest Management, New Delhi: Society for Promotion of Wastelands Development, 1993

Peluso, N., *Rich Forests, Poor People: Resource Control and Resistance in Java*, Berkeley: University of California Press, 1992

Peters, P., 'Manoeuvres and debates in the interpretation of land rights in Botswana', *Africa* 62(3), 1992, pp. 413–34

Pigg, S. L., 'Inventing social categories through place: social representations and development in Nepal', *Comparative Studies in Society and History* 34(3), 1992, pp. 491–513

Poffenburger, M., 'The resurgence of community forest management in the Jungle Mahals of West Bengal', in D. Arnold and R. Guha (eds), *Nature, Culture, Imperialism: Essays on the Environmental History of South Asia*, Delhi: Oxford University Press, 1995

Poffenburger, M. and B. McGean (eds), *Village Voices, Forest Choices: Joint Forest Management in India*, Delhi: Oxford University Press, 1996

Rangarajan, M., 'Imperial Agendas and India's Forests: The Early History of Indian Forestry', *Indian Economic and Social History Review* 31(2), 1994, pp. 147–67

Rival, L., 'The growth of family trees: understanding Huaorani perceptions of the forest', *Man* 28(4), 1993, pp. 635–52

Roe, E., 'Development narratives, or making the best of blueprint development', *World Development* 19(4), 1991, pp. 287–300

Roy, B. K., *From Wasteland to Wealth: The West Bengal Way*, Calcutta: Directorate of Forests, 1992

Roychowdhury, A., 'The woods are lovely . . .', in *Down to Earth*, 3(17), 1995, pp. 25–30

Sahlins, P., *Forest Rites: The War of the Demoiselles in Nineteenth Century France*, Cambridge, Mass.: Harvard University Press, 1994

Schama, S., *Landscape and Memory*, New York: Alfred Knopf, 1995

Schmink, M. and C. Wood, *Contested Frontiers in Amazonia*, New York: Columbia University Press, 1992

Scott, J. C., *Domination and the Arts of Resistance: Hidden Transcripts*, New Haven: Yale University Press, 1990

Sivaramakrishnan, K., 'Colonialism and forestry in India: imagining the past in present politics', *Comparative Studies in Society and History* 37(1), 1995, pp. 3–40

—— 'Forests, Politics and Governance in Bengal, 1794–1994', Unpublished Ph.D. thesis, Yale University, 1996

Steedly, M. M., *Hanging Without a Rope: Narrative Experience in Colonial and Postcolonial Karoland*, Princeton: Princeton University Press, 1993

Stoler, A. L., '"In cold blood": hierarchies of credibility and the politics of colonial narratives', *Representations* 37, 1992, pp. 151–89

Stone, L., 'The revival of narrative: reflections on new old history', *Past and Present* 85, 1979, pp. 3–24

Taylor, M., *Community, Anarchy and Liberty*, Cambridge: Cambridge University Press, 1982

Tennekoon, S., 'Rituals of development: the accelerated Mahavali development program in Sri Lanka', *American Ethnologist* 15, 1988, pp. 294–310

Thomas, K., *Man and the Natural World: Changing Attitudes in England, 1500–1800*, London: Allen Lane, 1983

Thompson, E. P., *Whigs and Hunters: The Origins of the Black Act*, New York: Pantheon, 1975

Tsing, A. L., *In the Realm of the Diamond Queen: Marginality in an Out-of-the-way Place*, Princeton: Princeton University Press, 1993

White, H., 'The question of narrative in contemporary historical theory', *History and Theory* 13, 1984, pp. 1–33

Woost, M., 'Nationalising the local past in Sri Lanka: histories of nation and development in a Sinhalese village', *American Ethnologist*, 20, 1993, pp. 502–21

Postface

Postface: The Life of
Trees . . .

Jacques Brosse

. . . To Live with Trees[1]

I have been asked to draw this book to a close with a few concluding remarks, a responsibility I find of disproportionate magnitude. I am, after all, no more than an amateur who has spent almost all his life among trees, who has planted and grown many, and who has studied them in their natural environment, at home or abroad (Brosse 1997). I can perhaps justify my writing this postface by saying, as did James Fernandez in his contribution (Chapter 4), 'It is not hard for me to commune with trees.'

My purpose is not to comment on these pertinent studies, written by specialists from England, France, the United States, the Netherlands, and Norway, and also from Australia, Japan and India, whose inter-communicating and complementary works cover more or less the whole surface of the globe. These contributions, moreover, draw on a number of fields, and most especially anthropology. What strikes me most initially is that these scholars do not adopt the detached tone that, too often, is used in universities, but, on the contrary, often start from personal experience – theirs, as much as that of the people whose understanding of trees they have investigated. This respect for the beliefs of the other, for her own mind, goes hand in hand with a notable change in the way in which nature is now approached.

The question asked at the start of the preface by Laura Rival, originator and animator of this important conference, is: 'To which symbolic ends are trees used?' The answers given by the contributors, who have approached tree symbolism from very different perspectives, is that 'trees are used symbolically to make concrete and material the abstract notion of life', and that 'trees are ideal supports for such symbolic purposes precisely because their status as living organisms is ambiguous' (Laura Rival, Chapter 1). I would like to add that this is precisely why trees remain intriguing, mysterious . . . Besides, is it not that 'ambiguous' and 'mysterious' are precisely what defines the 'sacred'? Trees are not mysterious simply because of their timelessness, or because they appear to undergo cycles of death and rebirth. They are mysterious, rather, because they communicate with the deepest elements, their roots within the earth, their cymes into the sky, which they seem to unite, hence making possible the communication between the two invisibles, above and below.

Is it not, having followed one's first, spontaneous, impressions, that the presence of a tree corresponds to this 'disquieting strangeness' evoked by Freud? Is it not what was felt by those who, in times past, penetrated the 'sacred grove', this original temple, which, as Uchiyamada (Chapter 8) shows, has not entirely disappeared from the planet? He talks about the *kaavu* of the Travancore Untouchables: 'To them, these trees are both "sacred" (*sudham*) and "fearful" (*bhayam*)' – not exclusive terms . . . 'They also describe their nature in terms of "life force" (*shakti*) and "fault" (*doosham*).' All this is not without recalling the two trees in the garden of Eden: the tree of life, and the tree of knowledge of good and evil. Isn't this the mysterious and transcending ambiguity of the 'sacred', of which, for humans who still live in the midst of trees, who are still 'savages', in the original sense of *silvaticus*, the tree is the personification *par excellence*? A point of view that centuries of militant rationalism have not managed to extirpate entirely from human consciousness, and that we find sometimes manifested amongst these late-comers – or, rather, these precursors – the poets, artists, mystics, and dreamers. This is the theme that I would have personally chosen.

In his time, Carl Jung, who asked his patients to draw or paint their inner states, noted, not without surprise, that many of them spontaneously, and without knowing or understanding the symbolism at work, represented their inner state of consciousness as a tree. Having studied these images, Jung realised that they often corresponded with critical periods in life, and that they constituted privileged symbols of the 'ego represented in a process of individuation'. After having consulted comparative studies in religion and mythology, he came to understand why human consciousness so often gave rise to tree imagery. Jung's approach sprang back to my memory when I was asked to analyse paintings of trees in the *naïf* style, from different parts of the world (Brosse 1990). It became clear to me that these paintings were best interpreted as self-portraits; witnesses to the painters' aspirations and anxieties, they were inscribed in what in nature is most mysterious and protective, and has most force: the tree.

Traces of such latent symbolism are to be found in the works of poets and painters alike. One only needs to cite Rainer-Maria Rilke (1942) who, in his *Fragments in Prose*, wrote that 'he felt almost imperceptible vibrations passing from within a tree into him, with most gentle movements. He felt as if his entire body was a welcoming soul, and said to himself that he was being led to the other side of nature.' Having abandoned oneself to the 'slow general will', the world, thanks to the tree as intermediary, becomes spontaneously intelligible; in meditation, one finds the origins, the genesis of all life. Isn't this what happened, after all, to Buddha Shâkyamuni by the Nairanjanâ River in Uruvela (Bodh-Gayâ), under the tree of the Awakening (the *Ficus* called *religiosa*)?

That a natural affinity exists between the tree and the artist is precisely what was stressed by one of the greatest inventors of a new pictorial language, Paul Klee, in his famous 1924 lecture *On Modern Art*, delivered in Jena where his work was being exhibited. Klee, who sees nothing more important for the artist than his 'earthly rooting' coupled with 'cosmic intimacy', compares the creative process to the tree, and proposes that the modern artist does not purposefully deform her experience of nature and life, but, like the trunk of a tree, transforms experience naturally, for 'no one expects that a tree forms its superior limbs in exactly the same fashion as its roots. The artist, like the tree trunk, collects what comes from the depths, and transmits it. The position of the artist is modest; he does not execute or order, but mediates. He has no beauty of his own, the beauty of the branches only transits through him.' It is worth noting that Klee's inspiration here is Goethe (1790), the too poorly known naturalist Goethe, author of *Versuch die Metamorphose der Pflanzen zu Erkläre*.

I thought I had completed my research on trees when, three years ago, a young Franco-German photographer, Thomas Heuer, requested that the author of *Mythologie des Arbres* (Brosse 1989) see his work. As soon as he opened his portfolio, I was utterly fascinated, stupefied, almost ill at ease. He had photographed red, orange or bright blue trunks and branches (I was reminded of Mondrian's *The Red Tree*), and pink, lilac or light blue leaves whose structure was similar to the structure of the branches, the whole standing out against a sky streaked with passing stars, in which the planets' orbits were visible. Were these images really trees? The trick, as the young photographer explained to me, was all in the duration of the pause (several hours); but, as I soon realised, it was also in the attention, care and patience of this man, who was spending night after night with 'his' trees. Thomas Heuer, without realising it, had arrived at this achievement: he had revealed the invisible, the bioluminescence of trees. This was later confirmed by specialists who were working on this subject, after they saw these magical pictures.

Now that we have established that trees can communicate through channels that we cannot yet explore, everything remains to be discovered. What our ancestors perceived, what we no longer perceive, is another reality, far richer than ours. One of modern man's problems is that he misses one sense, that of the 'interdependence between people and other animals', interdependence that extends, as Maurice Bloch (Chapter 2) notes, to plants as well. This leads him to cite *The Savage Mind*, written by my friend Claude Lévi-Strauss (1962), who, playing on the double meaning of the French word *pensée* (mind and pansy), brilliantly illustrated the cover of his book with a 'wild pansy'. And it is with a quote from this prodigious anthropologist and philosopher that I wish to end:

> For despite the ink spilled by the Judeo-Christian tradition to conceal it, no situation seems more tragic, more offensive to heart and mind, than that of a humanity coexisting and sharing the joys of the planet with other living species yet being unable to communicate with them. One understands why myths refuse to consider this an original flaw in the creation and see in its appearance the event that inaugurated the human condition and its weakness (Lévi-Strauss with Eribon 1991: 139).

Notes

1. Text translated (from French) by Laura Rival.

References

Bachelard, G., *L'Air et les Songes*, Paris: J. Conti, 1943
Brosse, J., *Mythologie des Arbres*, Paris: Payot, 1989

Brosse, J., *L'Arbre et les Naïfs. Arbre Symbolique et Peinture Naïve*, Paris: Eds Max Fourny, Art et Industrie, 1990

Brosse, J., 'La forêt d'hier . . .' in *Hommes et Plantes*, 21 (Spring Issue), 1997

Goethe, J. W. von, *Versuch die Metamorphose der Pflanzen zu Erkläre*, Gotha, 1790

Klee, P., *On Modern Art* (trans. Paul Findlay), London: Faber, 1966 [1924]

Lévi-Strauss, C., *The Savage Mind*, Chicago: University of Chicago Press, 1962 [2nd edn 1966]

Lévi-Strauss, C. and D. Eribon, *Conversations with Lévi-Strauss* (trans. Paula Wissing), Chicago: University of Chicago Press, 1991 [1988]

Rilke, R.-M., *Fragments en Prose*, Paris: Gallimard, 1942, pp. 109–10.

Notes on Contributors

Maurice Bloch is Professor of Anthropology at the London School of Economics and Political Sciences (University of London), and a specialist in ritual and religion. He has conducted extensive fieldwork in Madagascar, and has published numerous articles and books on the Merina and Zafimaniry. His most recent publication, *Cognition, Memory and Literacy* (Westview Press 1997) reflects his growing interest in the interface between culture and cognition.

Pascale Bonnemère, a researcher of the CNRS, is a member of CREDO (Research and Documentation Centre on Oceania) in Marseilles, France. She has worked among the Ankave-Anga of Papua New Guinea for the past ten years. Her present research interests focus on the concept of personhood, life-cycle rituals, food taboos and ethnobotany. She is also pursuing a comparative ethnographic study of the Anga peoples. She is the author of several professional articles on the Ankave, and has recently published *Le Pandanus Rouge. Corps, Différence des Sexes et Parenté chez les Ankavé-Anga* (1996, Paris: Maison des Sciences de l'Homme).

Jacques Brosse is a French intellectual, who has written numerous books on trees and tree mythologies. During his long and eventful career, he has also been a diplomat, a publisher, and a disciple of Taisen Deshimaru. He has taught Zen Buddhism for the last twenty years.

Roy Ellen is Professor of Anthropology and Human Ecology at the University of Kent at Canterbury. He has conducted fieldwork in the Moluccan islands of Eastern Indonesia, among the Nuaulu of Central Seram (periodically since 1970 to the present) and in the Gorom-Geser archipelago (1981, 1986), and also in south-east Sulawesi and central Java (1976) and Brunei (1991). He is the author of numerous papers on the ecology of small-scale societies, ethnobiology, and inter-island trade in the Moluccas. His recent books include *The Cultural Relations of Classification* (1993), and *Redefining Nature* (1996, co-edited with K. Fukui).

James Fairhead is Lecturer in Anthropology at the School of Oriental and African Studies, University of London. He has extensive research experience in West and Central Africa, especially the Democratic Republic of Congo and the Republic of Guinea. His anthropological enquiry has focused on agricultural knowledge and practice, environmental history, ecology, agrarian social change and the social construction of environmental knowledge. Recent publications include *Misreading the African Landscape* (co-authored with Melissa Leach, 1996) and journal articles on development issues in Africa.

James Fernandez is Professor of Anthropology at the University of Chicago. His fieldwork on cultural revitalisation has been conducted in three parts of Africa, Equatorial (Gabon, Cameroon and Rio Muni), South-eastern (Natal), and West (Guinea Coast). He is presently working on shifting lifeways from agro-pastoralism to mining and post-industrialisation in Cantabrian Spain (Asturias). He has published widely, both articles and monographs on all these research areas.

Rodolfo Giambelli currently works as a Social Forestry and Rural Development Consultant. He holds a M.Sc. in Social Anthropology from the London School of Economics, and a Ph.D. in Anthropology from the Research School of Pacific and Asian Studies of the Australian National University at Canberra. He has carried out research fieldwork in Nusa Penida and Bali, and has undertaken consultancy work throughout Indonesia and South-east Asia.

Signe Howell is Professor of Social Anthropology at the University of Oslo, Norway. She was trained at the Institute of Social and Cultural Anthropology of the University of Oxford, and has conducted fieldwork in Malaysia and eastern Indonesia. In addition to numerous articles and papers, her publications include *Society and Cosmos: Chewong of Peninsular Malaysia* (1984, 1989), as well as the edited volumes *For the Sake of Our Future: Sacrificing in Eastern Indonesia* (1996), and *The Ethnography of Moralities* (1996).

John Knight is a Research Fellow at the International Institute for Asian Studies, Leiden, The Netherlands. He has published a number of journal articles and book chapters on Japanese mountain villages.

Melissa Leach is a social anthropologist and Fellow of the Institute of Development Studies at the University of Sussex, where she directs the Environment Group. She has extensive research experience in West Africa (Sierra Leone and the Republic of Guinea). Her anthropological research has focused on environmental history, ecology, gender–environment relations, agrarian social change and the social construction of environmental knowledge. Recent publications include *Rainforest Relations* (1994), *Misreading the African Landscape* (co-authored with James Fairhead, 1996), and *The Lie of the Land* (1996).

Marie Mauzé is a researcher of the CNRS, Paris, and a member of the Laboratoire d'anthropologie sociale. She has conducted fieldwork with the Kwakwaka'wakw (Kwakiutl) in British Columbia since 1980. She has published articles in various journals (*L'Homme, Gradhiva, Journal des Américanistes, The European Review of Native American Studies*), has authored *Les Fils de Wakai. Une histoire des Lekwiltoq* (1992), and edited *Present is Past. Some Uses of Tradition in Native Societies* (1997). Her current interests are in the field of the anthropology of art.

Laura Rival is currently Lecturer in the Department of Anthropology at the University of Kent at Canterbury. Her main research interests are the theories of learning and knowledge acquisition; Amerindian conceptualisations of nature and society; historical ecology; Latin American nationalisms and politics of culture and identity; and the impact of national development policies on indigenous peoples. Her doctoral research was among the Huaorani Indians of the Ecuadorian Amazon (1989–1990, 1991, 1994, 1996), on whom she has written a number of ethnographic articles and papers. She is currently preparing a monograph titled *Trekking Through History. The Huaorani of Amazonian Ecuador*.

Krishna Sivaramakrishnan is a Post-Doctoral Associate in the School of Forestry and Environmental Studies at Yale University. He holds a Ph.D. in Anthropology, and has graduate qualifications in the fields of Environmental Studies and Modern History. He has published various articles on the history and politics of forest management in

Bengal, India. The title of his forthcoming book is *Governance and Environmental Change in Woodland Bengal, 1767–1947*.

Yasushi Uchiyamada is currently a Senior Researcher in Social Anthropology at the Foundation for Advanced Studies in International Development, Tokyo, Japan. He obtained his Ph.D. from the London School of Economics and Political Sciences (University of London). He has published a few articles based on fieldwork amongst Untouchables in Kerala, South India, and is currently preparing a book on land, spirit possession, Untouchables and late modernity in South India.

Angie Zelter has been a grassroots campaigner all her life. Her peace and environmental campaigning, which uses non-violent direct action and civil disobedience, has taken her to Brazil, Sarawak, Canada and Fennoscandia to protest against repressive global timber extraction. She took part in the East Timor Ploughshares action to disarm a Hawk fighter plane due to be exported to Indonesia, and is currently working for *Reforest the Earth* with the Nuxalk Nation in BC, Canada, to stop clear-cutting in their territory.

Index

Lightning Source UK Ltd.
Milton Keynes UK
UKHW02f2356040118
315541UK00005B/190/P